'Euro-Asia' at the Crossroads

'Euro-Asia' at the Crossroads

Geopolitics, Identities and Dialogues

Editors

Jyrki Kakonen
Sanjay Chaturvedi
Anita Sengupta

In Association with
Centre for the Study of Mid-West and Central Asia,
Panjab University, Chandigarh, India
Jean Monnet European Centre of Excellence,
University of Tampere, Finland
Mahanirban Calcutta Research Group (CRG), Kolkata, India

SHIPRA

ISBN: 978-81-7541-600-0

First Published in India in 2011

'Euro-Asia' at the Crossroads: Geopolitics, Identities and Dialogues

Published by:
SHIPRA PUBLICATIONS
H.O.: LG 18-19, Pankaj Central Market, Patparganj,
Delhi-110092, Tel: 91-11-2223 5152, 2223 6152
Br.Off.: 4617/18, Ansari Road, Darya Ganj,
New Delhi-110002, Tel: 6594 6453, 9810522367
E-mail: info@shiprapublications.com
www.shiprapublications.com

Acknowledgements

First and foremost our gratitude goes to distinguished colleagues who have contributed to this volume. We wholeheartedly thank them for their scholarly contributions to this volume, patience, understanding and stimulating companionship.

For institutional support we are grateful to Ms Krista Varantola, Chancellor, University of Tampere, Professor Kaija Holli, Rector, University of Tampere, Professor R. C. Sobti, Vice Chancellor Panjab University, Professor Ranabir Samaddar, Director, Mahanirban Kolkata Research Group (CRG) and Professor H.S. Vasudevan, Director, Maulana Abul Kalam Azad Institute of Asian Studies, Kolkata.

We would also extend our sincere thanks to the faculty and staff of the former Department of Political Science and International Relations, University of Tampere, Jean Monnet European Centre of Excellence, University of Tampere, Centre for the Study of Mid-West and Central Asia, Panjab University, Mahanirban Kolkata Research Group (CRG) and Maulana Abul Kalam Azad Institute of Asian Studies, Kolkata.

A special debt is acknowledged to Mahanirban Kolkata Research Group (CRG) for its generous support to this book project. We are enormously thankful to Professor Ranabir Samaddar, Director, CRG, whose insightful suggestions greatly improved the book's final version.

Our special thanks to the Embassy of Finland in New Delhi, which has been a source of great inspiration and sustained support for cooperation and collaboration between institutions of higher learning and research in Finland and India. We would like to place on record our deep sense of gratitude to the following Ambassadors of Finland to India: H.E. Mr. Benjamin Bassin, Mr. Glen Lindholm, Mr. Asko Numinnen and Ms. Terhi Hakala.

Special thanks to Ms. Tytti Erasto, Research Scholar, University of Tampere and Mr. Chandan Awasthi, Research Scholar, Centre for the Study of Mid-West and Central Asia, Panjab University for their research and editorial assistance.

It has been a pleasure to bring out this book under the prestigious imprint of Shipra Publications, Delhi. We are especially thankful to Mr. D. Kumar of Shipra Publications for making the production process swift and smooth. We would also like to thank copyeditor Ms. Rita Banerjee for her excellent work on the manuscript.

Contents

Introduction

Jyrki Kakonen and Sanjay Chaturvedi

The central message of this volume is that at the dawn of the twenty-first century, the continent of 'Euro-Asia' finds itself at the crossroads; a historic juncture from where various alternative futures are indeed possible, provided there is enough political will around, supported by both the appreciation of historical inter-civilizational exchanges and dialogues and the bold vision of shared futures. Consequently, wide-ranging alternative imaginations of the identities of places and peoples inhabiting and sharing this vast and diverse continent are also possible. Underlying such a contention is the assumption that in the absence of such alternative visualizations of Euro-Asia (being guided by non-domination as the fundamental principle of governance at all levels) dialogues anchored in the politics of autonomy, and aiming at social transformation, gender justice and ecological-human security, may not be possible at all.

Themes addressed by various contributions to this volume straddle both Europe and Asia, and in one way or the other touch upon the intricate interplay between the "geo-economics of hope" and the "geopolitics of fear" on this vast and diverse continent. The insertion of a hyphen between 'Euro' and 'Asia' by us in the title of the volume is rather deliberate. On the one hand, it conveys our intent to differentiate this concept, to the extent possible, from the overwhelming military-strategic connotation of the term 'Eurasia'—Eurasia as a geostrategic space. On the other hand, a hyphenated relationship between 'Europe' and 'Asia' underlines our understanding of Euro-Asia as predominantly a socio-economic as well as political-cultural space of continental proportions.

After all, we also need to bear in mind that the history of mobility on this continent is much older than the histories of Westphalian territoriality, singular 'national' identities and rigid borders. Instead of remaining within the established limits of bounded territoriality, this volume aims at shifting the focus to the more inclusive concepts of flow and mobility and to identify the diversity of ideas, imaginations, human practices, and social institutions that apparently form boundaries but from another perspective also unite this vast and diverse continent.

An understanding of Euro-Asian diversity is an essential prerequisite for initiating and sustaining a dialogue of civilizations on a continent shared by both Europe and Asia. What is common to various chapters in this book is that each chapter reminds us in its own way that instead of searching for 'unity in diversity' on this vast continent, we should try and understand the 'diversity in unity'; that is how diverse understandings of unity have come to inform each other in conversation or dialogue with one another.

Mapping Euro-Asia: Cartographic Consciousness and Geopolitical Narratives

In academic as well as popular discourses, as Henri Lefebvre (1991) has argued in *The Production of Space*, the word 'space' is often used in a somewhat casual manner. A more apt and functional understanding of the world-order-space could well be that it appears to be a space constitutive of and constituted by interplay among wide-ranging "spaces of places" as well as "spaces of flows": a *space of diverse spaces*, which, given its plural nuance, questions rather simple and straightforward ways of imagining, constructing and performing space. Having noted that, the fact remains that the dominant spatiality of the 'world order', for most of the twentieth century, has been approached and analysed primarily in general terms of the meta-geographies of continents, and more specifically within the 'reasons' of the sovereign-territorial state actors.

What is Asia and where is it situated? By whom, when and why was the boundary between Europe (which geographically speaking is a peninsula of Asia) and Asia drawn? Various contemporary discourses such as "EU as a normative power" and the "Rise of Asia" tend to give the impression that both Europe and Asia are two distinct and homogenous geopolitical entities. Pekka Korhonen, while critically reflecting on the metageography of Euro-Asia in this volume, argues perceptively that we should be aware of our own cartographic consciousness and the manner in which they give rise to our mental maps. We need to continuously interrogate the ways in which unconscious sets of spatial-cartographic tools are being deployed by various actors and agencies, as they seek to arrange their knowledge of the world, and in the process also continue to (re) locate their respective positions in the dominant spatial hierarchy. What remains at the core of the interplay between the material and the symbolic understanding of a particular 'worldview' at a particular given time, therefore, is more or less a mythical set of categories of ancient or more recent origin, with the help of which the world is arranged into regions or sub-regions containing characteristics based on a mixture of social, political, racial, cultural and even economic narratives.

As John Agnew[1] has perceptively pointed out, there is no such thing as 'a view from nowhere'. Once this is acknowledged, the narratives feeding into (as well as deriving out of) notions of Europeanness (*the* European values or norms) or for that matter Asianness (*the* Asian values) become somewhat problematic. Korhonen argues and illustrates that once names ascribed to the continental and the oceanic layouts acquire a firm grip on our global-regional spatial imagination they are not easy to abandon. He reminds us of how the narratives of "enlightenment" and "conquest" were not only attached to the name of Europe; they also helped construct an imagination of Asia that stood opposed to almost everything that defined Europeanness. If it was a "civilizational" narrative that was deployed as dichotomous metageographical norm to differentiate between Europe and Asia during the fifteenth and sixteenth centuries,[2] it is the geo-economics discourse that is being currently used as a metageographical element to conceptualize the major differences within Asia on the one hand and between Europe and Asia on the other. The 'New Asia' comprises largely the eastern maritime states of Asia (from Japan to Singapore) and it is they who have more or less monopolized the metageographical visualization of 'truly Asia'. This is quite similar to the manner in which Western Europeans have tended to monopolize the dominant understanding of what Europe is all about.

And yet it is possible to argue and illustrate, as Rudolf Wastl does in his contribution to this volume, that the dividing line in cartographic representation between Europe and Asia has changed many a time and has failed to contribute to the construction of a functional geographical entity called Europe. Europe, argues Wastl, has been and will continue to be constructed, portrayed, and interpreted in different ways depending on a particular actor's point of view. A key question here, according to him, is how can we make geography work together with analytical and visualization tools to find understandable spatial matters and to construct a new model of better and connected Euro-Asia?

One of the striking features of international relations for over two hundred years has been the pursuit of primacy and the domination of some countries by others. In their widely acclaimed book entitled, *Mastering Space*, John Agnew and Stuart Corbridge point out that, "a geopolitical discourse signifies the rules and conceptual resources that political elites use in particular historical contexts to 'spatialize' the international political economy into places, peoples and disputes."[3] Of course not all the power elites have equal leverage on how global political-economic space is to be visualized and represented. It is those yielding authority in Great Powers or within the hegemonic state (if there is one) that have the power to write and impose the dominant geographies of international relations. Moreover, geopolitical reasoning, often presented in the garb of super-visions transcending time and space, operates through the active simplification of complex social-cultural realities. "This is how places and their inhabitants can become 'security commodities', readily subject to invasion, control and bombing."[4]

Geopolitical Imaginations and Conceptualizations

The *realm of geopolitics* is a highly contested realm, marked by the various competing territorial as well as non-territorial logics of power. There is a strong possibility that the emerging world order may continue to be seen in terms of what Brenner has described as "global territorialist approaches."[5] According to these approaches, global space is represented "in a state-centric manner, as a privilege territorial container within which globalization [as well as the world order] unfolds, rather than analysing the historical production, reconfiguration, and transformation of this space."[6] However, a major weakness of such a conceptualization lies in its reluctance to acknowledge that "territory is no longer bound within a single state...late capitalism extends the mathematical, calculative understanding of territory to the entire globe."[7]

What provides yet another layer of complexity and contestation to the geopolitical realm of the emerging world order is the issue of 'geocentrism'. As Richard Peet points out, "all centrisms see the world through the delusions of their own self-importance. Geo-centrisms see the world through the collective myths created about the Central We and the peripheral They. At worst, as with the above list of clichés, these myths combine ignorance with hatred, and dominance with fear."[8] Peet's argument is that what we are currently witnessing is the transformation of a Eurocentrism that celebrated the dominance of West Europeans in world affairs into an "even more virulent geo-cultural form that worships the freedom, democracy and lifestyle of the United States."[9] According to this new ideology of Americentrism, "everything that is important happens first in the United States."[10]

Once approached through geocentric worldviews, global space comes to be visualized in terms of cocentric circles of decreasing significance. If power continues to create space(s) on a continuous basis (rather than the other way round) then the rising powers of Asia, especially India and China, are also likely to create their own cocentric spaces or "spheres of influence". How India and China, with their increasing energy insecurities, choose to manage their competitive-collaborative relationship, in the years and decades to follow, will be of crucial importance for the international system. May be what we are going to witness is overlapping circles of various centrisms, in the making of which Asian powers will play a major role; a pattern which may or may not *fit* that easily into the totalizing, hierarchical spaces of the emerging world order.

At a more fundamental level, critical perspectives on the realm of geopolitics raise the proverbial billion dollar question of who stands to gain (or lose) what, when, *where*, and *why* from the emerging world order? We hope that a serious and systematic search in this direction, as attempted in this volume, will create the necessary theoretical scope, to begin with, for a critical enquiry into the ways in which world order space is imagined, represented as well as resisted in geopolitical struggles, and in everyday life.

How do we explain that most of the dominant geopolitical discourses tend to frame 'Central Asia' in exclusively geopolitical terms of the 'old' and the 'new' 'great games'? 'Central Asia' or 'Central Eurasia' is perhaps the most excessively imagined place on the face of the globe today. A ruthless pursuit of the so-called 'vital' interests of resource geopolitics, ably supported by the rhetoric of disciplining places and peoples in the name of western-style democracy, too has unleashed a process that insists on creating winners and losers with conflicting political agendas. Marginalized as well as trivialized by such 'resource wars' are the perspectives and voices that nevertheless dare to challenge the 'new' strategic geography of corporate-style war making as well as the maps that are drawn more on the basis of resource concentrations than political boundaries.

It is significant to note that over the past decade and more, there has been a noticeable, rather dramatic growth of interest in geopolitics in post-Soviet Russia.[11] While it is true that this development can be seen as part of a broader international "renaissance" of geopolitics, as Bassin and Aksenov point out,

> Russia's new preoccupation with the subject is distinctive in a variety of respects. Perhaps most notably, geopolitics never had any status as an academic discipline in Russia, and thus—in contrast to the situation in Germany or France—there is no formal tradition upon which current interest could draw and develop. Very much to the contrary, geopolitics was denounced throughout the Soviet period as a *lzhenauka* or false-science, and the study, indeed the very mention of it was relegated beyond the limits of political acceptability. This proscription began to crumble in the 1980s as part of the liberalisation of Mikhail Gorbachev's *perestroika*, at which time "political geography" gained gradual acknowledgment.[12]

Mackinder is receiving a great deal of attention and visibility in Russia today as the most important proponent of 'classical' geopolitics. His ideas about the 'Geographical Pivot of History' and 'Heartland' are being mentioned and/or cited in virtually all geopolitical texts, and enthusiastically mobilized in geopolitical discourses. In many Central Asian republics too various citations of Mackinder's theory are being used to construct geopolitical narratives in an era of renewed great power interest in the region.

Sanjay Chaturvedi argues and illustrates how against the backdrop of a global renaissance of geopolitics, hinted at above, contemporary Central Eurasia is gradually being turned by the security-strategic communities of major actors engaged in the so-called 'New Great Game' into a site of excessive geopolitics, marked by the 'clash' of geostrategic imaginations. He points out that a clash of imaginations is not about how the major actors imagine Central Asia and implant maps of meaning on such a diverse and complex landscape but also how they read certain meanings into each other's visions and imaginations. His analysis shows that the interplay between the geoeconomics of hope and the geopolitics of fear is most pronounced in Central Asia, and carries enormous implications for both ecological-human well-being and energy-climate security considerations in the region and beyond. Chaturvedi concludes by commenting on the problems and prospects of realizing anti-geopolitics in Central Eurasia, an alternative imagination of politically organized spaces marked by civility and tolerance for diversity and difference.

The following chapter by Anita Sengupta is much more optimistic about the future of Euro-Asian cooperation. Her key argument is that contrary to the impression that there is today a revival of the great game, principally between three major players, Russia, China and the US in the Central Asian region, cooperation and multilateralism seem to be the watchwords of diplomacy for Eurasian powers. If this is the case then the continuing interpretation of the history of the region in terms of an intense rivalry for control over the so-called "heartland of the world" is rather questionable. According to Sengupta, no major geopolitical conflict now divides the powers of the Eurasian heartland and there is a new rapprochement over the region. While, on the one hand, this calls for a reinterpretation of the viability of the great game theories, on the other, it calls for a new look at the emerging multilateralism in the region. Accordingly a number of questions assume significance. How viable is multilateralism in the Central Asian region and what is the extent to which the states themselves are willing to be part of multilateral process? What are the attitudes of Russia and China towards multilateralism in general? How about the viability of Russian and Chinese-led multilateral processes in the Central Asian region given the reality of US presence? Seeking answers to these questions, as skilfully attempted by Sengupta, should lead us towards a better understanding of how the concept and practices of security in the multilateral arena itself might be changing on a broader Eurasian level. The prospects of such multilateral cooperation no doubt are related to the ability of actors concerned to engage in critical self-reflection about the dynamics and dilemmas of the sense of belonging. In other words, the issues related to the question of identity loom large before Euro-Asia at the crossroads.

Dynamics and Dilemmas of Belonging

In the post-Cold War era no other thesis on identity geopolitics in the context of globalization has generated so much of controversy and contestation among academia and policy makers, as the 'clash of civilizations' argument by Samuel P. Huntington. Our intention here is not to repeat the critique of this thesis, ably discussed elsewhere[13] but to introduce, as concisely as possible, the critical engagement by Ayla Göl with Huntington's thesis in her perceptive contribution on Turkey's search for national identity in this volume.

Is Turkey, geographically located between 'Europe' and the 'Middle East', a bridge between the West and the East, between Europe and Asia? If yes, in what respect? If not, why not? According to Samuel P.

Huntington, Turkey, rather than a bridge, had become a 'torn' country that "has a single predominant culture which places it one civilization but its leaders want to shift to another civilization."[14] Equally interesting is the connotation Huntington provides to the very idea of a 'bridge', arguing that as an artificial creation connecting two solid entities, it is a part of neither and hence 'torn'. He concludes that the Muslim character of Turkish society and Islamic legacy of the country are incompatible with Westernization and modernization.

Mark Bassin's critical assessment of the 'clash of civilizations' thesis points out that similar to the dominant visualization of Cold War blocks (characterized largely through state-based typologies such as 'superpowers,' 'allied states,' 'client states,' 'non-aligned states,' 'neutral states', 'gateway states,' 'dominoes,' and 'shatter belts') Huntington's typology for his post-Cold War civilizational blocks is *state-centric.*[15] Acting as the political-geographical pivot of the civilizational block are with the so-called 'core states', which, by virtue of the relative power and 'cultural centrality' possess the right to 'represent' other 'member states' of the respective civilizational block. The remaining constituent parts of a civilizational block include 'cleft countries' (states whose population is significantly divided between two or more civilisations, such as India, Indonesia, Ukraine); 'torn countries' (states belonging to one civilization whose leadership attempts to move it to another, such as Russia, Turkey, Mexico, Australia; and finally 'lone countries', which belong to no larger civilization, such as Haiti, Ethiopia, and Japan.

What is the significance of Huntington's ambivalent engagement with geography? According to Bassin, "It can be argued that the inconsistency of Huntington's deployment of geography—the unresolved tension between a Realist acknowledgement of geography as an 'objective' and autonomous element of the political process on the one hand and the affirmation of the primacy of subjective, non-geographical factors of social psychology on the other is itself entirely consistent with a 'fault line' that has been characteristic for at least one important tendency in American security discourses in the twentieth century...it may be possible to begin to speak of a peculiarly American form of 'torn' geopolitics, 'torn' not civilisationally but rather between the simultaneous recognition of and refusal to recognise the fundamental place of geography in politics."[16]

Göl argues that Huntington's claims in the context of Turkey's relations with the West are historically as well geopolitically incorrect. She also questions several key assumptions underlying the 'clash of civilizations' thesis in general, and their application in particular to

Turkey's location, orientation, identity and role in regional and global affairs. There appears to be a selective and deliberate manipulation of historical 'evidence' and 'memory' when, for example, Huntington talks of Turkey's "antagonism" with the West. May be he is referring here to the 'golden age' of the Ottoman empire, while failing to acknowledge that that the Sublime Porte—*Bab-i-Ali*—was geopolitically part of the Concert of Europe and developed close relations with the West through war, trade and diplomacy, since the fifteenth century. Contrary to what Huntington is inclined to believe there is no evidence of strong anti-western feelings in Turkish politics.

In our view, Göl's contribution raises a number of fundamental questions about geopolitics, spaces and identities in Euro-Asia, especially in the wake of the unfortunate event called 9/11 and its equally, if not more, unfortunate aftermath. How accurate, for example, is the essentialist view of Islam that the "democracy deficit" in the Muslim world is largely due to religious or cultural factors? Can there be a Muslim democracy? If not, why not?

Our next case study by Daragh McDowell raises yet another set of pertinent questions about geopolitics, spaces and identities with regard to the Russian Federation and Central Asian Republics; entities that are totally devoid of the experience of Westphalia territoriality in the form of a 'nation-state'. The issues concerned here appear to be far more complex than state-centric geopolitical imaginations could possibly grasp or even visualise. They also reveal, in their own ways, the power of narratives. According to Marc Howard Ross, narratives may be defined as "frameworks for action" through which members of particular identity groups "understand the social and political worlds in which they live, and explain the conflicts in which they are involved."[17] Narratives, then, "are the stories that members of social and political group tell about themselves and relations with selected 'others' to create a sense of collective identity and shared purpose."[18]

The onset of the so-called 'Colour Revolutions' in post-Soviet Central Asia compelled the Central Asian Republics in transition to take a closer and critical look at their respective emerging trajectories of geopolitical (re) orientations and alliances in both the regional and global contexts. The daunting tasks of nation-building and state-building were further complicated by the lack of a concrete ideological basis for the conduct of 'foreign' policies. The western mission of "promoting democracy" was met by various responses including the articulation of the concept of 'sovereign democracy' in Russia. According to Andrei Okara, 'sovereign democracy' highlights international problems in the first place. "These are global competition, the struggle for energy resources, attempts by some countries to restrict the sovereignty of other countries, 'coloured revolutions' etc. But the goal is roughly the same—to furnish the power wielding camp with grounds for claiming the exclusive rights to upkeep its preponderant status and legitimize itself in the eyes of the nation and world community."[19]

Daragh McDowell's chapter deals with Russia-Kazakhstan relations, particularly in the light of events such as 9/11, the 'Colour Revolutions' and the birth of the concept of 'sovereign democracy'. In his view, this relationship underlines that this bilateral relationship is perhaps one of the most important factors in the evolution of the politics of Central Asia and Eurasia as a whole. According to him a vast majority of western scholarship on this subject is driven by the materialist paradigms, focusing on Russia's geo-economic or strategic links with Kazakhstan and other Central Asian republics. In his view, the normative factors underpinning Russia's relations with the Central Asian republics in general and Kazakhstan in particular have not received the attention they demand as well as deserve. He shows how both Russia and Kazakhstan political elites have constructed certain narratives of a normative 'Eurasian' identity, which are also being deployed for both internal-domestic purposes and those of foreign policy. McDowell argues that 'sovereign democracy' is the political side of the 'Eurasian' identity and can be seen as an attempt to form a common ideology to provide 'Eurasianism' with a normative basis.

Dialogues and Autonomies

In the aftermath of the East-West Cold War, what kind of a world order is emerging? What are the prospects of a paradigm shift from domination to non-domination as the fundamental principle of governance at all possible (and not just state) levels across the globe? What is the evidence to suggest that the key objective of the emerging world order is to realize the 'good life' for the entire mankind? Is it feasible, or even desirable, to realize a *good* life in the absence of values such as tolerance, civility, dignity and humanism?

If the above mentioned values also qualify as liberal *universal* values, then it is more of a reason that they should be pursued with vengeance by all those who believe in emancipatory transformative politics. A serious and systematic search for the kind of practices and institutions that are needed to translate these universal values and visions into reality, is likely to confirm in our view, the desirability as well as feasibility of a number of parallel autonomous (alternative?) *orders* (global, regional and sub-regional) from below, demanding acknowledgment of spaces of their own making as well as a spacing of their own choosing. The geographies of such orders are likely to be rather skewed and overlapping in comparison to the bounded spatiality of the dominant discourses of a unipolar, imperial *Order* forged and forced from above.

It is often forgotten by some that the continent shared by Europe and Asia has been a site of some of the outstanding cultures of exchanges, dialogues and tolerance. Maria Rosa Menocal[20] has provided an inspiring account of medieval 'al-Andalus' or Andalusia; the rise and fall of the great Muslim civilization of Spain against the backdrop of how Christianity, Judaism and Islam once flourished side by side, tolerating one another and borrowing language, art and architecture from each other. According to Menocal, "This was the chapter of Europe's culture when Jews, Christians and Muslims lived side by side and, despite their intractable differences and enduring hostilities, nourished a complex culture of tolerance."[21] The reminder that emerges loud and clear from nearly 800 years of history of ethos of tolerance and symbiosis is this: what *once* was and what could *be*. To quote Menocal,

> What happened? How and why does a culture of tolerance fall apart? How did a people come to abandon a culture rooted in an ethic of yes and no, so readily able to love and embrace the architecture or the poetry of political enemies or religious rivals, so willing to read good books regardless of the library they came from? All the answers are themselves bundles of contradictions. The deal was both very easily done, it seems, and yet it was accomplished only with great difficulty. The outcome was all too predictable from very early on, yet it was also sudden, from one day to the next, and quite unimaginable at the time. *Events could have turned out quite differently indeed. Perhaps all that can be said with any conviction is that it is in the combination of spectacular successes and failures presented by the history lies tales of both warning and encouragement.*[22] (Emphasis given)

The issue of continental dialogue and unity has become increasingly important in recent years, for unlike during the Cold War, the relations between Europe and Asia can no longer be viewed as being of 'secondary' importance. Even a cursory glance through various country strategy papers of the European Commission (e.g., India 2007-2013; a New Partnership with South East Asia 2003; China 2007-2013), reveals that a great deal of emphasis is being placed on initiating and sustaining 'dialogues' in various spheres.

With interaction between Europe and Asia broadening as well as deepening, we are likely to witness overlapping zones of cooperation and interdependence, both formal and informal. Commerce and trade are common interests that have always bound this continent together and they will continue to do so. This is not to suggest however that geo-economics is replacing geopolitics. Much of this has to do with expanding Asian markets and energy considerations, which are likely to further increase trans-continental commercial flows in the future. There are also shared problems, such as environmental degradation, climate change, and poverty. Many of these problems require shared solutions. In order to identify common interests and solutions for the Euro-Asian region, a common ground must be found. While it is clear that this cannot be done with the help of classical geopolitical notions such as 'spheres of influence', or 'coalition of the willing' what is not that obvious is the nature and location of that 'common ground'. Similar to conventional cartographies, the traditional scale seems to be a rather poor guide to understanding spaces of flows and what Rudolf Wastl has referred to in his chapter in this book as "multilayered organizational" spaces.

Ranabir Samaddar argues in his chapter that most of discussions on Eurasia are dominated and dictated by geopolitical images and memories that they invoke are those of power and pursuit of primacy; echoing the sounds of galloping horses of an Alexander or Genghis Khan. Given such a context, it is not surprising perhaps that even the definitions of 'regions' and 'sub-regions' invariably remain overloaded with geopolitical connotations. For Samaddar, in the context of popular and contentious politics of contemporary times, such geopolitically manufactured images and threat narratives as 'flash points', 'zones of percolating violence', and 'black holes', seem 'sickeningly banal'. It is important therefore to re-visualize Euro-Asia as a site of many overlapping existences both below and above the state where many autonomies are working out their continuous as well as contentious existences as fundamental principles of reorganizing society.

What is the so-called 'genuine' autonomy all about? What are its constituents and how do they hang together? Are these constituents, historically and culturally, invariable universals, or are they relative to context? How do we ensure that none of the various competing knowledge claims to autonomy, flagging 'national' or 'regional' or 'local' interests, monopolizes the right to speak authoritatively about particular places and peoples? How do we preempt a situation whereby a particular hegemonic knowledge claim gets generalized and naturalized, far beyond the immediate spatial as well as temporal context in which it was initially made? How can the fundamental democratic *right of having one's moral worth recognized* be ensured for one and all, especially for those who remain on the margins of both the dominant discourses on autonomy and the practices that flow from them?

Samaddar argues that if governmentality produces difference from the top, then autonomy is the mark of negotiating difference from below. For him, "autonomy is therefore not an exceptional principle of democracy conceded to some belligerent section of society or some areas or groups of population…it is the organizing principle of the emerging political society, autonomies in perpetual dialogue among themselves, linked by respective responsibilities to retain the autonomous places in a dialogic universe." In our view, the relevance and resonance of Samaddar's critical engagement with the ethics and the politics of autonomy can (and should be) be revisited in the light of the South Asian experiences of Sri Lanka, Nepal, India, Pakistan and Bangladesh, or the European experiences of Basque, Kosovo, and Northern Ireland.

In contrast to the visualization of Euro-Asia as a "space of interacting autonomies," and "dialogues across differences," we continue to hear various monologues of superiority and differences based on the so-called civilizational-cultural attributes, the most dramatic being Huntington's clash of civilizations thesis. Also, more recently, from the streets of Germany to the French polling booths, from the Polish Parliament to the Danish Government, the rise of extreme right parties in Western and, more recently, Central and Eastern Europe has received widespread attention in the media and has been the subject of much academic debate.[23] In various parts of South Asia too we have seen various groups of what Anthony Smith has tellingly described as "Chosen People," flagging vociferously (and in some cases even violently) identities marked by religious purity.

These are just a few of the major challenges facing what John M. Hobson has described in his contribution to this volume as "the dialectical-dialogues of civilizations" marked by symbiosis and mutual learning. These dialogues have been historically characterized by the myriad ways in which each civilization develops through the borrowing and assimilation of resource portfolios that emanate from other civilizations. After all, the

Renaissance owes a huge debt to the contemporary Muslims. How can (and why do) many Europeans tend to forget also the significant contribution that the Chinese made to the pivotal British industrial and agricultural revolutions?

Hobson forcefully questions the image of Europe clashing, colliding with other civilization; the image that is conventionally thought to mark Europe's history, past and present and further reinforced by the popularity in the 'West' of Huntington's clash of civilizations thesis. Hobson points out that "the paradox cosmopolitan-Eurocentrism" underlying the idea of a "Manichean clash of two great antithetical civilizations of Christianity and Islam" by arguing that precisely at a time when the Europeans were engaged in military confrontation (the Crusades), with Islam, they not only continued trading with Muslims but they were avidly borrowing a wealth of Islamic ideas, technologies and institutions that in turn propelled Europe's imperial movement forward. Hobson shows how Europe's dialogical cosmopolitanism went hand-in-hand with a desire to appear monologically separate, uniquely inventive, culturally superior and above all exceptional—the very essence of Eurocentric identity.

How do we explain the persistent tendency among some to focus only on European 'clashes' with Islam while conveniently glossing over many symbiotic cosmopolitan dialogical interactions that have taken place between the two? Will the European Union, as a civilian-normative power, be in position to effectively question and contain such tendencies and trends so that a more humane and just world could be realized through diplomacy and dialogue? This question, in our view, assumes greater significance when approached in the context of growing cartographic anxieties over various scenarios of chaos and disorder as articulated, for example, by Robert D. Kaplan:

> Imagine cartography in three dimensions, as if in a hologram. In this hologram would be the overlapping sediments of various group identities such as those of language and economic class, atop the two dimensional color distinctions among city-states and the remaining nations, themselves confused in places by shadows overhead, indicating the power of drug cartels, mafias, and private security agencies that guard the wealthy in failing states and hunt down terrorists. Instead of borders, there would be moving "centres" of power, as in the Middle Ages. These power centres would be both national and financial, reflecting the sovereignty of global corporations. Many of these holistic layers would be in motion. Replacing fixed and abrupt lines on

> a flat map would be shifting patterns of ecoregions and buffer entities. To this protean cartographic hologram one must add other factors, such as the growing populations, refugees, migrations, soil and water scarcities and...vectors of disease. Henceforward, the map of the world will never be static. This future map—in a sense, the 'Last Map'—will be an ever-mutating representation of cartographic chaos. On this map, the rules by which diplomats and other policymaking elites have ordered the world these past few hundred years will apply less and less.[24]

The highly alarmist imagined geographies that underpin Kaplan's vision (evoking an imaginary of chaos, unpredictability, instability and conflict) seem to be a hallmark of what some scholars would describe as a "disconcerting era."[25]

According to Ferguson and Mansbach, "Many of the most important normative concerns raised about the post-international world, including those opposed to globalization, are explicitly or implicitly linked to the broad concern that people, including those in democratic societies, are losing their ability to control their own lives or to choose how to live them. This is, in other words, a growing democracy deficit."[26] They would further argue that, at a time when the shape of the post-Westphalian global politics remains obscure, "the United States' ability and propensity to act unilaterally in recent years and to control, impede, weaken, or even destroy international institutions tempts one to conclude that it alone could reverse many of the trends of postinternationalism. This would be premature and, in our judgement, unwise conclusion because much of the United States unique unilateral capability seems better adapted to resisting change than to guiding it, moving it in different directions, or managing it." In their view, since American norms, interests and identities would suffer the most in the event Kaplan's vision of chaos were to materialize, the US policy will soon overcome the "neoconservative" period and replaced by some kind of moderate nationalism.

On the other hand, there are scholars like Hall Gardner who would argue that "there is a real risk of a potential 'clash of democracies' between an expanding EU and the global interests of the United States."[27] According to Gardner it is not inevitable that the United States and the EU will 'fight' with each other but it more unlikely than otherwise that "the two may be unable to coordinate policies due to their divergent interests, the different ways in which they rank 'common' values and norms, as well as the different ways in which the two formulate foreign policy."

Jyrki Kakonen adds a new dimension to the ongoing debate on the nature and scope of emerging EU-US multifaceted equation by seeking answers to the following pertinent questions: Can the EU, as a civilian-normative power, provide an alternative to the hegemony of the United States of America in the Euro-Asian space? What are the major interests of the EU in Asia? How does the EU see its own role in Asia? Has the EU been able to carve out a niche for itself in Asia that is distinct from that of the USA? In what ways can the EU possibly contribute towards the realization of less violent future *in* and *for* Asia without being perceived by the others as paternalistic or patronizing? Kakonen takes a critical look at some of the key EU documents on Asia in order to find out whether the EU is indeed seriously providing elements for an alternative order in Asia, and examines the extent to which its worldview and visions are influenced by the theories of classical geopolitics. According to him, in the mental maps of the EU policy makers, India, in contrast to China, is being seen more as an equal partner. Could it be that the EU is late in the sense that India now appears more inclined towards forging a strategic partnership with the US?

Rajen Harshe argues in his chapter that any conception of 'Eurasia' can hardly be indifferent to the possible ties between the European Union and India. This echoes the emphasis placed on multifaceted India-EU relations in the European Commission (EC) document entitled, "The European Union and India: A Strategic Partnership for the 21st Century". It says in part,

> We live in a 'global village', in which the threats and opportunities that confront one region or nation have an impact on all others. Global leaders such as the EU and India must therefore work together to defuse the dangers of modern life and optimise the possibilities it offers. EU-India global cooperation, based on shared values and philosophies, works well. It is helping to counter terrorism, transnational crime and drugs, protect the environment, democracy and fundamental rights and ensure that globalization's benefits are evenly distributed.
>
> In a rapidly evolving international order of new groupings and challenges, India and the European Union (EU) are both world leaders, and so called to play major roles within their respective regions and beyond. The EU and India are the world's two largest democracies; the EU is the world's biggest economy; India is

> the second most populous nation and the fourth biggest economy in purchasing power parity terms.
> We share many common values and beliefs, such as commitment to democracy, pluralism, human rights, the rule of law, and independence of judiciaries and the media. This makes us natural partners as well as important factor of stability in the modern world order.

Harshe, while acknowledging the significance of common values as well as reciprocal interactions between India (as a sovereign state actor) and the EU (as an international organization of considerable magnitude), cautions against carrying any comparison between the two entities too far in view of fundamental differences that clearly separate them. Having said that, Harshe goes on to argue that the common challenges faced by both the EU and India with regard to energy security, human security and terrorism demand and deserve further broadening and deepening of their relationship. Harshe, while talking about the burgeoning prospects of development cooperation, also talks about emerging frontiers of EU-India cooperation including the Galileo-Satellite project in the realm of outer space.

Notes

1. J. Agnew, *Geopolitics: Re-Visioning World Politics* (London and New York: Routledge, 1998).
2. Agnew, *Geopolitics*.
3. J. Agnew and S. Corbridge, *Mastering Space* (London: Routledge, 1995), 48-9.
4. Agnew and Corbridge, *Mastering Space*.
5. N. Brenner, "Beyond State-Centrism? Space, Territoriality, and Geographical Scale in Globalization Studies," *Theory and Society* 28 (1999): 39-78.
6. Brenner, "Space, Territoriality," 59.
7. S. Elden, "Missing the Point: Globalization, Deterritorialization and the Space of the World," *Transactions of the Institute of British Geographers* 30 (2005): 16.
8. R. Peet, "From Eurocentrism to Americentrism," *Antipode: A Radical Journal of Geography* 37 (2005): 942.
9. Peet, "Eurocentrism to Americentrism," 937.
10. Peet, "Eurocentrism to Americentrism."
11. Mark Bassin and Konstantin E. Aksenov, (2006) "Mackinder and the Heartland Theory in Post-Soviet Geopolitical Discourse," *Geopolitics* 11, no. 1 (2006): 99-118.

12. Bassin and Aksenov, "Post-Soviet Geopolitical Discourse," 99.
13. For a discussion of this thesis, see M. Bassin, "Civilizations and Their Discontents: Political Geography and Geopolitics in the Huntington's Thesis," *Geopolitics* 12, no. 3 (2007): 351-74; M. Gismondi, "Civilization as Paradigm: An Inquiry into the Hermeneutics of Conflict," *Geopolitics* 9, no. 2 (2004): 402-24.
14. Samuel P. Huntington, *The Clash of Civilizations and the Remaking of World Order* (New York: Simon & Schuster, 1996), 138.
15. Bassin, "Huntington's Thesis."
16. Bassin, "Huntington's Thesis."
17. M.H. Ross, "The Political Psychology of Competing Narratives: September 11 and Beyond," in *Understanding September 11*, Calhoun Craig, Paul Price and Ashley Timmer (eds) (New York: New Press, 2002), 303.
18. N.C. Funk, and A.A. Said, "Islam and the West: Narratives of Conflict and Conflict Transformation," *International Journal of Peace Studies* 9, no. 1 (2004): 3.
19. A. Okara, "Sovereign Democracy: A New Russian Idea or a PR?" *Foreign Affairs* 2 (July & September 2007).
20. M.R. Menocal, *Ornament of the World: How Muslims, Jews and Christians Crated a Culture of Tolerance in Medieval Spain* (Boston, New York, London: Little, Brown and Company, 2002).
21. Menocal, *Medieval Spain*, 11.
22. Menocal, *Medieval Spain*, 266.
23. A. Mammone, E. Godin, and B. Jenkins, 2008. "The Extreme Right in Contemporary Europe," (Editorial), *Journal of Contemporary Europe* 16, no. 3 (2008): 323-6.
24. R.D. Kaplan, 1996. *The End of the Earth: A Journey into the Frontiers of Anarchy* (New York: Random House, 1996), 336-7.
25. Y.H. Ferguson and R.W. Mansbach, *Remapping Global Politics: History's Revenge and Future Shock* (Cambridge: Cambridge University Press, 2004).
26. Ferguson and Mansbach, *Remapping Global Politics*, p. 324.
27. H. Gardner, *American Global Strategy and the "War on Terrorism"* (Aldershot: Ashgate, 2005), 161.

1

On the Metageography of Euro-Asia

Pekka Korhonen

The main purpose of this chapter is to try to understand from a long historical perspective the changes taking place in our understanding of the concept of Asia within the larger geopolitical entity of Eurasia. Even the most omphalopsychotic of European researchers cannot by now have failed to recognize that something is happening in Asia, that 'Asia is rising' and moving forward with great developmental energy.[1] This economy-based perspective towards Asia is nowadays commonplace, and there is no point in going once again through the statistics here. Instead, I try to take a look at the metageographical assumptions that we have when we discuss Asia as a geopolitical phenomenon. By metageography I mean the usually unreflected and often unconscious set of spatial conceptual tools with which people arrange their knowledge of the world. This results in a more or less mythical set of categories of ancient or more recent origin, with which the world is arranged into regions containing characteristics based on a mixture of social, political, racial, cultural, religious, and economic narratives. The result often tends to approach what we can call geographic concordance, where disparate phenomena are supposed to exhibit the same variation in space, so that different regions systematically acquire essentiality. For instance, 'Europeanness' is supposed to permeate everything in the region named Europe, and likewise 'Asianness' is the basic characteristic of the region named Asia. To be able to set the current discussion into a perspective, I shall employ a really long temporal framework for analysing changes in the concept of Asia, starting from ancient Greek geography, over two millennia ago.

In this approach I am much indebted to Martin W. Lewis's and Kären E. Wigen's book *The Myth of Continents* (1997), where they systematically try to analyse the jumbled mass of historical data attached to continental names. One of their conclusions is that we might well do without the old continental scheme altogether, and instead reclassify the world using other criteria, such as functioning politico-economic groupings of states. This is what is actually taking place in practice, but purely functional names for integrative organizations, such as the Organization for Economic Cooperation and Development (OECD) or the International Monetary Fund (IMF), which were fashionable in the immediate post—World War II situation, are not used nowadays. In spite of all the hype of globalization and the speed of communications, geographic proximity still is one of the basic ingredients in the creation of functional communities. In other words, regionalism is a strong element in functional cooperation. One cannot help noticing the prevalent use of the old continental names in contemporary discussions, with Africa, America, Asia and Europe being not only constantly maintained in national and international discussions, but also reinforced by the creation and strengthening of regional interstate organizations, such as the European Union, the African Union, the Free Trade Area of the Americas, the East Asia Summit, or the Asia Europe Meeting. Old continental names seem to have such a tight grip of our world spatial imagination that they cannot be discarded.

Nevertheless, the metageographical assumptions connected with them certainly should be clarified. This article attempts to find clarity on the geopolitical uses of Asia, both historically and at present. The approach is that of conceptual history; the source material is both cartographical and textual, covering both Asian and European discussions on the subject. However, as I am in practice familiar only with discussions in Western Europe and East Asia, I will limit myself to analysing these only.[2]

Ancient Greek Geography

Many of the basic concepts of our contemporary geography are derived from ancient Mediterranean thinking. The central metageographical concept was the basic division of the world into water and land, which cartographically lead into the depicting of continents as islands in the middle of the World Ocean. Another important meta theoretical notion is the contrast between civilization and barbarity, which in many kinds of forms has accompanied the narratives connected with continents. Humans lived on the continents, making their living out of various occupations, especially in the centre of the world, where the continents met, and where the Egyptian, Mesopotamian, Phoenician and the younger Greek cultures were situated. The farther one travelled from the eastern Mediterranean area—either over land or over sea—the more monstrous it became. The habitable world was supposed to have been composed of three continents, namely Asia, Libya and Europe. The Romans later changed the name of the second continent to Africa. These ideas about the naming of continents date from three millennia old eastern Mediterranean geography, whose first concepts were developed in Mesopotamia and Egypt, and which later were adopted by classical Greek authors.[3]

Because of the importance of the notions of civilization and barbarity, these three continents were evaluated also along this dimension. By stretching the concept of geopolitics outside of its strict usage as foreign policies of nation-states, we can also call this practice 'geopolitical' in the sense that different places were ranked higher and lower with it. John Agnew's term civilizational geopolitics[4] could perhaps be used here, but it is important to notice that the evaluations differed drastically from the nineteenth century valuations that Agnew studied.

The first systematic analysis of the continents that have survived was made in minute literary form by Herodotus (484-424 BC), who was an Asian Greek, born in Halicarnassus in Caria, as a subject of the Great King of Persia. Herodotus claims that he does not know who divided the world into Asia, Libya, and Europe, or who gave to these continents the names of ladies. The division simply looked ancient to him, and it was evident that the names were used not only by the Greeks, but also by Persians and other inhabitants of Asia. Libya as a continent was bounded by the Nile in the east, the Mediterranean in the north and the World Ocean in the south and west.[5] Asia was a place similar to Libya, namely blessed with high culture, warm climate and abundant harvests. The river Nile separated Asia from Libya, and the mythical river Phasis, from Europe. An additional metageographical element seems to have worked here, namely cartographic symmetry; Phasis was a theoretical extension of the Mediterranean and Black Sea towards the east. Both Libya and Asia were small, but Asia perhaps was smaller—so small that it was basically covered at any time by a single empire, like those of the Median, Scythian and Persian empires, which all were said to have encompassed all Asia.[6] Likewise, the later Macedonian conqueror Alexander the Great was also said to have ruled all Asia. The centre of Asia was Persia, surrounded by the lands of the Medes, Saspires and Colchians to the north, Assyria, Arabia, Palestine and Egypt in the south, and India in the east. Asia was inhabited from the eastern banks of the Nile all the way to India, but after India there existed only uninhabited deserts, and Herodotus did not have any information about them, or what lay beyond them, but he did not think that Asia would extend far to the east.[7] Asia was the most well known of all the continents, and excepting the eastern deserts, with nothing but residual waste lands imposed conceptually on its area.

Map 1.1

Europe was the greatest anomaly, because it seemed to be indefinitely vaster than the other two continents. It spanned the length of them both, and no one knew where it ended in the west, north, and east.[8] Europe thus appeared to be incomparably broader than either Libya or Asia, containing all residual land that could not be meaningfully placed into the other two continents. That residuary here implies barbarity in contrast with the images of civilization attached to Libya and Asia. Europe was a cold and dark place, while Asia was populated by civilized people, Europe was populated by mythical beings, such as Arimaspians, who had only one eye in their head, and who were very warlike. In Europe lived also men who were completely bald, and there were also rumours of men with goat's feet, living in distant mountains, and about people sleeping six months of the year.[9] Considering humanlike beings, most of Europe was populated by Scythians, who were divided into many nations and spoke different languages. The general term Scythian was not an ethnic denomination, but rather described a way of life, that of nomadic people moving around after pasture with their herds of horses, cows and sheep over the grasslands and forests of Europe. Scythians were ferocious people. A Scythian drank the blood of the first man he had slain. Scythians used to take the scalps of their killed enemies, some even making garments to wear after collecting many of them.[10] Europe was thus essentially a place of barbarity, occupying the lowest place in the hierarchy of continents.

It was only at the time of the Roman Empire that the continental division was changed so that Europe acquired some civilizational characteristics and a smaller size, while the area of Asia necessarily became expanded because of this. The most influential geographer proposing this kind of division was Strabon (63 BC-AD 19), a Hellenic Greek, but a Roman subject. As the centre of the Roman Empire was in Italy, the status of Europe had to be elevated, and Strabon did this by simply proposing a south-north boundary between Asia and Europe, running from the Nile via the Mediterranean and Black Sea to the river Tanais (Don). That definition made Tanais flow symmetrically with the Nile and the former east-west symmetry was thus replaced with south-north symmetry. The Don was not exactly on the same meridian as the Nile, but not far from it.[11] As a consequence, Asia became the continent holding all the residual land that could not be placed elsewhere, but that did not mean that it as a whole would have become uncivilized.

Strabon continuously considered Egypt to be more civilized than Rome in the Mediterranean area, although he had to write carefully about

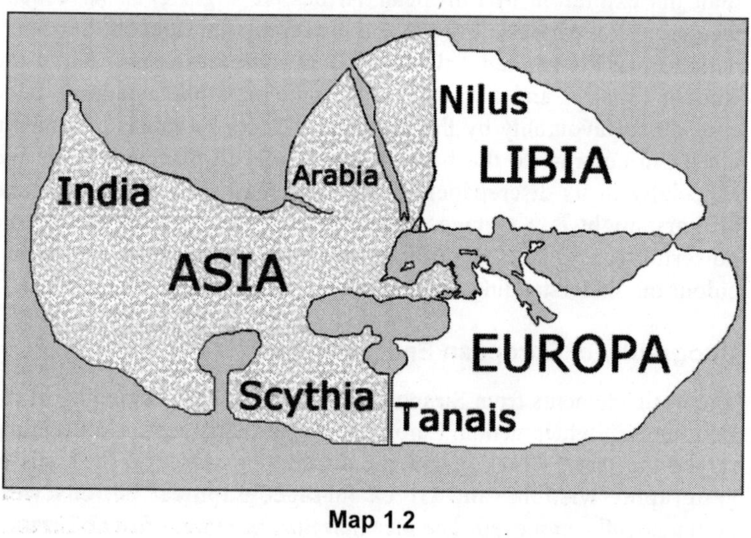

Map 1.2

the subject. Being politically correct he defined Europe as a place characterized by the excellence of people and governments, contributing most for the other continents. Such an admirable place also had to be favourable in terms of nature, and thus Strabon limited Europe—cutting out the mythical far north not fit for human beings—so that almost all of it appeared habitable, suitable for human life.

Besides Egypt, there was only one other place that exceeded Europe in blessedness, and that was India. Strabon called it the greatest of all nations and happier than any other.[12] India was not only fertile, but its farmers were good and its fighting men were excellent. Indians were living under orderly government, ruled by the best of men. Indians never set out on warlike expeditions outside of their own country, because of their respect for justice. The land was organized properly in castes just like it had been presented in Plato's *Republic*, with farmers, herdsmen, artisans and merchants plying their respective trades, the soldier class taking care of all military activities, and learned overseers and scholars taking care of public affairs. All rulers and administrators were chosen from the class of scholars. Indians were lean, tall and much lighter in movement than other people.[13]

Strabon's scale of grading areas in terms of civilization was not systematic, but the discrepancies can be explained politically. He praised Europe when he was writing about it, and he praised some other places when writing about them, but clearly his praise of India was stronger than his exultation of European virtues. It might even have been dangerous not to praise Europe and especially the Romans. Strabon's native town Pontus had only recently become incorporated into the Roman Empire, and anti-Roman arguments would not have been considered favourably by the new rulers. India served as a romantic utopia in contrast to the harsh Roman rule. In Strabon's text, and especially in its discrepancies, one can clearly see that power and military might is a metageographical element; perspectives of the powerful tend to strongly influence the way geopolitical evaluations colour our understanding of geography.

Geography of European Enlightenment

The basic elements from Strabon, all the way till the beginning of the Period of Enlightenment in Europe during the early eighteenth century, stayed the same. Greek geographers were considered as the basis of geographic wisdom, and Greek metageographical notions were systematically employed. The idea that Europe represented civilization and Asia its opposite is of much more recent origin than people usually realize. The fact that the Portuguese and later the Spanish were able to get some foothold in Asia from the sixteenth century onwards did not mean that they did not respect Asian cultures. It was only in the realms of religion and seafaring where they thought of themselves as better than Asians. Economically, and in terms of political organization, Asia appeared systematically superior to what the Europeans had.[14] This began to change during the period of the European Enlightenment, Agnew tells the story well, but I would here like to point out the importance of Swedish and Russian collaboration in this turning point of world idea history.

The seminal text attaching Enlightenment thinking to the concepts of Asia and Europe was that of Philip Johan Stralenberg's (1676-1747) *Das Nord und Ostliche Theil von Europa und Asia*, published in Stockholm, in 1730, and translated into English in 1738, as *Russia, Siberia, and Great Tartary (Russia Observed)*. The rhetorical re-description presented in this book was in many senses dramatic, as it for the first time in millennia departed from the descriptions of the Greek ancients. The most well known feature of the book was its re-description of the boundary between Europe and Asia. Characteristic of the situation was that the new Enlightenment narrative spread from the west to east. Europe was the place inhabited by the people whose astounding achievements in the development of sciences, technology, and especially overseas conquest, dwarfed the achievements of all previous generations.[15] Europe was the continent of overwhelming progress, and progress became the new metageographical element shaping the conceptualizations of continents.

The characterization of Europe as progress-centred, was especially a reference to places along the maritime states bordering the Northern Atlantic, the Netherlands, Britain and France. They definitely were European, and nations to the east participated in Europeanness to the extent that they also could be depicted as progressive achievers of great deeds overseas. Pure geographical definitions were found wanting in this ideational climate, not only because they were found to be empirically inaccurate, but also because they did not contain this narrative of progress. Besides, during Stralenberg's time, the boundary issue had already come under discussion. The classical Greek practice of placing the boundary at river Don was not satisfactory, because the Don was not a very long river, and clearly did not divide the land mass into two separate halves. In maps drawn during the sixteenth and seventeenth centuries, religious criteria sometimes replaced classical geographical ones, in the sense that there was a tendency to consider Turkey and Tartaria, or the area under Mongolian rule, as clearly non-European, and the little known kingdom of Muscovia was considered as similar with Tartaria.

The Catholic Hapsburg and Polish Empires, and the Protestant Swedish Empire, on the other hand, clearly were understood as European.[16] In several maps, though not in all, this led to the solution that the Dnepr was adopted as the practical boundary between Europe and Asia, the boundary then going from the upper course of the Dnepr to Lake Ladoga and the White Sea. The boundary thus became a political and religious one, with empires and kingdoms professing the western Catholic and Protestant faiths forming Europe, and everything else being Asia. Stralenberg toned down the use of religious criteria—although of course pointing out that even the Russian Orthodox religion is Christian. Instead, he ostensibly returned to geographic criteria, but in a way that announced the ending of the relevance of geographic criteria in geopolitical argumentation. This is not altogether clear at first sight, because he apparently returned to pure geographic arguments. He nevertheless discarded the basic ancient metageographical notion of continent as a large piece of land separated from others by water. Instead of the Don, Stralenberg wanted to use a mountain range as the boundary between Europe and Asia, declaring:

> From the Ice [Polar] Sea between the mouths of Petšora and Obi Rivers rises a mountain range, which the ancients called *montes Riphæos*, but Russians call it *Kamenoi* or *Weliki Pojas*, which means the Stony or Great Mountain Belt, or they even call it the Belt of the Earth.[17]

Stralenberg is not a poetic writer, and his sentences seldom rise to a level of elegance, but this opening sentence of the new conceptualization displays a rare event of a purposeful attempt to use rhetorical *pathos* to move the minds of his readers. Here Stralenberg writes in a strongly metaphorical way, creating a mental picture of a magnificent stony wall dividing the continent into two halves. *Montes Riphæos* was a name used by ancient Greeks to denote the extreme northern reaches of mythical Scythia. This Stralenberg took to mean the Ural Mountains. That name meant in Stralenberg's time only the southern regions of the area, but later superseded other Russian names. Stralenberg's text was even more metaphorical in view of the fact that the Ural Mountains are not very high, and large areas of the supposed mountains is simply hilly country, between the Russian and Siberian plains, but in his argument the magnificent Belt of the Earth, which connected the Ice Sea with warmer southern climates, was suitable to act as the boundary between Europe and Asia. This reconceptualization simply stated that because it was futile to search for an indisputable boundary formed by water, you should look for something else, and that something else was the Ural Mountains with their grandiose Russian names. Thus Stralenberg effected the dropping of the ancient metageographical notion of Asia and Europe as separate continents in the geographic sense. Yet, even if they were not real continents, they should conceptually be kept strictly apart. This needed argumentation that sounded more geographic. Stralenberg proceeded with the *logos* part of his re-description by giving empirical reasons for accepting the Belt of the Earth as the boundary. I'll present some of them, enough to show his line of argument:

1. In Europe, big rivers run in many directions, such as Veiksel, Düna, Dwina, and Petšora to the north; while Dnepr, Don, and Volga run to the south. In Asia the big rivers, namely Ob, Lena, Irtysh, and Yenisei, run only to the north.
2. The European side of the Ural Mountains is drier, while the Asian side is wet, swampy and full of trees.
3. Rivers on the western slopes of the Urals flow to the west, while the rivers on the eastern slopes flow to the east.
4. In European rivers there are lax and crabs, but in Asian rivers these cannot be found.
5. There grow spruce, oak and hazel in Europe, but larch and fir in Asia.
6. Along European riverbanks you can find small stones of various colours, but in Asia you find grey rock.

We can see that although Stralenberg presented many arguments, they really are not very convincing, if we consider the issue at hand to be re-drawing the boundary between Europe and Asia. Some of the 'facts' he mentions are irrelevant, such as the direction of the flow of rivers, and some of them are even dubious, such as his biological data. The whole *logos* of his argument is oddly empty, distorted and incoherent.

Inferring from the fact that the *pathos* of the argument rested largely on the magnificence of the Russian name for the Urals, it is quite possible that the idea originated from the Russians, and that Stralenberg acted only as a spokesman and publicist for it. The Ural Mountains were a perfectly logical civilizational boundary from a Russian point of view, because they had long served as the boundary between Russia and Siberia, which in the Russian imagination had clearly been distinguished from each other.[18] Russia represented the traditional area of agricultural economy under the practical rule of the Czar, while Siberia was a wild area to the East populated by pagan nomadic populations, hunters, and Russian fur traders, who could not be effectively governed by anyone. What later emerged as the generally accepted European and Asian boundary was originally an intra-Russian division of civilization and way of life.

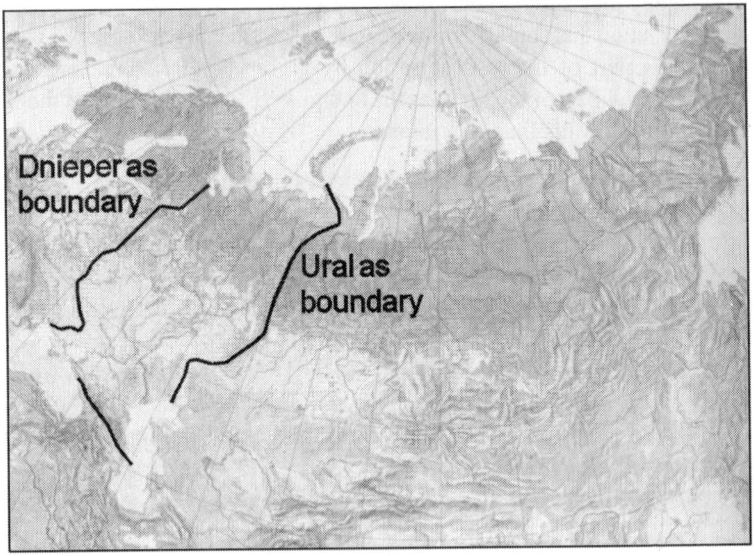

Map 1.3

As a matter of fact, the idea has been credited to Vasiliy Tatishchev, an historian and geographer in the service of Czar Peter I, and as has been pointed out, this is one of the first instances in Russian history when Europe was taken into use as a speech act, whereby Europe was talked and written into existence, in connection with Russia.[19] Compared with the prevalent Western European idea of the Dnepr as the political and civilizational boundary, removing the boundary to the Urals had the effect of moving the rapidly westernizing Russia under Peter I from Asia to Europe. This is the political sense of Stralenberg's rhetorical re-description of the Euro-Asian boundary.

As Mark Bassin argues, in pre-Petrine Russia the orthodox concept of Moscow as the Third Rome had served both as the ideological and geopolitical definition, setting Russia apart from both Europe and Asia, which were irrelevant concepts. Classical Greek geographical theory had been known in Russia, but the continental boundary issue was treated simply in a scholastic manner, with the Don being taken without qualms as the boundary, simply because the whole question of placing the country geographically either in Asia or in Europe was politically and religiously irrelevant. Russia was an Orthodox Christian realm, pure and solitary. With the ascent of Peter I the situation changed drastically during the first quarter of the eighteenth century, exactly when Stralenberg was in Tobolsk as a prisoner of war.

The Petrine ideology adopted western civilizational categories, and with them acknowledged the absolute pre-eminence of Western European civilization. The Petrine reforms—from the ban of beards, and requirement for a German dress at court, to constructing the new capital of St. Petersburg a thousand kilometres west from Moscow—attest to the comprehensiveness of the ideological change. Situating Russia within the Europe-Asia division also became an important political issue. Tatishchev, an ardent supporter of the Petrine reforms, had been given the task by Peter I to construct the geography of the new reformed Russia, and he had also been in contact with Stralenberg, first during his captivity and later in Sweden. Stralenberg seems to have been the first to publish the idea in print; Tatishchev's manuscripts for his geography seem to have become ready for circulation among the Russian elite only during the 1730s, when Tatishchev also wrote a commentary on Stralenberg's book.[20] It is probably impossible to determine indisputably who first came up with the idea of using the Urals as the Euro-Asian boundary, but it seems absolutely clear that the political impulse for the re-description came from the Russians, with Stralenberg simply complying with it.

How should we then interpret Stralenberg's rhetorical redescription in a geopolitical sense? From a later perspective one could understand the situation in terms of the expansion of Europe. Western European colonial empires were definitely expanding at this time, as was also Russia with the victorious wars of Peter I, and it would be easy to equate the two. Western European conceit towards the rest of the world was increasing in leaps and bounds, as was also Russian pride of their own achievements. After the victory over Sweden in 1721, Peter I abandoned the old idea of Muscovia as Czardom, and instead the rank of the ruler was proclaimed to be *imperator*, not mere Czar, and simultaneously Russia was ceremonially proclaimed to be an *imperiia* or colonial empire, similar in rank with Spain, France and Britain.[21] During the nineteenth century

Siberia also was consistently 'Asianized' in Russian discussions, with colonial images relating to its emptiness in terms of population, its exotic ethnic composition, and its economic value as a provider of 'soft gold', namely the expensive furs, whose monetary importance as Russian export articles resembled that of Spanish gold and silver derived from the American colonies. The Russian Empire was conceptually divided into a European Russian metropolis and its Asian colony in Siberia, and similar orientalized language was used about Siberia as western colonial empires used of their own colonies.[22]

However, this represents the mature phase of an established discourse; the situation at hand during the Petrine period was that of the necessity to establish the terms of the discourse in the first place. With the acceptance of the cultural and epistemological superiority of Europe the principal evaluation making audience of Russian rhetoric also shifted to the West. The re-description of the boundary was specifically a Russian argument. Russia first had to be accepted as a European country, and only after that could it pose as a European empire, colonizing vast tracts of Asia. In terms of naming, Russia initially had to move rhetorically westwards, until its physical movement eastwards could be interpreted as European expansion. With Stralenberg's and Tatishchev's rhetorical re-description. Russia left Asia and entered Europe. Stralenberg's book attracted considerable attention around Europe, because first-hand knowledge of Russia as a new great military power in the East had been scarce, and during the subsequent decades it was translated into English (1738), French (1757), and Spanish (1786).

While the narrative of enlightenment and conquest was thus attached to the name of Europe, Asia began to resemble everything opposite, a place to be conquered and colonized. Geography as such became irrelevant in Eurasian geopolitical discussions, civilizational politics clearly becoming the overriding metageographic elements, although this tended to be clothed under the use of geographic language, in the same way that Stralenberg had done. From this time onwards for a couple of centuries, geographic concordance, with the exception of the Oriental Renaissance of the nineteenth century,[23] began to influence nearly everything written about Europe and Asia. This historical phase has nevertheless been studied so thoroughly by others[24] that I shall not touch it here.

Post-War American—Asian Geography

The next period when really interesting changes began to happen was the post—World War II situation, as Western European narrative spinners found themselves in a quite different situation compared with the eighteenth century. The colonial empires crumbled, and European states ceased to be great powers. The concept of the West itself changed.[25] The United States, as the new world hegemonic power, assumed the central position within that concept, and the rest of the West meant a disparate collection of American allies in the Cold War, from Norway and Turkey to Japan and Australia. Simultaneously, Western Europeans lost their previous monopoly for defining themselves, and American discussion on Eurasia became a strong, if not altogether dominating, influence. Americans had little interest in ancient European beliefs, but instead named the Eurasian landmass according to their own geopolitical interests, as an American geographer pointed out in 1951, in an all out rejection of old European naming practices:

> Is the huge landmass of Eurasia one continent or two? The common practice is to slice the Union of Soviet Socialist Republics in two parts along an arbitrary line [...] This so-called continental boundary in the general vicinity of the Ural Mountains follows no significant division of topography, drainage, climate, soils, land use, culture, or history. [...] Europeans have looked eastward to Asia, hence the usage of Near East and Far East. These directional terms have no significance to the people of Asia itself, or to Americans. Accordingly they are not used in this volume [...][26]

Even from a purely geographic standpoint, Americans were not only looking at the Eurasian landmass from the west, behind the backs of Europeans, but also directly from the east, over the Pacific Ocean, and already this fact made much of old European geography of less value for them. In addition, as a great military and economic power with varying interests towards all different political divisions of Eurasia, Americans simply needed more finely tuned divisions than Europeans during the colonial period had needed. The Urals as a boundary, and even the necessity for a boundary between Europe and Asia became largely irrelevant. That definition survived in school geography and family atlases, but the Soviet Union became such an overriding geopolitical entity that it began to acquire the characteristics of a new 'continent'. Especially in maps using the Mercator projection, the Soviet Union became a huge portion of land dwarfing everything else in the landmass, and this happened in a similar way in western as well as Soviet maps. The Ural

Mountains returned to being an inner boundary within the Union of Soviet Socialist Republics.

From American discussion also the name Middle East superseded names like Western Asia, Near East, or Levant, and as a consequence Europe practically ceased touching Asia. As Europe became militarily and politically small, there was no longer any necessity to honour European naming practices, and its geographic area could be contracted to the "Western peninsular Eurasia."[27] It is an interesting fact that this corresponded roughly with the same area where it had been conceptualized during the sixteenth and seventeenth centuries before Stralenberg's reinterpretation.

Map 1.4

The metageographical notion of a continental dichotomy in Eurasia was destroyed by the Americans. The Old World became composed of five politically and functionally meaningful 'continents', namely the old one of Europe, Asia and Africa, and the new ones of Middle East and Soviet Union/CIS. Partly this phenomenon also reflects the fact that residual areas—unknown, uninhabited, and needed by no one—exist no more. This makes the concept of Asia again smaller, corresponding with the thinking of Herodotus, although the exact geographic location of Asia is vastly different. Early twentieth century discussions about Asian unity by such figures as the Japanese art historian Okakura Tenshin and the Indian poet Rabindranath Tagore were still departing from Stralenberg's definition of Asia, and it is exceedingly difficult to find some kind of cultural unity for the whole area east of the Urals. The results are necessarily thin.[28] Breaking the old idea of conceptualization, freed Asians of the necessity to try to find some commonalities with the Russians and Arabs. For instance, the Japanese Ministry of Foreign Affairs has verbally since the 1960s, and graphically since the early 1990s, used a five-fold division of the old world, shown in the map. This is a practical division, which reflects the divisions within the ministry itself. For the purpose of being meaningfully able to conduct its affairs, it has been divided into sections, where knowledge of history, culture, customs, languages, politics, economics, etc., has been concentrated. For any kind of practical administrative purposes Stralenbergian geography does not work, and thus it has been discarded.

The practical result of all this is that Asia has become geographically a much smaller place than contemporary Europeans tend to think, which is directly linked to the fact that there exists an accompanying conscious effort to attach also the properties of an actor to the name of Asia, i.e. Asian regional organizations can nowadays be created. In continental geopolitics, size is essential, as only smallness implies the capability to act. Action involves heavy amounts of multilayered international cooperation and integration, and the larger amounts of sovereign nation-states you have integrating with each other, the messier the results tend to be. Thus, nowadays, under the name of Asia is generally placed countries from Pakistan eastwards and Mongolia southwards, the Pacific and Indian Oceans forming the eastern and southern boundaries. This can sometimes be quite difficult for Europeans to grasp. For instance, despite all evidence that the geopolitical language describing the meaningful divisions of Eurasia has changed, Göran Therborn in his recent discussion of the concept of Asia simply thinks that Asians are wrong, and he knows better what should be counted into Asia.[29]

How to Conceptualize Contemporary Asia

So we have nowadays a smaller Asia than we did before. It is smaller especially in terms of geography, but not really much smaller in terms of population. Even this kind of definition of Asia contains more than half of humanity, and political, military, economic, religious, linguistic and cultural divisions between Asia tend to be serious. We are not talking about an EU-like structure at all. If the European Union can be defined as an organization, where states give up part of their sovereignty for the purpose of creating a larger whole, which would be stronger and more important in world politics than the constituent states separately, in Asia, at least in the case of most states, regional cooperation is taking place precisely to enable the states become stronger as sovereign states, and to consolidate themselves as nations. Of course common bargaining power towards outsiders also has to be taken into consideration, but that is in practice possible only for certain Asian subunits, such as ASEAN, but hardly for Asia as a whole.

More than an integrated area, Asia is a collection of security complexes. One of them is in the south, composed of India and its neighbours, especially Pakistan and China; one in Southeast Asia including Australia and New Zealand, although within ASEAN there hardly has been any violence between countries for decades, but most countries have had disputes with China. The third security complex is situated in Northeast Asia, being composed of Japan, the two Koreas, Taiwan and China, with Japan having varying levels of tension with all of them. China, as the territorially largest state, and being also the most imperialistically oriented, in Hans Morgenthau's old realistic sense, is part of all these security complexes. Because Asia is not a unity, and because both small-scale and large-scale military violence always looms in the possible action horizon, outside powers, especially the United States, have considerable influence in the area.

Asian unity can hardly be seen at the level of citizens, who tend to identify either with their states, or smaller ethnic and regional units within their states. Only at the level of national intellectual, economic and political elitist discussions, Asian cooperation has been thriving during the past two decades. This discussion in its modern form is not old. It is based on the somewhat older discussion of Pacific integration, which started to emerge in Japan in the 1950s, and which led to the establishment of organizations such as Pacific Economic Cooperation Council (PECC) in 1980, and Asia Pacific Economic Cooperation (APEC) in 1991.[30] The basic axis of these organizations has been Japanese and US cooperation with a number of smaller American and Pacific Asian countries. Asia began to be themed around in discussions of economic integration from the middle of the 1980s onwards, for two reasons. For the first, the United States with its economic health being spoilt during the Reagan administration, took an increasingly hostile stand towards the rapidly growing Pacific Asian states with large trade surpluses with the United States. For the second, China entered the economic configuration of the region with force, and this changed also the geopolitical situation. The theoretical economic viability of the Asian side of the Pacific system increased, while a clearly political dimension was added to the tensions with the United States. In addition, Chinese participants entering discussions had influence also on the rhetoric, because they systematically used the term Asia, instead of the Pacific.

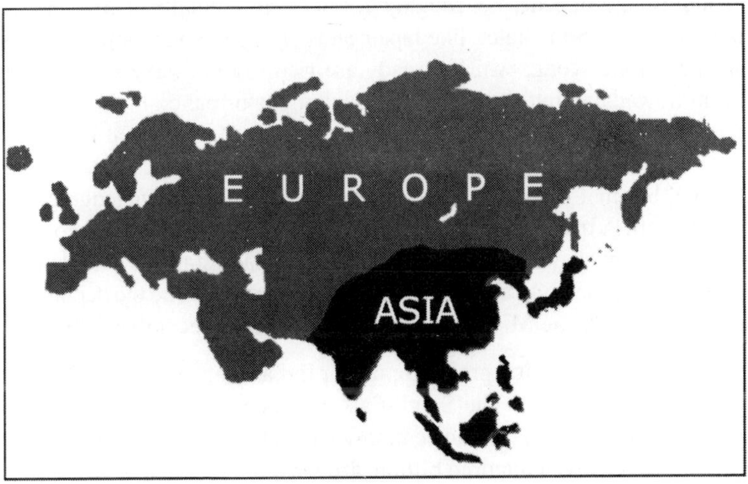

Map 1.5

In a sense the new Asian discussion has meant a return to dichotomous metageographical concepts, because the discussion seldom touches the niceties of sharp divisions in other parts of the world than Asia. The discussion mainly takes place at the eastern maritime states of Asia, and they have, so to speak, monopolized the use of the concept of Asia, much like Western Europeans have tended to monopolize the use of Europe. East Asian states, from Japan to Singapore, represent economic success, and thus they form the nucleus of organizational and rhetorical activity. While concentrating on speaking about Asia as a small region capable of organizing, they at the same time necessarily treat the rest of the Eurasian continent as a residual category, and unless specific names are given to that area, as the Japanese Foreign Ministry does, the non-Asian part of the landmass necessarily has to be Europe. Europe also unfailingly comes up in discussions when it turns to history, because only the West, meaning Europe in the past and the United States backed by the European Union nowadays, is a factor strong enough to create a meaningful conceptual unity in Asia. With some personal experience I can say that many Europeans find it rather startling to find themselves placed into a residual category, but that is the way the world changes.

Simultaneously, a new metageographical element is added. This time it is not civilization, politics, or religion, but economic performance. Many Asian states may be poor, but the norm defining inclusion to that chosen group of countries is economic growth of the order of doubling the economy in a decade, i.e. roughly 7.2 per cent annually. This is not an ideal; this is a norm. States, like Japan, and corresponding political entities, such as Hong Kong, which already are rich, do not have to fulfil this norm nowadays, but they have had such a performance in the past. All poor states either have to attain the rate of growth, or they at least have earnestly to strive for it. In practice there are exceptions, such as Myanmar/Burma, but that does not destroy the existence of the metageographical norm itself. A true Asian country is an economically successful country, but defined by way of a process, and not as a steady state, as would be the case in EU Europe. As evidence for the argument I can cite the declaration of the Indian Prime Minister Manmohan Singh in December 2005.

> I find there is a great support for India's engagement and India's involvement. The South-East Asian countries recognise that a fast-growing Indian economy with a Gross National Product of over seven hundred billion, growing at the rate of seven to eight per cent, has (a) beneficial impact on growth processes in South-East Asia as a whole.[31]

According to Singh, getting closer to East Asia has been an important goal of Indian diplomacy ever since the formation of its Look East policy in the early 1990s, and now after clearly fulfilling the Asian metageographical growth norm, India can approach East Asia with confidence, relying on the support of the ASEAN countries in the process.

Asian Regional Organizations as Name Politics

Prime Minister Singh uttered those words on his way to participating in the first East Asian Summit, which was held in Kuala Lumpur, on 14 December, 2005. It has been called an historical event, because it was the first time such a meeting of Asian heads of states took place under such a name. The organizational etymology of this meeting goes back to the tumultuous year of the post-Cold War period, when new forms of constructing the international situation in the Asian Pacific area were being sought. In 1991, the Malaysian Prime Minister Mahathir Mohamad proposed the formation of an East Asian Economic Caucus, which would have been composed of ASEAN, Japan, South Korea and China, and which would have been led by Japan. It was also described as a caucus without Caucasians by pundits. At that time the organization was not established, principally because the United States vehemently opposed the creation of a potentially important international organization, where it was not a member, and which also potentially could have adopted an anti-American agenda. As a consequence the Japanese government refused to go along with Mahathir's proposal, and the idea was buried as such, but over the years it developed into an arrangement called ASEAN+3 (or APT), where leaders of Japan, South Korea and China used to have a special meeting with ASEAN leaders in connection with ASEAN's annual summit meetings. ASEAN+3 started to convene during the Asian Financial Crisis in 1997 to discuss mutual help in handling the situation. The main point of this arrangement has been to gather together and discuss mutual financial, trade and security relations, while avoiding a name that would suggest an anti-American organization. Over the years ASEAN+3 has acquired the character of steady cooperation not only on head of state, but also at ministerial and bureaucratic levels.

A somewhat related forum has been the ASEAN Regional Forum, established in 1993, dedicated to discussing security and political matters, and which nowadays includes, in addition to ASEAN, Australia, Canada, China, European Union, India, Japan, Democratic Peoples' Republic of Korea, Republic of Korea, Mongolia, New Zealand, Pakistan, Papua New Guinea, Russian Federation, Timor Leste, and the United States. It is an open-ended process, where new members constantly have been added over the years, the only criterion being that the activities of members should have some bearing on security issues in Northeast and Southeast Asia.

Thus also the EU is a member. Many Asian international organizations tend to grow in size in terms of membership and geographical area exactly because the principle of exclusivity is applied with utmost care, especially towards great powers. The purpose of these organizations is the management of mutual interdependences, and that is best done by gathering state representatives together to talk. No spectacular achievements or grand decisions are usually made in these meetings, and that is not even their purpose. As it is said in the ARF home page, "cultivation of habits of dialogue" among potentially conflicting states is one of the basic goals of the organization. Decisions should be made by consensus, which means that major decisions cannot be made at all. Decision making is not the purpose of ARF, but rather "moving at a pace comfortable to all," which means a very low pace.

In addition, both ARF and APT have been successful organizations in their own terms because their activities have been organized around ASEAN rather than any great power, and that is symbolized also by their names. There is no official leadership, and no special goal, except the creation of stability in the area for the purpose of economic development and state consolidation. ARF meetings, just like the APT meetings, are venues for multilateral as well as bilateral diplomacy. They are not actors by themselves, but diplomatic space for state representatives to act according to a formal set of rules. They are thus examples of international society.

The idea of placing APT activity openly under a clear name displaying Asia resurfaced after a decade, when Mahathir's successor, Malaysian Prime Minister Abdullah Badawi, suggested discussions about the idea of an East Asian Community, at the 2004 ASEAN+3 meeting. The name East Asian Community is a direct reference to the European Economic Community/European Union, and potentially would have meant the creation of an exclusive regional organization, which perhaps could become an actor, and not only a venue. Badawi won immediate backing from China's Prime Minister Wen Jiabao. Both China's recent interest in multilateral diplomacy and resurfaced anti-American feelings were important factors in renewing the discussion. China has to an extent replaced Japan as a possible leader in the area, and at the same time it cautiously seems to be trying to create a sphere of action independent of the United States. The Shanghai Group, with Russia, Kazakhstan and Central Asian states is one example of this, and China's agreement to form a free trade area with ASEAN by 2010 is another.

On the other hand, there has been widespread exasperation with the United States during the administration of George W. Bush. They have not shown any special interest in Asia, and especially since September 2001, American foreign policy has concentrated on the War against Terrorism, which has little meaning to Asian countries as such. The Bush administration has used even the annual Asia Pacific Economic Cooperation (APEC) summits for spreading its anti-terrorist agenda as a global strategy, while practically all Asian members would have been willing to regard terrorists as a police matter, requiring no doubt some amount of international collaboration, but nothing more. Instead, Asian countries would have liked to concentrate on trade, investment and finance issues within APEC, which would have been much more sensible for them. By concentrating on the War against Terrorism, the United States during the first half of this decade succeeded in losing a considerable amount of its political influence in Asia, and irresponsible American economic policies, possibly placing the whole global economic system into jeopardy, and thus potentially seriously harming also the Asian states, have eroded also American ideological influence.

Badawi's original idea seems to have been only to place ASEAN+3 under a new name and increase its scope and depth. Subsequent diplomatic manoeuvering by Japan seems to have made considerable changes in the membership. To balance China's rising influence in the area, it demanded that also India, Australia and New Zealand, are allowed to participate, and especially in Australia, fairly strong governmental circles had, ever since Mahathir's original proposal, demanded access to existing East Asian organizational arrangements. This finally became possible after Australia and New Zealand signed with ASEAN a *Treaty of Amity and Cooperation. The name of the meeting was agreed to be East Asian Summit (EAS), although it might as well have been called simply Asian Summit because of its geographic composition.*

The agenda of the inaugural meeting was not very ambitious. In practice the summit meant only a few hours of common talks of Asian leaders, plus ample possibilities for bilateral diplomacy. Clearly, the EAS did not start on the road to form itself into a tight regional organization capable of united action, but rather the events seem to point towards another ARF—type venue. Japan's Prime Minister Koizumi Junichiro declared before and also during the conference that the continuation of good relations between Japan and the United States is a precondition for Japanese participation in Asian integration,[32] which perhaps indicates that Asian integration still is a worrisome project outside of it. The leadership of the United States tends to regard any attempts to distance the superpower from Eurasian geopolitics with suspicion.

The term 'community' did not appear in the final communiqué of the meeting, but instead the EAS decided to establish itself as a permanent meeting.[33] The only other concrete decision from the meeting was another joint declaration of combating the avian flu.[34] Apparently also the question of the location of future meetings was discussed, the result being that they would not be held in any of the major regional major locations, such as China, but always in connection with ASEAN summits in some ASEAN country. Thus, although the name changed, the organizing ethos remained the same. The same can be said of the second EAS held in Cebu, the Philippines, on 15 January, 2007. This time publicity around the summit was much lower than during the inaugural conference, but discussions seem to have been more concrete, centreing on ways to maintain rapid economic development, especially regarding problems of energy security.[35]

Activities in Asian international organizations as a norm are not dramatic, but rather extremely boring. Nothing especially interesting seems to take place, but a new organization is added, or a change of the name of an existing organization takes place, once or twice in a decade. No one is in a hurry, except perhaps outside participating powers such as the United States, and all activities tend to follow the sacred norm of 'moving at a pace comfortable to all', and especially to those that want to move slowly. That does not mean this is not serious business. The temporal framework simply is wide. A state has to react to events fairly rapidly, within days, weeks or months, normally, and it has the capacity to do that.

A relatively tight and established international organization, such as the European Union, works in a somewhat slower temporal framework, but nevertheless it has the capacity to contemplate budgetary decisions and policy alternatives in such diverse fields as common foreign policy, agricultural policy, or the Bologna process in education at the pace of a year. In Asian international organizations the smallest meaningful temporal unit of analysis may be a decade, and a longer meaningful unit is that of a generation. This temporal framework can be discerned very clearly for instance in the speech that Prime Minister Wen Jiabao gave at the East Asia Summit.

> Looking ahead, we are full of confidence. Our goal is to double China's per capita GDP of 2000 by 2010, and after that, to bring China's GDP to US$4 trillion and its per capita GDP to US $3,000 in another 15 years. This will turn China into a country of moderate prosperity. [...] For China to be fully developed, it will take the unremitting efforts of several generations, or even a dozen generations of the Chinese people. China thus needs a

> durable and peaceful international environment that enables it to concentrate on economic development.[36]

The temporal sense is very natural. The goal of attaining the level of moderate prosperity is within reach. If everything goes all right, that stage could dawn in 20 years from now, i.e. within a generation, and within the life time of most Chinese living at present. Not only are most of Asian states still in a transition process from weak to strong states, in Barry Buzan's terms, but economically most of them either are still growing or have until recently been growing at a pace of more or less doubling or tripling their GNP in a decade. The relative capacities of Asian states can change a lot during a decade, and there is no wish to harden the system in any way that would inhibit that. Because a collection of loose discursive structures works, nothing is broken, and there is no reason to fix anything drastically. Because rapid change is taking place at the state level, the organizational level can move forwards to greater levels of complexity very slowly.

Notes

1. Gerard Delanty (ed.), *Europe and Asia beyond East and West* (London and New York: Routledge, 2006).
2. See also, Pekka Korhonen, *Ajia no Nishi no Sakai*, (Kyoto: International Research Center for Japanese Studies, 2000)]; Korhonen, "Aasiaksi nimetty tila," *Kosmopolis* 33, no. 1: 9-37; Korhonen, "The Concept of Asia," in *At the Crossroads of Europe, Asia and Africa*, Zeki Kütük (ed.) (Turku: University of Turku, Department of Contemporary History Researches 29), 103-23.
3. Martin Bernal, *Black Athena. The Afroasiatic Roots of Classical Civilization*, vol. 1, *The Fabrication of Ancient Greece 1785-1985* (New Brunswick, NJ: Rutgers University Press, 1987); *Black Athena. The Afroasiatic Roots of Classical Civilization*, vol. 2, *The Archaeological and Documentary Evidence* (New Brunswick, NJ: Rutgers University Press, 1991).
4. John Agnew, *Geopolitics. Re-visioning World Politics* (London and New York: Routledge, 1998), 85-7.
5. Herodotus, *Herodotus*, IV [Loeb Classical Library, Cambridge, Mass. and London: Harvard University Press, 1990 (c. 440 BC)], 42.
6. Herodotus I, 104-6, 130.
7. Herodotus IV, 37-41.
8. Herodotus IV, 45.
9. Herodotus IV, 13-36.

10. Herodotus IV, 64-73.
11. Strabon, *The Geography of Strabo*, vol. 2 (Loeb Classical Library, Cambridge, Mass. and London: Harvard University Press, 1968-82), 4, 5-7.
12. Strabon, vol. 2, 5-32.
13. Strabon, vol. 15, 1, 59-73.
14. Andre Gunder Frank, *ReOrient: Global Economy in the Asian Age* (Berkeley: University of California Press, 1998); Pekka Korhonen, "Asia's Chinese Name," *Inter-Asia Cultural Studies* 3, no. 2 (2002): 253-70.
15. W.H. Parker, "Europe: How Far?" *Geographic Journal* 126 (1960): 280.
16. Parker, 281-4.
17. In original: *Erstlich erhebet sich zwischen der Mündung gedachten Pytziora und Obi Strohms und von dem Eiß-Meer ab, ein Gebirge, so die Alten montes Riphæos, die Rußen aber Kamenoi oder Weliki Pojas (das ist: steinerne oder grosse Felsen-Gürtel, ja wohl gar Poyas Semnoi, das ist Gürtel der Erden), nennen.* Ph. J. von Strahlenberg, *Das Nord und Ostliche Theil von Europa und Asia*, Studia Uralo-Altaica 8 Szeged: Attila József University, 106.
18. Mark Bassin, "Inventing Siberia: Visions of the Russian East in the Early Nineteenth Century," *American Historical Review* 96 (1991): 7.
19. Iver B. Neumann, *Russia and the Idea of Europe. A Study in Identity and International Relations* (London and New York: Routledge, 1996), 2-12; Martin W. Lewis and Kären E. Wigen, *The Myth of Continents. A Critique of Metageography* (Berkeley: University of California Press, 1997), 27-8.
20. Bassin, "Inventing Siberia," 4-7; Marc Raeff, "Russia's Perception of Her Relationship with the West," *Slavic Review* 23 (1964): 13-19.
21. Bassin, "Inventing Siberia," 5.
22. Mark Bassin, "Russia Between Europe and Asia: The Ideological Construction of Geographical Space," *Slavic Review* 50 (1991): 763-75.
23. Raymond Schwab, *The Oriental Renaissance. Europe's Rediscovery of India and the East, 1680-1880* [New York: Columbia University Press, 1984 (1950)].
24. See Bernal, *Black Athena*, vol. 1; Edward Said, *Orientalism. Western Conceptions of the Orient* (London: Penguin, 1995); Victor Kiernan, *The Lords of Human Kind. European Attitudes to Other Cultures in the Imperial Age* (London: Serif, 1995); Lewis and Wigen, *The Myth of Continents.*
25. Patrick Thaddeus Jackson, *Civilizing the Enemy. German Reconstruction and the Invention of the West* (Ann Arbor: The University of Michigan Press, 2006).
26. George B. Cressey, *Asia's Lands and Peoples. A Geography of One-Third the Earth and Two-Thirds Its People* (New York, Toronto and London: McGraw-Hill, 1951), 12.

27. Cressey, *Asia's Lands and Peoples*, 13.
28. Pekka Korhonen, "The Political Geography of Okakura Tenshin," *Nichibunken Japan Review*, no. 13(2001): 107-27.
29. Göran Therborn, "Post-Western Europe and the plural Asias," in *Europe and Asia beyond East and West*, Gerard Delanty (ed.) (London and New York: Routledge, 2006), 31-2.
30. Pekka Korhonen, *Japan and the Pacific Free Trade Area* (London and New York: Routledge, 1994); Korhonen, *Japan and Asia Pacific Integration: Pacific Romances 1968-1996* (London and New York: Routledge, 1998).
31. Manmohan Singh, Media Briefing by Prime Minister Dr. Manmohan Singh on board Special Aircraft to Kuala Lumpur to attend 4th India-ASEAN Summit and 1st East Asia Summit, 2005, http://meaindia.nic.in/, visited 10.01.2006.
32. Junichiro Koizumi, Press Conference by Prime Minister Junichiro Koizumi Following the ASEAN+3, Japan-ASEAN and EAS Summit Meetings, 2005, http://www.mofa.go.jp/region/asia-paci/eas/press0512.html, visited 10.01.2006.
33. East Asian Summit, Kuala Lumpur Declaration on the East Asia Summit, 2005, http://www.mofa.go.jp/region/asia-paci/eas/joint0512.html, read 10.01.2006.
34. East Asian Summit, East Asia Summit Declaration on Avian Influenza Prevention, Control and Response, 2005, http://www.mofa.go.jp/region/asia-paci/eas/joint0512-2.html, visited 10.01.2006.
35. Gloria Macapagal Arroyo, Chairman's Statement of the Second East Asia Summit, 2007, http://www.mofa.go.jp/region/asia-paci/eas/state0701.html, visited 22. 04. 2007.
36. Wen Jiabao, *China's Peaceful Development: An Opportunity for East Asia*, 2005, http://www.fmprc.gov.cn/eng/wjdt/zyjh/t228273.htm, visited 10.1.2006.

2

Euro-Asia: Cartographic Representations and Imaginations

From a European Perspective

Rudolf Wastl

Continents are usually considered to be the first sub-division of our world on a global scale and surrounded by water. But Europe and Asia are different. Europe is like a peninsula on the western end of the Eurasian landmass, but is nevertheless known as a continent. Europe and Asia were constructed as spatial entities mainly by physical criteria, but also in order to portray a relatively strong and well developed Europe, as separate and different from the remaining landmass, in the last centuries. The dividing line in cartographic representations has changed several times and has not really contributed to the construction of a functional geographical entity called Europe.

With the enlargement of the European Union (EU) Europe and its eastern boundary have been dealt with more often and have been used as an argument for and against further enlargements especially in political discourse. An example which characterizes this use was when the Prime Minister of Turkey, Erdogan, on his visit to Germany to promote the Turkish request of an EU membership, claimed, "Geography teaches that Turkey is a part of the European continent."[1] Precisely such calls on geography to provide a clear cut delineation of Europe lead us once again to deal with the following questions:

1. How was Eurasia divided between Europe and Asia by geographers and cartographers over the last centuries and is it still the case?

2. Is another regionalization of the world on a global scale, such as world regions, more appropriate?
3. Can a clearly defined Europe be constructed by overlaying several European institutions and organizations?
4. How is Europe in a broader global sense imagined by Europeans and to what extent do these imaginations fit with the ones presented here?

These questions will be addressed geographically and cartographically. This approach provides a comprehensive perspective of the essay by analysing existing maps, and the drawing of new maps to explore it from different points of view. Initially the formal continental division of Europe and Asia will be explored by analysing atlas maps from Asia, Europe and the US. In the second part, Europe as a functional entity will be constructed in the sense of a regional approach. This will be done by analysing Europe as a world region as well as the different institutional and organizational concepts of Europe. For this purpose different cartographic representations will be provided to explore multiple perspectives of Europe. Because of the significant changes in the political order, the scope of 'multilayered organizational Europe' over the last 22 years also will be discussed. Finally, the results of an empirical study concerning the imagined geographies of Europe will be compared with the existing cartographic representations.

Geographic Europe: The Continental Division of Europe and Asia

Europe is one of the traditional continents, but the idea of a landmass completely surrounded by water does not apply. In this case, the European continent is not natural because the boundaries of Europe are not naturally defined. They were and still are questionable, and are often adapted to political, economical, social and other realities, i.e. they are culturally constructed.

The Austrian geographer E. Lichtenberger argues that the awareness of Europe in the modern age began as a confrontation of the Christian Occident versus the Ottoman Empire.[2] With the Europeanization of the world, the eastern boundary had been shifted eastwards until 1730, when the Swedish scholar Philipp Johan von Strahlenberg suggested it on the main range of the Ural Mountains and along the Manych depression. Korhonen argues that it was at this time a perfectly logical boundary from the Russian point of view with the effect of moving the rapidly westernizing Russia from Asia to Europe.[3] In the middle of the nineteenth century, the German Geographer Carl Ritter and the French Elisée Reclus suggested setting it slightly east of the mountain range along the rivers Ob and Toboi (not clear. Found no such river) because this dividing line is the lowest above sea level. In most cases, physical features were and still are being chosen for the boundary although the continent itself is fragmented in terms of physical geography. According to old globes and world maps, the eastern boundary on the Ural Mountains has been accepted more or less up to now even though it has been scrutinized critically all times, for example by the German geographer Hettner at the end of the nineteenth century.

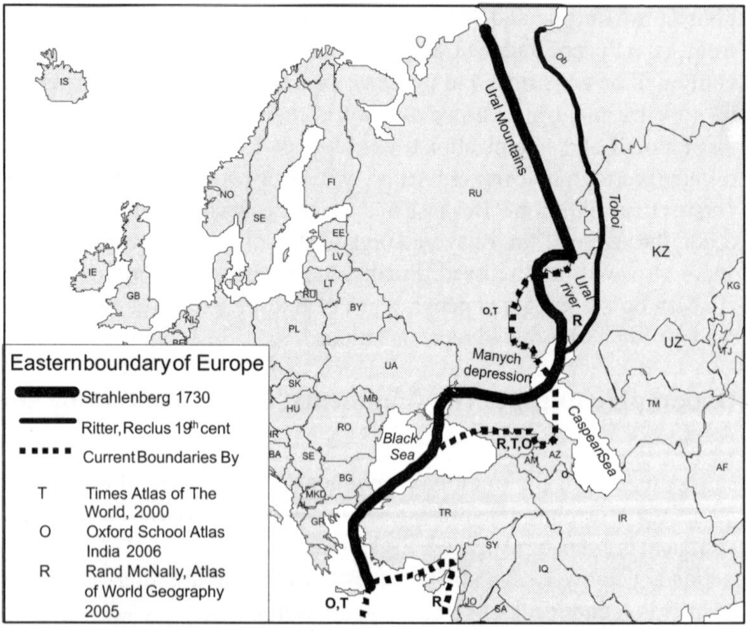

Fig. 2.1: Continental or geographic Europe in selected representations

Continental classifications are mostly portrayed on globes and atlas maps. They seem to describe "realities" in an objective way with a view from above. Although they do not portray a "reality" but rather an "imagined reality" of the map designer, the publisher or another map patron,[4] it makes them powerful tools to shape understanding. Especially when used by students for the first time in their life, atlas maps contribute more intensively to the imagination of the world than any other kind of media. That is the reason why school atlases from different continents were analysed in a short sample. The question was: If and in what way were Europe and Asia differentiated in actual atlases? The results can be summarized and characterized by three types:

1. Political and physical atlas maps of Europe and Asia present the countries and physical features of both continents to their full extent without the continental division. Examples are the Dierke Weltatlas as well as the Perthes World Atlas used primarily in European schools.
2. This basically follows the previous point. The continental division is visualized by a striking dividing line. Europe is described as a cluster of peninsulas and islands extending from northwestern Asia. Examples are the atlases edited by the National Geographic Society.
3. Political and physical maps portray only the content for the designated continent while other parts are blank or only shown with a basic map. The Ural Mountain Range serves as dividing line. In a few cases Russia is presented twice—in the map for Europe as well as Asia. Examples are the Rand McNally Atlas of World Geography used in the US, the Dorling Kindersley Student Atlas used in UK and the Oxford School Atlas used in India.

In the European atlases, the map content does not end with a dividing line between Europe and Asia. But a formal continental division obviously still exists in slightly different positions in school geography, at least in the English speaking world. In some US atlases only natural features are used as the dividing line, for example, the Ural Mountains, the Ural River and even the main range of the Caucasus which divides Georgia and Azerbaijan into European and Asian parts. This corresponds widely to the traditional idea of naturally divided continents. On the other hand, state borders are also partially used as the western border of Kazakhstan in the Indian atlas. This corresponds more to the idea of dividing different functional entities.

However, considering that Russia and the former Soviet Union were divided between two continents, and that continental Europe is not identical with any European functional region, this kind of boundary has little or no effect on everyday life. But it has a certain influence on the image of Europe and Asia and on the self-image of the people. In practice geographic Europe is usually used for statistical purposes and to describe the world in manageable continental regions but also to argue politically for or against the EU membership of Turkey or maybe Russia. However, a definite eastern boundary of Europe as a continent cannot be provided by geography.

World Regions: A Functional Approach

Having seen that a formal and natural environment based conceptualization of Europe and Asia certainly is in use but not necessarily congruent with spatial interaction and organization, another regional approach shall be discussed, namely, the concept of world regions.

Well known US geographers use this concept as a spatial classification scheme for textbooks on world geography. Marston *et al.* define world regions as large-scale geographic divisions based on continental and physiographic settings that contain major clusters of humankind with broadly similar cultural attribute such as Europe, Latin America or South Asia.[5] Cultural and political differences are also used to distinguish between world regions instead of exclusively physical features. World regions are described as dynamic, with changing properties over time and fluid boundaries or transitions zones instead of permanent, sharp boundaries.

A little different from Marston *et al.* Bradshaw arranges world regions by emphasizing cultural characteristics combined with functional and political interaction within world regions and with other regions.[6] He describes Europe as the home of mainly Christian religious groups, capitalism and modern industrial technology and argues that Europe increasingly is defined as comprising those countries that identify themselves as present or potential members of the European Union.

From a different point of view, De Blij and Muller portray Europe as territorially small and politically fragmented, but disproportionately influential in global affairs.[7] Some consideration that the EU might challenge the dominance of the United States in global affairs could be derived from this description.

Besides these differences, the eastern boundaries of the investigated world regions of Europe are only partly different in several textbooks. All include the EU with 27 member states and the other states of the Balkan Peninsula—some also include Belarus, Ukraine and Moldova (see Fig. 2.2). The western part of Russia is represented as outside of Europe. Russia is usually described as the dominant part of another world region such as the Commonwealth of Independent States by Bradshaw. The

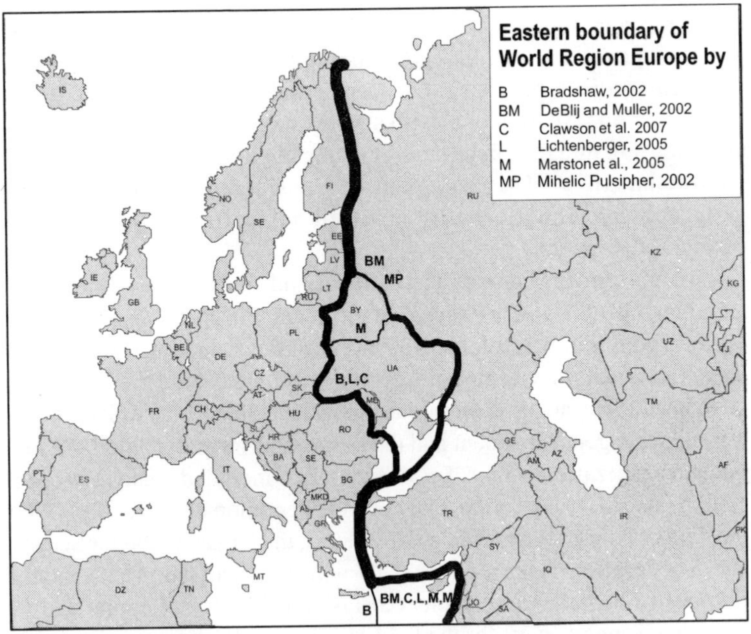

Fig. 2.2: Eastern boundaries of world region Europe in selected textbooks

remaining parts of Asia he describes as Southern and Eastern Asia as well as Northern Africa and South-Western Asia. Similar to his description the Asian continent is subdivided into four or five world regions in all investigated textbooks. Turkey is positioned outside of Europe in all cases.

Varied boundaries for geographic Europe as well as different and varied ones of the world region Europe clearly show that geography cannot derive a clear cut eastern boundary of Europe for physical, cultural political and other phenomena together. Europe can be constructed, portrayed and interpreted in different ways depending on the actor's point of view. The following section will focus on Europe as a functional region based on organizational linkages.

"Institutional" Europe: A Multilayered Project without Common Boundaries?

Considering the Cold War era and the enlargement of the EU, Lichtenberger provides a more functional approach.[8] She conceptualizes Europe as a project on supranational level for legislation, administration, economic and social affairs above the participating nation states to promote peace as well as economic and social development. This European project, the EU, is not seen as static, but in progress, in two directions: on a spatial level with several stages of enlargement and as an increasing integration by strengthening the EU institutions and other contractual ties. EU-Europe can be considered as one of several geographical, functional or institutional entities, visualized by cartographic layers.

To portray the idea of institutional and multilayered Europe the membership of states of several significant European institutions or organizations will be explored where several fields and intensity levels of cooperation will be addressed. According to Lichtenberger's description three institutions are used on supranational level: the EU as well as the EU related Schengen Agreement and the European Monetary Union. Another major organization which for decades has included many European countries, with strong contractual ties and integration effects is NATO. For the field of politics, on the cooperative level, the Organization for Security and Cooperation in Europe (OSCE) will be discussed. The Union of European Football Associations (UEFA) for the area of sports and the Eurovision song contest for the field of culture will be discussed as well.

In many cases, the membership of states in international organizations is visualized in tabular form. According to the suggestions of Crampton the complex and multilayered institutional Europe will be visualized in three steps in order to make spatial relationships visible by using multiple perspectives and multiple map displays.[9] In the first one, the spatial dimensions of each institution will be addressed, showing smaller and larger concepts of Europe in a series of analytical maps. In a second step the membership of states to different organizations will be emphasized with a cartogram. In the final step, the level of integration over time will be visualized with a European integration index.

According to an order from the smallest to the largest spatial extension of organizations the European Monetary Union is to be addressed first. At the moment only 16 out of 27 EU countries fulfil all criteria and are thus members of the Monetary Union and using the Euro as official currency. Within the next years other EU countries will join it.

Besides 22 EU countries as well as the non-EU members Iceland, Norway and Switzerland are full members of the Schengen Agreement. The Schengen area enables free movement without border control within the area, while the outer border is controlled more intensively. Two EU countries Ireland and the United Kingdom participate only partly and still maintain their own border regime. The EU members Bulgaria, Cyprus and Romania do not fulfil the criteria yet and might join the Schengen area later. Both the European Monetary Union and the Schengen Agreement support common interests on supranational level and are closely connected with a strong integration process from the EU.

Since the beginning of 2007 and for its 50th anniversary, the European Union has 27 member states. The process of integration is supported by a package of measures such as common symbols, standards and directives as well as exchange and cooperation programmes of various types. But in everyday life the EU is also present in cartographic form, portraying statistical and empirical data concerning, e.g., unemployment rate or university access in the EU member states in the news and other media.

These three European institutions have the strongest integration effects because of their supranational character. But nevertheless they don't form a unified whole (see Fig. 2.3) and their boundaries change when new members join. Besides these EU-related organizations focusing on the legislative and administrative integration of their member states, other organizations representing a larger Europe have considerable effects on the integration and conceptualization of Europe.

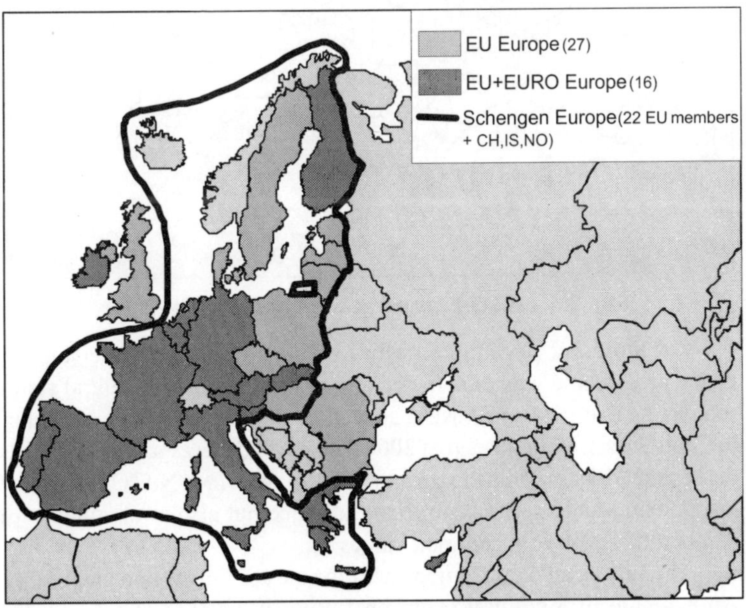

Fig. 2.3: European Institutions 2009

The first organization to mention is NATO, established as the military alliance of Western Europe, the United States, Canada and Turkey at the beginning of the Cold War deterring its opponents by providing an enormous military power. After the collapse of the Soviet Union and the Eastern European military alliance, the Warsaw Pact, NATO has expanded very quickly. It has expanded more rapidly throughout Eastern Europe than the EU and now includes not only the former Warsaw Pact members in Eastern Europe but also in the former Soviet Republics Estonia, Latvia and Lithuania.

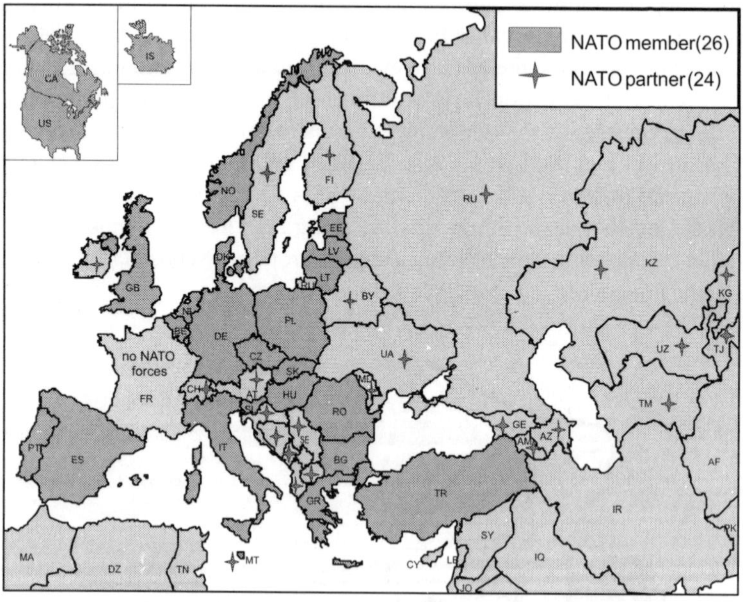

Fig. 2.4. NATO-Europe at the beginning of 2009

For those not planning on a full membership, the Partnership for Peace programme was established and was joined by the neutral states such as Switzerland and Austria as well as the former Soviet Republics in Central Asia. With the end of 2006, Bosnia and Herzegovina as well as the separated states Montenegro and Serbia have joined NATO PfP. Today NATO is not only seen as a military alliance but also as an alliance of democratic states with common values.

The European organizations next in size are Eurovision and UEFA. An example of a cultural event on European level is given with the Eurovision Song Contest. The European Broadcasting Union organizes a song contest once a year. Most European countries participate but Turkey and Israel participate as well. In 2007, Georgia, Armenia and Montenegro as well as Serbia took part for the first time.

In terms of sports, the Union of European Football Associations (UEFA) supports European interaction by running national and club competitions such as the European Football Championship. Compared to the Eurovision song contest Kazakhstan and Azerbaijan are also members of UEFA. In both cases, a wider Europe is represented also including Israel and Turkey.

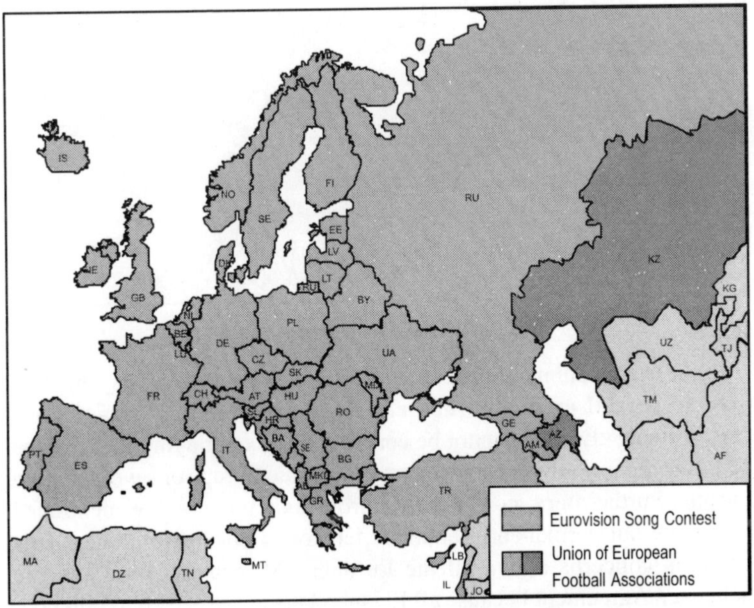

Fig. 2.5: European cultural and sport organizations

The largest European organization to be mentioned here is the Organization for Security and Cooperation in Europe (OSCE). With 56 members, it also includes the US and Canada as well as the former Soviet Republics in Central Asia, the latter on historical reasons. With the foundation in 1975 OSCE served as a platform for confidence-building measures primarily between NATO headed by the US and the Soviet Union dominated Warsaw Pact. Today OSCE acts as a significant platform for conflict prevention, crisis management, arms control and anti-trafficking.

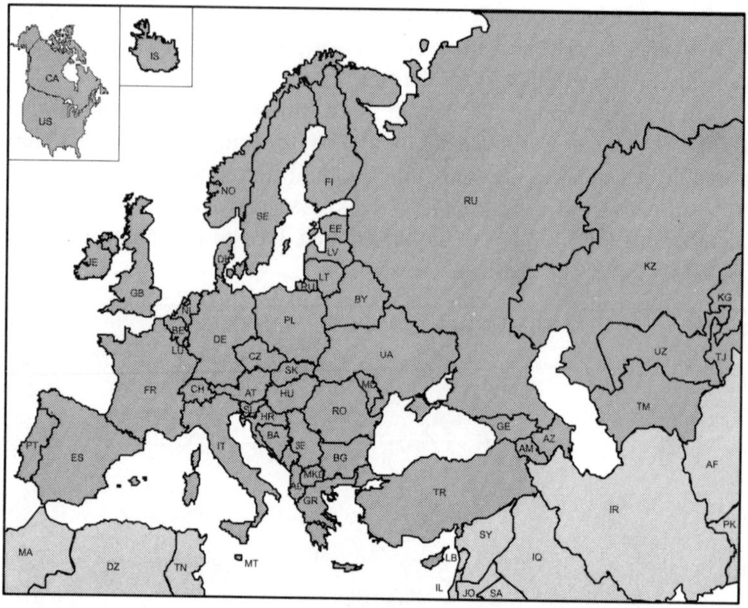

Fig. 2.6: OSCE—Europe 2009

The examination of European institutions and organizations with their diverse spatial extension has clearly indicated that a single one "institutional" Europe cannot be constructed by overlaying them. None of these organizations exactly covers geographic Europe or a world region Europe. Furthermore, considering Europe as a process, the mentioned layers are not permanently bounded territories but flexible ones. This situation concerns above all the European Monetary Union and the Schengen Agreement because all EU members are expected to join both institutions.

Up to this point, the spatial extent of each institution or organization was portrayed by using single maps. With another cartographic representation the intensity of an organizational integration into Europe is summarized and visualized. Every country is portrayed with a rectangle of the same size and its membership to an organization by a respective bar. With this cartogram (Fig. 2.7) while the number of memberships to organizations is focussed on, the spatial extent of the states and organizations is not taken into consideration.

The countries with more intensive organizational entanglement are located in the western part forming a kind of core area from Portugal via

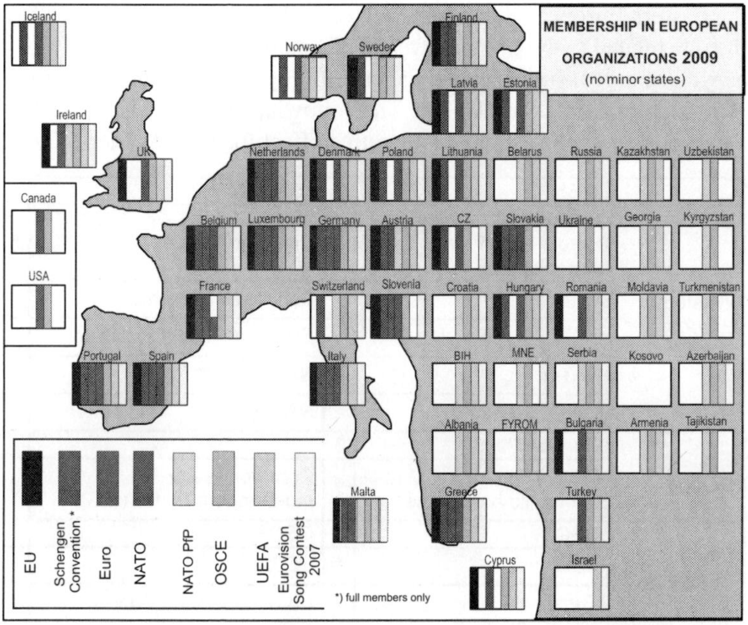

Fig. 2.7: Membership of states in selected European institutions and organizations 2009

Germany up to Finland. The less integrated ones are located in the eastern and south-eastern part appearing as a kind of periphery, or even a transition zone to Asia such as the countries east of the EU. Once again, the cartogram reveals a fragmented Europe without clear boundaries but fluid transition zones.

Having examined the integration effect of states into Europe through each individual state's membership to an organization in 2009, now the integration effect will be portrayed in a series of synthetic maps to represent snapshots over time. For this purpose, the mentioned organizations were weighed according to their assumed integration effect and summed up as an integration index. The method of an index and the used weight of index factors can be discussed from different perspectives but it serves well to summarize and visualize the time line of different levels of integration. It starts with the divided Europe in 1985 and continues to the new world order of 1995 and 2007. Taking the starting point to be the Cold War and the divided Europe at this time, the index covers the Western European and EU related integration. It also covers the Eastern European integration related to the former Soviet Union and the one related to the Commonwealth of Independent States (CIS) today as well as organizations covering entire Europe already during the Cold War such as OSCE and UEFA. The following weighted index factors correspond with the assumed integrating effect for 1985 and 1995/2007.

	1985	F	1995/2007	F
Western Europe	European Community or European Free Trade Association	3	European Union	5
			Schengen Agreement	3
			European Monetary Union	3
	NATO	3	NATO	3
			NATO PfP	2
Eastern Europe	Warsaw Pact	3		
	Council for Mutual Economic Assistance	3	Commonwealth of Independent States (CIS)	3
Entire Europe	OSCE	1	OSCE	1
	UEFA	1	UEFA	1
	Eurovision Song Contest	1	Eurovision Song Contest	1

Fig. 2.8: European integration indices 1985, 1995, 2007

The divided Europe of 1985 is clearly visible and Western European integration was mainly driven by the European Community and NATO, on a lower level. In 1995, after the fall of the Iron Curtain, the former Soviet allies in Eastern Europe and even some former Soviet Republics joined NATO PfP and Western European ties were strengthened while Eastern European ties have been weakened. In 2007, the EU and its related institutions have intensified Western European integration on a supranational level. The portrayed Western Europe excepting Turkey also corresponds to the world region by Bradshaw and some others. Regarding Europe as a functional region with intense organizational interaction obviously leads to similar spatial extension of world regions based on cultural and political conditions.

In summary, it may be said that Europe can be regarded as a multilayered institutional and organizational entity on different levels of integration with a core area in the western part and a kind of transition zone to Asia without a permanent bounded territory and quick organizational development. In addition, it can be recognized that not a single European institution/organization covers the same territory as one of the world regions or the described continents of Europe. This conclusion leads to the next question: "To what extent do the imagined geographies of Europe fit to the represented ones?"

Imagined Geographies of Europe: An Empirical Study[10]

To test these imagined geographies an empirical study was done in Austria, Switzerland, Czech Republic and China. 423 university students participated and about one third of them were geography students. This is not representative for all Europeans and Asians but it is a good sample for a first impression. Central European participants had a physical map of Europe, western and south-western Asia and the northern part of Africa from different atlases—Chinese students had either a physical or a political map of Eurasia. In all the maps, state borders were included, as well as the names of larger states and major cities. They were asked, "In your opinion, which parts should belong to Europe and not to Asia?" Chinese students were asked "In your opinion, which parts should belong to Asia and not to Europe?" Then they were asked to draw the suggested dividing line on the map. In a second question, they were asked to reveal the reasons for their decision.

The result is *consistent* only for the southern sector of the dividing line (see Figs. 2.9 and 2.10). Turkey is generally not imagined as a part of Europe. 86 per cent of Central European and 74 per cent of Chinese participants allocated Turkey to Asia arguing strongly that Turkey had a culture and religion different from Europe. This is exactly the opposite of the quoted statement of the Turkish Prime Minister.

The suggested dividing line in the northern part of the Eurasian landmass is *inconsistent*. Generally speaking Central European participants imagine a smaller Europe, Chinese a bigger one. The smallest was indicated by Austrians (Fig. 2.9) followed by Swiss, Czechs and students in Hong Kong; the biggest one in Zhuhai in Mainland China (Fig. 2.10). Some Chinese even included some Central Asian Republics and Iran in Europe.

In terms of features as dividing line three major ones were chosen:

1. 50 per cent of European and 53 per cent of Chinese participants decided for natural features as dividing line—the Ural Mountains and the Ural River. Most of the arguments were based unequivocally on natural feature and for others, mainly Chinese, because they had learned it in school.
2. The Russian state border primarily on the western but also on

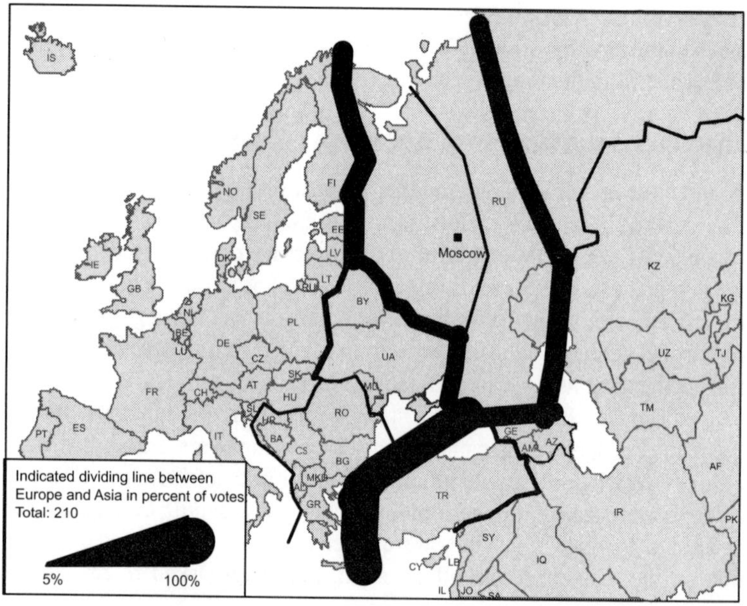

Fig. 2.9: Imagined dividing line between Europe and Asia by Austrian participants

the eastern side was indicated as dividing line. Chinese participants revealed that they did not want to separate Russia into two parts. 38 per cent of Central European participants assigned Russia completely to Asia. Their major reason was not the integrity of the state but the different political and economic situation present in Europe and Russia.

3. The eastern boundary of the EU 27 was also used as dividing line by up to 15 per cent of the respondents, mainly the Austrian participants.

Both imaginations along the western border of Russia and the eastern boundary of the EU 27 correspond widely with the earlier discussed concept of world regions. Also the argument for placing the dividing line on political and economic reasons indicates the functional approach of a division. This was primarily used by European students.

Chinese students usually followed a different approach. Their arguments were not based on economic and political reasons but rather on cultural ones like lifestyle, language, music and surprisingly on colour of skin (10 per cent).

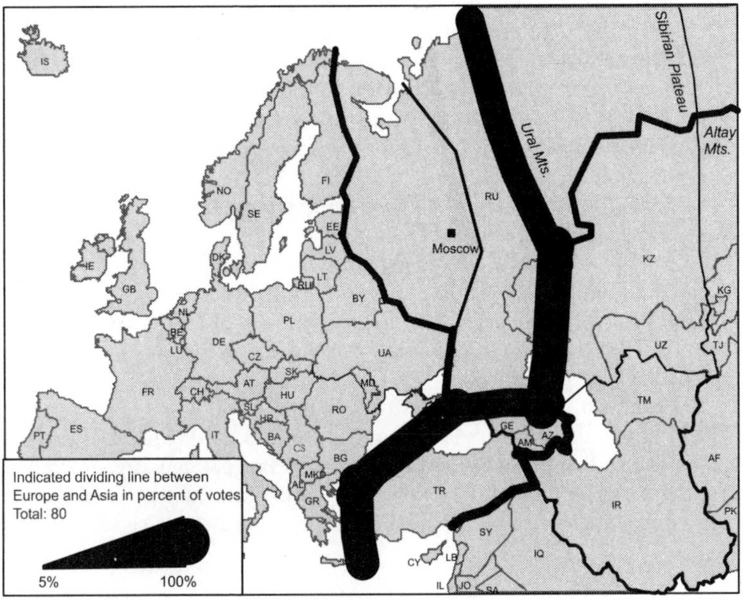

Fig. 2.10: Imagined dividing line between Europe and Asia by Zhuhai participants

Conclusion

All in all, many different conceptualizations of Euro-Asia can be seen. The traditional division of the Eurasian landmass in two separate continents to arrange geographic knowledge of the world seems to have come to a final stage. Obviously, it is still present in school geography, some atlases and imaginations. Other imagined geographies such as world regions have appeared, strengthened by a more functional approach without clearly and strictly bounded areas, but rather as multilayered and fluid regions with strong political, economic and cultural connections to each other. Geography works together with analytical and visualization tools to find understandable spatial patterns and to construct a new model of a better integrated and connected Euro-Asia.

Notes

1. *Der Spiegel* 41 (2004): 29.
2. Elisabeth Lichtenberger, *Europa—Geographie, Geschichte, Wirtschaft, Politik* (Vienna: Primus, 2005), 14.

3. Pekka Korhonen, "On the Metageography of Euroasia: Are there 'Two' or 'Three' Continents on the Eurasian Landmass?" Paper presented at the international conference *Revisiting "Euro-Asia" Cultures, Connections and Conceptualisations*, Chandigarh, India, 13 February 2006.
4. W. Jeremy Crampton, "Maps as Social Constructions: Power, Communication and Visualization," *Progress in Human Geography* 25, no. 2 (2001): 241.
5. Sallie Marston *et al.*, *World Regions in Global Context*, 3rd ed. (Upper Saddle River: Pearson, 2008), 5.
6. Michael Bradshaw, *World Regional Geography*, 2nd ed. (New York: McGraw-Hill, 2002), 14.
7. H.J. De Blij and Peter Muller, *Geography: Realms, Regions and Concepts*, 11th ed. (New York: John Wiley & Sons, 2006), 20.
8. Lichtenberger, *Europa.*
9. Crampton, "Maps as Social Constructions," 244.
10. I kindly thank my research partners Doris Wastl-Walter (University of Berne), Petr Dostal (Charles University, Prague) and Werner Breitung (University of Hong Kong and Sun Yatsen University, Guangzhou) for doing the respective empirical investigation at their university.

3

The Geopolitics of Domination and the Clash of Imaginations in Central Eurasia: Continuity and Change

Sanjay Chaturvedi

We might think of imaginative geographies as fabrications, a word that successfully combines 'something fictionalized' and 'something made real' because they are imaginations given substance.[1]

Geopolitically, America is an island off the shores of the large landmass of Eurasia, whose resources and population far exceed those of the United States. The domination by a single power of either of Eurasia's two principal spheres—Europe or Asia—remains a good definition of strategic danger for America—Cold War or no Cold War—for such a grouping would have the capacity to outstrip America economically, and, in the end, militarily.[2]

Eurasia is the world's axial supercontinent. A power that dominated Eurasia would exercise decisive influence over two of the world's three most economically productive regions, Western Europe and East Asia. A glance at the map also suggests that a country dominant in Eurasia would almost automatically control the Middle East and Africa. With Eurasia now serving as the decisive geopolitical chessboard, it no longer suffices to fashion one policy for Europe and another for Asia. What happens with the distribution of power on the Eurasian landmass will be of decisive importance to America's global primacy and historical legacy.[3] (Emphasis given)

Against the backdrop of the long-drawn shadow of the East-West Cold War, that was officially pronounced as over with the collapse of the Soviet Union in the late 1980s, we seem to be passing through an era of excessive geopolitics, marked by the forceful assertion of geographies of domination and the underlying "violence of abstraction"[4] in certain parts of the globe. And yet *again* it is the same old part of the Eurasian space called 'Central Asia' (New Central Asia), marked by increasingly fuzzy boundaries, that seems to have emerged as the 'geographical pivot' of competing (at times even clashing) imaginative geographies of the so-called 'New Great Game'.[5]

The major argument in this paper is that as the twenty-first century unfolds, we are likely to witness growing contestation over the meaning of Eurasian space. After all, "space is an effect of practices of representation, valorization, and articulation; it is fabricated through and in these practices, and is thus not only a domain but also a 'doing'."[6] The 'new' strategic salience of Eurasia, therefore, needs to be approached and understood not simply in terms of "spaces of places"—ranging from 'local' to 'national' to 'global'—but "spaces of flows, practices and representation" which challenge the conventional understandings of a static geographical scale, and in turn compel foreign policy, military and commercial establishments as well as analysts to rethink their mental maps, and correspondingly reorient themselves. Moreover, I wish to argue and illustrate that in the post-Cold War era, the quest for energy security in Eurasia,[7] consciously or unconsciously, is getting implicated in rapidly converging geographical imaginations related to the geopolitics of energy resources, "militant Islam,"[8] "clash of civilizations" and terror (ism). The implications of such convergence, especially in the aftermath of the tragic events of September 11, are likely to be far reaching for peace, conflict-resolution and international cooperation in the region.[9]

I would like to clarify at the outset that for purposes of this paper, when I look at Central Eurasia (or for that matter Eurasia), I deliberately approach and understand it not as very precise but as a dynamic, functional and contested *space* (extending from Central Europe to East Asia and from Siberia to the Himalayas) formed by various imaginative geographies of major powers (the old and the new), deployed in pursuit of primacy. And what I understand by "clash of imaginations" is not simply how the major powers imagine Central Eurasia and implant maps of meaning on such diverse and heterogeneous landscapes but also how these actors read certain meanings into each other's imaginative geographies.

Visualized in this manner, Central Eurasian space looks like a canopy open on all the sides and compels us to further explore how power continues to create space(s) on a continuous basis, rather than the other way round.[10]

What is happening *in* and *about* 'Central Asia' is also quite revealing in terms of how through imaginative geographies "regions are spoken into existence,"[11] which indicates that, "it is external agency that *speaks* the Central Asian region into existence—to the extent that it is international actors that are involved in articulating the boundaries of the region and positioning Central Asian countries into a category of states that share similar characteristics. In this setting, the suggestion is that a multiplicity of international actors has been involved in packaging and repackaging the geographical and geopolitical ramifications of Central Asia."[12] What is worth exploring is how, as suggested by the first epigraph above, imaginations (as outlines for example in the second and the third epigraph) are given substance through the geopolitics of domination and geographical struggles. In other words, what demands investigation is how the 'real' is being disciplined and manipulated in such a way that it fits into the imagined.

The Geopolitics of Domination and Geographical Struggles: The Material and the Symbolic

Geopolitics, according to some scholars, is about "geographical struggles over power, space, and resources."[13] It is also about how the world is to be imagined, understood and represented in the theory and practices of statecraft. According to Yves Lacoste, "Whatever its territorial extension (global, continental, state, regional, local), and the complexity of the geographical data (relief, climate, vegetation, distribution of population and activities), a geopolitical situation is defined, at a given moment in historical evolution, by rivalries between powers on a large scale, and by relationships between forces in different parts of the territory in question."[14] It is important to note, as Lacoste points out, that states engaged in the pursuit of primacy often find themselves entangled in power rivalries. At the heart of many such rivalries are contested claims to the possession and control of certain territory.

According to yet another definition (in my view one of the most insightful ones, and of particular relevance for this paper), the essence of geopolitics is that it is politics and not geography; a geographical politics, that is, "politics in which concepts and ideas about a geographical area (for instance, the territory of the fatherland) play an important, often decisive role. Political Geography tends to be descriptive; it is 'geography as an aid to statecraft'. Geopolitics on the other hand, tends to be prescriptive. In other words, it wants to be statecraft itself'. If we review the history of geopolitics—from Ratzel through Mahan, Kjellen, Mackinder, Haushofer, De Gaulle, and Kissinger—we notice that most of those who contributed to the store of geopolitical thinking were themselves deeply committed, whether professionally or not."[15] Critically approached, "geopolitics is a discourse concerned between power-knowledge and social and political relations."[16] According to ÓTuathail,

> The focus of critical geopolitics is on exposing the plays of power involved in (a) grand geopolitical scheme.... Fundamental to this process is the power of certain national security elites to represent the nature and defining of dilemmas of international politics in particular ways.... These representational practices of national security intellectuals generate particular scripts in international politics concerning places, peoples and issues. Such 'scripts' then become part of the means by which [great power] hegemony is exercised in the international system.[17]

According to Derek Gregory imaginative geographies at the same time imply, "Representations of other places—of peoples and landscapes, cultures and 'natures'—that articulate the desires, fantasies and fears of their authors and the grids of power between them and their 'Others'."[18] As I will argue and illustrate in the following section, imaginative geographies, therefore, create and legitimize certain 'worlds', which, in some cases, may be marked by geo-economic hopes or geopolitical fears, or both.

Eurasia in Classical Geopolitics: The Seduction of the 'Heartland'!

Sir Halford Mackinder (1861–1947), a British political geographer, is undoubtedly an outstanding example of how imaginative geographies, rooted in imperial impulses, are carefully woven around both ideological and material threads in order to produce a theatrical effect of perceived threats and dangers emanating from certain spaces, and how, in the process, such spaces are transformed (both discursively and through practices) by the 'role' they were recruited to play by the powers that be. Mackinder viewed "the rise of Eurasian continental states as the greatest threat to

British world hegemony."[19] While admitting the historical importance of sea power in the rise and decline of great powers, he grudgingly acknowledged that at the beginning of the twentieth century there was the possibility of a Eurasian land power (be it Russia, Germany or even China, and especially an alliance of the first two) gaining mastery of the resource-rich "Geographical Pivot of History" (which he later named as Heartland) and thus outflanking the importance of the maritime world. As Cohen points out, "the impact of Mackinder's thinking spanned half a century, and ideas were the cornerstone for generations of strategic policy makers. His view of the world became the basis for Lord Curzon's imperial strategies in South Asia and South Russia, for German *geopolitik* between World Wars I and II, and for Western containment strategies of the post-World War II era."[20]

Mackinder imaginatively divided the globe into three primary strategic regions or zones. First and foremost was the Eurasian core that comprised the Geographical Pivot of History later renamed *Heartland;* the closed heartland of Euro-Asia. The *inner or marginal crescent* included the marginal regions, around the heartland's periphery, including Western Europe, the Middle East, the Indian subcontinent and most of China. And the *outer crescent*, consisting of those regions separated from the heartland and the inner crescent by the seas, including the entire Western Hemisphere, Britain, Japan, and Australia. Mackinder tried to persuade his British audience in 1904 that each of the three zones marked on the globe by him had a geographically determined role to play in global politics. Absolutely critical to the outer crescent states in the post-Columbian epoch (which, according to Mackinder, was going to be dominated by the heartland power) was the preemption of the rise of a powerful eastern European state, which would become the presumed gateway to the Heartland. Mackinder also perceived the flat, open northern plain as a natural highway to the vast potential of the Heartland, which, at all costs, had to be kept divided or fragmented, for: "Who rules East Europe commands the Heartland. Who rules the Heartland commands the World of Islands. Who rules the World of Island commands the World." In other words, Mackinder's advice to the declining British Empire was that no single state or a coalition of states should be allowed to dominate the Eurasian landmass, and the failure to do so would definitely result in the rise of a world empire.

Nicholas Spykman, a US scholar of international relations rejected the land-power thesis of Mackinder. For Spykman the Rimland (Eurasian coastal land including Maritime Europe, the Middle East, India, Southeast

Asia, and China) was the key to the struggle for world primacy and control on account of its rich resource endowment, populations and their use of interior sea-lanes. He criticized Mackinder for having overemphasized the potential of power-generating aspects of the Heartland, while underplaying the dynamic interplay between land power and maritime power. Spykman modified Mackinder's geopolitical reasoning and renamed the Eurasian landmass the W*orld Island.* He went on to argue that the Rimland was vulnerable to both land and sea power and therefore by virtue of necessity must be ready to respond to both types of forces. The patterns of global power balance were, according to Spykman, dictated by and large by the alliances *within* the Rimland and *among* Rimland and Heartland/outer crescent powers. Spykman replaced the now famous Mackinder dictum with his own: "Who controls the Rimland rules Eurasia. Who rules Eurasia controls the destinies of the World." Such utterances are typical of the geopolitics of domination.

Mackinder's Pivot-Heartland thesis has also been criticized by a number of analysts as overly simplistic, deterministic and one-dimensional. According to ÓTuathail,

> Underpinning this [Mackinder's] argument is an unquestioned ethnocentrism, an ethnocentrism that initially sustained the belief that certain regions of the world political map were blank, undiscovered, and unoccupied and is now proclaiming the world political map a close system of space, settled, occupied, and named. The barbaric chaos of unknown space has been replaced by the civilizational certainties of the scientifically unveiled, one and only true geography of the planet. In not recognizing that geography is as much a political domination and cultural imagining of space, Mackinder's "end of geography" thesis could be described as triumphalism blind to its own precariousness. All through, of course, it was precisely to alert the ruling class of the empire to the precariousness of the British hold on global space that he spoke. What Mackinder does not anticipate...is that the British, European, and more generally, Western domination of global geopolitical space would be challenged profoundly in the new century. The struggle over geography had only begun.[21]

Mackinder's Heartland thesis has its supporters and admirers too.[22] Colin S. Gray, writing 'in defense of the Heartland' would argue that "Mackinder's geopolitics is a superior example of grand theory" and it "may have been born out of his anxiety for the security and prosperity of the British Empire, but if anyone early in the twentieth century wrote in a definitively global context, it was he."[23] For Gray, "The Pivot-Heartland theory rested upon geographical realities. Such is the arrangement of the continents that potentially lethal menaces to the security of the West plausibly could come only from the Eurasian landmass. Some critical theorists may disagree, but Mackinder's concepts were hewn out of bedrock. The concept of the Pivot-Heartland is of course a constructed one, but it reflected material facts and truth about location."[24]

The 'New Great Game': Implanting New Maps of Meaning on Central Eurasia

After the disintegration of Soviet Union in 1991, the former five Soviet Republics of Turkmenistan, Kazakhstan, Uzbekistan, Kyrgyzstan, and Tajikistan have now emerged as sovereign, independent, entities.[25] Apparently, these republics were not ready for independent status and all that it demands and dictates in a globalising world, and were rather 'forced' into it. Even the people of Central Eurasia had not anticipated the sudden collapse of the USSR. According to some analysts, they did not perhaps know "whether to celebrate their liberation from the Soviet Union or to grieve the passing away of their protector and benefactor."[26]

The post-Soviet Central Asian republics have become objects of wide-ranging geopolitical interests, imaginations and representations, as the result of a new mapping of their space, people and resource endowment. In some imaginations, the disintegration of the Soviet Union has opened up a 'geopolitical vacuum' in Eurasian space, which historically speaking had constituted a 'critical buffer' between Russia, China and the Islamic world. The global media too has been building various future scenarios for the newly independent states of the region: speculating over their centrality and/or marginalization role in post-Cold War international relations, prospects of a regional union, membership in various political and economic 'blocks' and 'ties' to the Muslim East. Whether the new possible alliances and alignments in the region would include 'common market of Turkic states' (with an anti-Iranian orientation), a Turkic-Iranian alliance that challenges Arab interests, or a bloc of Islamic states opposed to both the West and Russia, continue to be debated with much curiosity and interest.

This renewed interest in Central Eurasia and various imaginations about the 'centrality' of the region are in some ways reminiscent of the nineteenth century Great Game (a term coined by Rudyard Kipling) between the Russian Empire and the British Empire. But the so-called 'New Great Game' is said to be characterized not only by a far greater number of players or participants but is seen as unfolding in a far more complex, globalizing, and competitive world (witnessing the Rise of Asia) of both state and non-state actors.[27] If the old Great Game was about high politics, colonialism and military conflict, then the 'new' one is said to be more about the scramble over resources, especially oil and gas, as well as various competing attempts to gain control over trade and transit routes. The manner in which once retarded, and even lost, economic, cultural and geopolitical ties between the Central Eurasia and the rest of Asia, including the Middle East, are being resurrected and restored will have a significant bearing on the future of the Central Asian states.[28] What provides an extraordinary complexity to the imaginative geographies that feed into and flow out of the so called 'New Great Game', is that various state and non-state actors (including United States, and Russia, China, Japan, Turkey, Iran, Saudi Arabia, Pakistan and India) as well as multinational corporations are introducing into the region their respective strategic perceptions, priorities and policies,[29] which are likely to impact both the present and the future of the polities and societies of Central Asia. For instance, in the context of the Cold War "ideological geopolitics,"[30] Iranian-Turkish or Saudi-Iranian or India-Pakistan equations did not matter much to the Central Asian states under the Soviet regime. All that has changed now; the dialectics and the dynamics of these 'rivalries' are likely to have some impact on the strategic perception, priorities and policies of Central Asian states. At present both the big powers, the US and Russia—and regional powers like Turkey, Iran, Pakistan and India—are pursuing and promoting their respective agendas of energy security in the context of growing contestations over the pipelines routes carrying Central Asian oil and gas.[31] A number of pipeline projects however remain mired in various fault lines.

The manner in which some of the leading state actors approach and 'construct' Central Eurasian space in their respective geopolitical imaginations is the subject matter of the brief discussion that follows. It needs pointing out that the intention here is not to cover the entire gamut of relations between the major players in Central Eurasia and the post-Soviet Republics (far beyond the scope of this paper), but to show how new maps of meaning are in the process of being implanted on the Central Eurasian landscapes. I wish to argue that these maps of meaning, and the geopolitical imaginations in which they are grounded, throw some light on the outside-inside perceptions, priorities and policies on Central Eurasia.

Iran, on the whole, seems to have adopted a *pragmatic* approach towards Central Asia. Some analysts are of the view that while Iran supports the upsurge of Islam in Central Asia, it does not intend to export the ideology of Islamic revolution to these states. Similarly, Iran is not playing up the linguistic factor with Tajikistan, which is the only Persian speaking country in Central Asia.[32] Iran also appears to be of the view that close linkages between Central Eurasia and West Asia would enhance the non-Arab content in regional policies, and thereby help Iran in moderating the numerical advantage that the Arabs possess.[33] Iran continues to emphasize its location both as the centre of the world energy map and as a bridge between Asia and Europe and Central Asia and the Caucasus. Such a pragmatic emphasis underscores the need for investment in the infrastructure field of energy transfer and north-south pipelines, development of railroad and road networks. However the deployment of the word 'region' for Eurasia by the foreign policy establishment of Iran seems to be marked by some kind of calculated ambiguity, which seems to vary from context to context. Against the backdrop of the fast deteriorating state of USA–Iran relations, marked by a huge deficit of mutual trust, Tehran has expressed serious concerns over "the installation of the missile defense shield in the region."[34] According to Shireen Hunter, "Iran's policy toward Central Asia and Caucasus has been security-driven. Thus Iran's highest priority has been to safeguard its security and above all its territorial integrity. This security-driven policy, coupled with the de-ideologization of Iran's overall foreign policy and growing importance of national interest, has emphasized state-to-state relations rather than close ties with the region's Islamist movements."[35]

Turkey, deriving maximum possible mileage out of its ethnic-linguistic affiliation with most of the Central Eurasian Republics (with the exception of Persian speaking Tajikistan), has been systematically aiming at establishing a firm 'foothold' in practically all domains. Shireen Hunter would argue, "A principal purpose of Turkey's foreign policy toward Central Asia, Caucasus, as well as some other parts of the post-Soviet space, has been to make Turkey the new hub and centre of a new version of Eurasianism."[36] This new version, given Turkey's NATO membership has a western orientation,[37] which seems to be resisted by Moscow, leading to some kind of a tension in Turkey-Russia relations. Another major goal of Turkey's 'skilful diplomacy' towards Central Eurasia appears to be the 'containment' of geopolitical influences exerted by wealthy Saudi Arabia, Iran and Pakistan.[38] Turkey's self-image appears to be that of a 'role model' for the Central Asian Republics struggling through economic transition, as well as some kind of a 'bridge' between them and the western market economies.[39] "In addition to Eurasianism, Turkey's policy towards Central Asia has been influenced by a mild and almost cultural form of Pan-Turkism."[40]

Pakistan, locked up in hostile relations with allegedly 'Hindu' India, appears to have welcomed the rise of the 'Muslim' Republics of Central Asia. Pakistan perceives itself well placed to offer to this richly endowed, but landlocked region, a convenient outlet to the sea. In return, Pakistan would expect Central Eurasian republics to provide her with some 'strategic depth', new 'Islamic allies', and 'collective security' partners in its conflict with India. Besides, Central Eurasia could possibly prove to be a valuable market for Pakistani goods. In Pakistan's geopolitical calculations, such perceived economic benefits combined with common Islamic ties should provide a 'natural' base for Islamabad to project its political influence in the region. However many would argue that Pakistan's capacity to influence events in Central Asia has been limited due to its own domestic turmoil and economic difficulties.

As far as India is concerned, the emergence of Independent Central Eurasia has presented before it both challenges and opportunities.[41] The collapse of the Soviet Union as a superpower has led to a number of security concerns for India. In the emerging strategic-security maps of India, issues such as border realignment, ethnic disputes, resurgent Islam, and civil war in some parts of Central Asia, are likely to undermine the territorial integrity of Afghanistan, provide further fillip to centrifugal tendencies in Pakistan as well as Iran and thereby make the Kashmir issue far more complex. India's strategic planners perceive serious consequences flowing from such a scenario for India's national security. In the Eurasian geopolitical calculus of India the growing Chinese presence and participation in the region's affairs, especially through the Shanghai Cooperation Organization (SCO) has received a great deal of attention and assessment.[42] According to some analysts, "In the event of the best case scenario unfolding, Central Asia would emerge as a bridge joining various regions and a meeting point of diverse cultures. The worst case scenario would be the major powers clashing over resources and spheres of influence that may destabilize the entire region with adverse fall out on (the) Indian security environment."[43]

Russia, struggling to overcome its imperial nostalgia, still perceives itself as some kind of a 'guarantor of stability' in Eurasia. Russia also seeks to protect and expand its economic presence in Central Asia, as a part of a larger effort to revive its regional economic, and hence geopolitical, influence. Despite the fact that all the five landlocked Central Asian republics now have the choice of seeking alternative energy supply routes through Iran, Pakistan, China, and Afghanistan, and not depend on Russia alone, Moscow continues to locate Central Eurasia squarely within Russia's "legitimate sphere of influence."[44] The presence of a numerically strong Russian diaspora in Central Asia, particularly in Kazakhstan, and the widespread use of the Russian language (the regional languages are yet to become the working languages of the Central Asian republics), provides Moscow with a geopolitical excuse to flag 'natural' ties with the new polities and old societies of Central Asia, and retain Russian presence and influence in the region.[45]

In Russia's current threat perceptions and related foreign policy pronouncements the geopolitical discourse of Islamic threat has overwhelmingly focused on the post-Soviet Tajik experience. Moscow has alleged that the Tajik opposition is externally inspired and sustained. No doubt Iran's role has been repeatedly mentioned or implied, but it is the Tajik-Afghan cross-border activities that seem to have provided Moscow with the pretext to justify Russia's military presence in Tajikistan, especially in the borderlands. For Russia, the Tajikistan-Afghanistan border constitutes "the border of the civilized world" on behalf of which Moscow is compelled to perform the role of a stabilizer security provider. A number of analysts remain fairly sceptical of USA and Russia co-operating in Central Asia in the medium to long term span. For example, Ilan Berman would argue that,

> Remedial measures, such as a cooperative counter terrorism strategy for the region or direct U.S. investment designed to revitalize Russia's ailing energy infrastructure, could certainly diffuse some of the pressure at least temporarily, but policy makers in Washington would do well to recognize the long-term incompatibility of U.S. and Russian regional priorities. For the Kremlin, remaining the dominant player in the post—Soviet space is not simply a matter of political prestige; this role has increasingly become an economic necessity. For the White House, meanwhile, the continued independence of the fragile regional republics, not to mention their pro-Western political orientation, remains critical to the long-term success of the global war against terrorism.[46]

The clash of imaginative geographies over Caucasia (between the Westerners and the Russians) is an excellent example of how places and their inhabitants are implicated in fabricated images, and stereotypes the pursuit of the geopolitics of domination. As Ronald Grigor Suny puts it so succinctly,

> Caucasia has been for Russians and Westerners a place marked by the exotic and (the) savage, majestic beauty and legendary heroes, attractive because of its differences, dangers, and distance from metropolitan centers. For centuries Russians travelling in Caucasia have depicted that mountainous land as a mysterious, even enchanted place, where the locals are savage and noble, the terrain majestic and wild, and the rivers always turbulent. Exoticizing Georgia, Armenia, and Azerbaijan even today has its dangerous effects in the occasional Russian demonization of Caucasians as bandits, terrorists, and cheats. Caucasia's most famous son, after all, was one of the greatest tyrants of the twentieth century, a global menace to Western values and its political and military hegemony—Joseph Stalin. But for Russians, and it turns out the West as well, the distances of the past have shrunk, and the allure of the exotic has largely been replaced by strategic concerns and the mundane politics of oil and gas. Caucasia has become a contested terrain, not only among the indigenous peoples, but also between its former imperial overlord, Russia, and ambitious new players, the United States, the European Union, and NATO. And an obscure conflict in a hitherto unknown place, South Ossetia, has led to a major rupture between the West and the revived "East."[47]

Against the backdrop of Caucasia becoming an area of contestation between East and West, like most of post-Soviet Eurasia, there appears to be a widespread fear in the corridors of power in Kremlin that the White House is yet to fully abandon the Cold War mindset and is bent upon isolating and containing a 'resurgent' Russia. Here is a clash between two strands of the post-Cold War geopolitics of domination, namely "Russia's Caucasian policy, which revolves around its long-term interest in re-establishing its regional hegemony in the so-called Near Abroad, and the United States' grander ambition for global hegemony."[48] Russia has resisted, with all emphasis at its command, the alleged penetration of the South Caucasus (the southern tier of the former Soviet Union, namely Caucasus and Central Asia) by the United States, NATO, and the European

Community. Backed up initially by 'soft power', "Russia's move is not a programme of imperial control, but rather a determined effort to contain or even roll back the influence of other powers, most importantly, the United States and NATO in the regions closest to Russia's borders."[49] After August 2008, a far more assertive Russia appeared to be conveying the message that it was prepared, if pressurized by the West, to use "hard power."[50]

Afghanistan, among the various regional actors of Central Eurasia, is widely perceived as "most strategically located."[51] A fragmented polity with multiple, conflicting centres of authority, Afghanistan is also seen as the dangerous place of poppy production, and 'staging ground' for various groups of Afghan Mujahidin trying to infiltrate neighbouring Tajikistan and forging various cross-border ideological (Islamic) and ethnic solidarities. In the eyes of both the Russian and Uzbek governments, Afghanistan is a source of material and ideological support for the ongoing civil war in Tajikistan. This has led to greater anxiety in and around Central Asia with regard to Tajikistan and Afghanistan, themselves becoming the objects of regional and extra-regional, military and political intervention. The developments in Afghanistan seriously undermine the prospects of this country acting as one of the 'gateway' states for access *into* and *out of* the land-locked Central Asian republics, especially into the Indian Ocean region. The prospects of the resurgence of age-old trading links and political ties between Balkh, Herat and other regions of Afghanistan with the rest of Central Eurasia too, are undermined.[52]

Due to its contiguity to Central Asia, overwhelming physical size, fast pace of economic growth, and nuclear-military might, China has emerged as a potential competitor for Russia and other major players in Eurasian geopolitics. China's relations with the new Central Asian states are said to be one of the key factors shaping the post—Cold War order in Asia and beyond. No longer bordered by a super-power, China today finds itself surrounded by a number of 'small' and 'vulnerable' states subjected to wide-ranging destabilizing factors and forces, including radical Islam. As one analyst puts it, "Until the collapse of the Soviet Union ignited an explosion of interest in Central Asia, most outsiders considered the region a political backwater, an amorphous place of exotic peoples whose time of greatest power had long passed and whose future could have little impact on international affairs. This perception began to change during the 1980s when China's concern over the stirrings of ethnic separatism in Xinjiang helped focus international attention on Islamic revivalism in Central Asia."[53]

China's growing interest and involvement in the Central Asian republics has prompted wide-ranging geopolitical speculations and assessments in various parts of the globe. A number of scholarly studies, including the one by Anita Sengupta,[54] have discussed at length the Chinese motives and motivations behind taking the initiative for the Shanghai Cooperation Organization (SCO); ranging from the perceived need to insulate Xinjiang from the possible spillover of political volatility on the other side of its borders, to ensuring uninterrupted access to the natural resource endowment of Central Asia (especially energy) and firmly establishing its own geopolitical niche in Eurasia before the US becomes excessively predominant with the help of NATO, and/or before Russia decides to reassert itself in its 'near abroad' policy. According to Feng Shaolei, "China also views the Central Asian states in the context of Eurasia. They have a linking role not only in a geographical sense but also in a political and cultural sense. Central Asia has been called a bridge between (the) East and (the) West. China is closely interested in the stability and prosperity of the region because turbulence around that bridge would affect the future of political and economic cooperation on the whole Eurasian continent. Political and economic stability in the Central Asian states is therefore very important for China."[55]

At the same time Russia, India and China, have been engaged in a dialogue in order to pursue common goals in an international geopolitical economy. With the intention of enhancing trilateral cooperation in a variety of fields, foreign ministers from China, Russia and India met in Wuhan, the capital of the central Hubei province on 14 November 2010. As the 10th of its kind, the meeting as was reported in the Chinese media, was an evidence of the further deepening of trilateral ties among Beijing, Moscow and New Delhi. The Chinese scholar Yu Jincheng, in an editorial titled, "Emerging Strategic Triangle" wrote in the *China Daily*:

> Due to the ever-growing influence of the countries in regional and world affairs, trilateral cooperation between the three countries offers opportunities for further development. As three of the BRIC (Brazil, Russia, India and China) members, China, Russia and India together account for 40 percent of the global population and their combined gross domestic product takes up more than 15 percent of the world's total. The three countries also enjoy a particularly advantageous geopolitical position, along with an abundance of labor and natural resources, as well as some scientific and technological advantages. The

> geographical location of the three nations also facilitates further deepening of trilateral cooperation.
> However, despite tangible advancements in recent years, China-Russia-Indian trilateral ties also face some difficulties. Mutual political trust among them should be further enhanced. Beijing and New Delhi are still plagued by some thorny issues in bilateral relations, such as border demarcation issues. The US factor in the triangular ties of China, Russia and India also cannot be ignored. Washington has been worrying that a strong relationship among the three emerging nations will pose a threat to its global dominance and thus has made unremitting efforts to boost its own ties with India in its attempts to contain China.[56]

The United States of America perceives Central Eurasian space largely through such geopolitical codes as 'stability', 'containment', and 'access' to key raw materials (especially oil), and prevention of nuclear proliferation. Despite the fact that the American commitment to implement these objectives is somewhat constrained, Washington continues to focus on the most important element, which is to "maintain stability" in Central Eurasia and contain the 'Islamic threat' and nuclear proliferation.[57] Some analysts in the United States have argued that the US 'engagement' is essential for Eurasia's political future and economic vitality. Such an argument is also rooted in a geopolitical imagination which projects Eurasia as a geo-economic space waiting to be exploited, and thus in need of 'guidance' from the West. Some even fear that lack of sustained commitment on the part of the United States might prove to be geopolitically advantageous to China in medium to long term basis.

It has also been emphasized by some American experts on Central Asia that the establishment of a 'friendly' regime in Afghanistan may not suffice and Washington will have to work out a long-term policy towards Afghanistan's northern neighbours. Michael Rywkin while talking about 'American Perspectives' has raised the following interesting questions.

> What does Central Asia really represent for us? A supplier of oil, gas, and non-ferrous metals whose problems are of no great importance as long as they do not jeopardize our energy supply routes? A strategic area that must be brought under our influence because of its location at the crossroads of the Russian, Chinese, and Middle Eastern worlds? As an alternative, would it be better to share influence over the region with Russia, both as a price for Russian cooperation in the war against international terrorism

> and because the Russian presence frees us from the need for a larger, long-term military presence?[58]

Yet another imaginative geography of Central Asia calls upon the US policy makers to acknowledge and treat the entire region as a 'pivotal state'. The pivotal states are to be selected on the basis of the following five criteria: population, geography, location, economic potential, physical size and capacity to affect regional and international stability. The argument then becomes that each criteria is significantly present in Central Asia.[59] If taken on an individual basis, no Central Asian state carries enough weight in terms of population or territorial size to qualify as 'pivotal'. But when the enormous energy-resource endowment is considered in conjunction with the possible 'domino' effects of a 'failed state', it becomes obviously compelling that Central Eurasia deserves America's focused attention and sustained engagement. Accordingly, the region should be considered as a whole due to its staggering economic potential and prospects of a future marked by general instability.[60] This is how 'imaginations are to be given substance': when, where and how?

In October 1999, the US Department of Defence decided to reassign senior command authority over American forces in Central Asia from the Pacific Command to the Central Command. This was an important pointer in the direction of a major shift in American geopolitical thinking.[61] Throughout the Cold War, Eurasia had been perceived as a marginal concern, firmly anchored within the Soviet sphere of influence, on the outermost edge of the Pacific Command's main areas of responsibility (China, Japan, and the Korean Peninsula). Today, the region stretching from the Ural Mountains to China's western border has become an object of the so-called 'New Great Game', due to vast reserves of oil and natural gas thought to lie *in* and *around* the Caspian Sea. It is the Persian Gulf region that has been the major responsibility of the Central Command. The addition of Central Asia suggests that this area is now under the close scrutiny of those responsible for ensuring the uninterrupted supply of oil to the United States and its allies.[62]

The growing visibility of landlocked Central Eurasia and its resource endowment in mainstream US geopolitical thinking appears to be having an important bearing on the larger geopolitical setting of the Indian Ocean region, or what Robert Kaplan would call "The Rimland of Eurasia."[63] During the Cold War, the strategic spaces that seemed to matter the most to the defence establishments were the zones of confrontation between the US and the Soviet blocs: central and southeastern Europe and the Far East. After the collapse of the USSR, however, the strategic appeal of this area has declined for the United States, with the exception perhaps of the demilitarized zone between North and South Korea. It is the Persian Gulf, the Caspian Sea basin, and the South China Sea that are demanding as well as receiving much greater attention from the Pentagon. To quote Michael Klare,

> Behind this shift in strategic geography is a new emphasis on the protection of supplies of vital resources, especially oil and natural gas. Whereas Cold War-era divisions were created and alliances formed along ideological lines, economic competition now drives international relations—and competition over access to these vital economic assets has intensified accordingly. Because an interruption in the supply of natural resources would portend severe economic consequences, the major importing countries now consider the protection of this flow a significant national concern. In addition, with global energy consumption rising by an estimated two percent annually, competition for access to large energy reserves will only grow more intense in the years to come.[64]

No sub-region on the Eurasian Rimland looms as large in the 'new' imaginative geographies as the 'Middle East', which in a recent study has also been termed as "Eurasian Energy Heartland."[65] The deployment of the geographical term 'Middle East' to it in the contemporary context of energy security, suggests remarkable continuity in the imperial-colonial mapping of the region. It is useful to recall that the term 'Middle East' was the result of earlier British imperial designations of the world which have been retained both on the maps and in the geopolitical imaginations of policy makers.

After the end of the Cold War, the geopolitical significance of the Middle East was relocated on the wider canvas of what was designated by Zbigniew Brzezinski as 'The Eurasian Balkans' on the 'Grand Chess Board'.[66] Brzezinski visualized Eurasia as "the chessboard on which the geopolitical moves and counter-moves for global primacy will continue to be made, and that this struggle involves geo-strategy—the strategic management of geopolitical interests." Further emphasizing that, "It is imperative that no Eurasian challenger emerges capable of dominating Eurasia and thus also of challenging America," he mooted the notion of 'Eurasian Balkans'. To quote Brzezinski,

> In Europe, The word 'Balkans' conjured up the images of ethnic conflicts and great-power regional rivalries. Eurasia, too, has

> its 'Balkans', but the Eurasian Balkans are much larger, more populated, 'even more religiously and ethnically heterogeneous. They are located within that large geographic oblong that demarcates the *central zone of instability*...and that embraces portions of southeastern Europe, Central Asia and parts of South Asia, the Persian Gulf area, and the Middle East...Eurasian Balkans are infinitely more important as a potential *economic prize*: an enormous concentration of natural gas and oil reserves is located in the region, in addition to important minerals, including gold.[67] (Emphasis given)

More recently, a new term, "Greater Middle East" (referred to by some as 'New Heartland') has entered the lexicon of the competing imaginative geographies of the Eurasian space.[68] The Greater Middle East is perceived to be occupying a 'pivotal' position at the juncture of Europe, Africa and Asia, and representing the 'sum' of the core Middle East, North Africa, the African Horn, South Asia and ex-Soviet Central Asia. It is said to be occupying,

> ...a crucial position with respect to some of the major issue areas of the cotemporary era. Those issue areas are energy sources and availability; *the proliferation of weapons of mass destruction (WMD) and their delivery systems; and the dangerous pairings* involving Israel and the Arabs, Iran and Iraq, and India and Pakistan. Surely, this region in its aggregate has come to be viewed by the contending and aspiring world powers—the United States, Russia, a united Europe, China—as a strategic prize, may be *the* strategic prize.[69] (emphasis given)

The Princeton Project on National Security, a three-year, bipartisan initiative to develop a "sustainable and effective national security strategy for the United States of America," in its final report titled, "Forging a World of Liberty under Law: U.S. National Security Project in the 21st Century," too is of the view that, "The rise of India and the resurgence of Russia have brought broader Eurasian great power politics into the expanded geopolitical space of Asia. A central part of this new power politics concerns the pursuit of energy, featuring India and China as competing consumers and Russia as a pivotal supplier."[70]

Neo-Liberal Geopolitics. Eurasia on 'Pentagon's New Map'

One of the most dramatic deployments of imaginative geographies can be found in the writings of Thomas Barnett, the author of the widely cited and discussed book titled, *The Pentagon's New Map*.[71] In this grand global visualization, humanity is partitioned into 'functioning core' and 'non-integrated gap'. The former comprises the majority of the world's population, either already integrated or fast integrating into the US-led globalization project; namely, North America, Europe both "old" and "new", Russia, Japan, China (although the interior is less so), India (in a pock-marked sense), Australia and New Zealand, South Africa, and the ABC of South Asia—Argentina, Brazil and Chile. Whereas "the Gap" consists of the following regions: the Caribbean, Central America (south of Mexico), South America (except for Brazil, Uruguay Argentina and Chile), Africa (except South Africa), the Middle East (including Turkey), the Balkans, Bulgaria, Romania, Moldova, Armenia, the Central Asian Republics, Afghanistan, Pakistan, Kashmir, Nepal, Bangladesh, the Muslim provinces of Western China, and all of Southeast Asia.

Connectivity, Barnett argues, holds the key to both peace and prosperity. Those unfortunate enough to be still disconnected are prone to violence and live under a variety of tyrannies, whereas those connected in the core are blessed with much better living conditions and ample freedom to follow their own course in life. To quote Barnett,

> Show me where globalization is thick with network connectivity, financial transactions, liberal media flows, and collective security, and I will show you regions featuring stable governments, rising standards of living, and more deaths by suicide than murder. But show me where globalization is thinning or just plain absent, and I will show you regions plagued by politically repressive regimes, widespread poverty and disease, routine mass murder, and—most important—the chronic conflicts that incubate the next generation of terrorists. These parts of the world I call the Non-Integrating Gap, or Gap.[72]

According to Barnett, the 'old Pentagon' is ill equipped to meet the challenge of the 'new' wars which are already upon the people in the US and other parts of the civilized functioning core. Instead of operating on the old geographic premises and outdated cartographies, Pentagon, argues Barnett, have been rendered irrelevant by the demise of the Soviet Union and the rise of globalization. What is needed therefore, argues Barnett, are the new maps truly reflecting a paradigmatic strategic transformation.

The imaginative geographies that underpin 'Pentagon's New Map' evoke and justify the deployment of American military forces in order to get rid of the isolated political regimes in the world. According to Barnett, "if we (US troops in their new roles as shrinkers of the Gap) draw a line around the majority of those military interventions, we have basically mapped the Non-Integrating Gap." Barnett proudly proclaims further: "...security is this country's [America's] most influential public-sector export...show me a part of the world that is secure in its peace and I will show you strong and growing ties between local militaries and the U.S. military. Show me regions where major war is inconceivable and I will show you permanent U.S. military bases and long-term security alliances." Furthermore, as far as Central Asia is concerned:

> Our recent moves into Central Asia signalled the sort of long-term export of security we ended up pursuing in Europe following the Second World War. I believe America will end up exporting security on that scale not just to Central Asia, but also to Middle East, Africa, the Caribbean Rim, and—yes—even South East Asia, a place where we swore we'd never return to after losing Vietnam.[73]

Barnett's thesis has invited thought-provoking reactions from critical geographers. Susan Roberts, Anna Secor and Matthew Sparke have forcefully argued that Barnett's work is their main example "of a more widespread form of *neoliberal geopolitics* implicated in the war-making."[74] What we find in this geopolitical world vision is the "neoliberal idealism about the virtues of free markets, openness, and global economic integration" linked to "an extreme form of American unilateralism."[75] They further "highlight how the neoliberal geopolitics of the war planners illustrated the contradictory dependency of multilateral neoliberal deregulation on enforced re-regulation and, in particular, on the deadly and far from multilateral re-regulation represented by the 'regime change' that has now been enforced on Iraq." Furthermore,

> In the neo liberal approach, the geopolitics of inter-imperial rivalry, the Monroe Doctrine, and the ideas about hemispheric control that defined Butler's era are eclipsed by a new global vision of almost infinite openness and interdependency. In contrast also to the Cold War era, danger is no longer imagined as something that should be contained at a disconnected distance. Now, by way of a complete counterpoint, danger is itself being defined *as* disconnection from the global system. In turn, the neoliberal geopolitical response, it seems, is to insist on *enforcing* reconnection.[76]

Conclusion: Prospects for Imaginative Counter-Geographies

In this paper I have made a modest attempt to argue and illustrate that there has never been, nor will there be, a single, 'fixed' geography of Eurasia or for that matter Central Eurasia but, in fact, multiple, dynamic *geographies*. Great powers of different eras have been making efforts to inscribe their culture-specific geopolitical imaginations onto the Eurasian space, reading in the process different meanings (geopolitical, economic as well as strategic) into the 'centrality' of Central Asia. The manner in which Central Eurasia has been described in discursive terms reveals how the geo (political) acts of transforming 'spaces' into 'places', or writing the geographies of international politics, involve selective uses of 'geographical knowledge'.

It is significant to note that even though the geo-historical context in which Mackinder theorized disappeared a long time back, his geopolitical ideas (even if Mackinder did not like the term geopolitics) continue to appeal to foreign policy establishments and strategic thinkers in different parts of the world. In a recent seminal study Anita Sengupta has shown, "how a model imagined at a particular juncture in history is revived to formulate a strategy in the context of (a) vastly changed scenario."[77] Most striking is the manner in which post-Soviet Russia, as shown by Bassin and Aksenov[78] has taken to geopolitics in general, and to Mackinder and his Heartland thesis in particular, after having been largely critical and dismissive of geopolitics throughout the Cold War. In the words of John Agnew,

> Halford Mackinder has had a posthumous existence that many of us might envy. Long after his earthly demise, some of his ideas, particularly that of the "geographical pivot of history," keeps coming back to life. Currently, some well-known pundits in US foreign policy circles, typically thought of as neo-conservative and keen on a 'muscular' US military presence around the world, have re-discovered Mackinder's geographical determinism as providing a seemingly naturalistic account for the approaching rebirth of the "yellow peril" (the rise of China) and offering as it did at the turn of the last century a timeless rendering of the challenges to the democratic maritime powers from the despotic land powers of Eurasia. The widely cited American journalist Robert Kaplan... for example frames the emerging "geography" of China's power almost entirely in these terms. It is timely, therefore, to have a new intellectual biography

> of Mackinder that not only critically engages with the central themes of his geopolitics but that does so by both situating them in the historical context of the early twentieth century and showing why they remain attractive in some quarters by dint of their effective depoliticization of the very world politics that they underwrite.[79]

Imaginative geographies and their geopolitical reductionism will continue to be tested by the complex and dynamic socio-economic, political and cultural transformations in Euro-Asia. As Gregory Gleason points out, "transitions of the scale of post-Soviet reform are not easily characterized and reduced to simple causal relations."[80] Yet, these imaginations or representations should not be taken lightly since they influence, and are in turn influenced, by the mental maps of policy makers visualising 'their' world in capitals of major powers. Although seductive as well as reductive, neither the discourse of 'block' centric geo-economics nor geographical imaginations, such as Greater Middle East/New Heartland/Eurasian Balkans/Demand Heartland, can fully capture and explain for example the multidimensional, multilevel complexity of energy flows. The 'centrality' of the strategic salience of Central Asia ought to lie in the acknowledgement by all—the so-called 'insiders' as well as 'outsiders'—that cooperation rather than conflict, has to be the norm, rather than the exception, while addressing the problems of growing human-energy-environmental insecurities.

Amartya Sen has a valuable insight to offer on how imaginative counter-geographies could possibly be initiated and strengthened by harnessing the forces of an emerging global civil society in Euro-Asia and beyond.[81] According to him the time is just right to rethink such taken-for-granted notions as 'Western' values and/or 'Asian' values. To quote Sen,

> The world has come to the conclusion—more definitely than should have been needed—that culture matters. The world is obviously right—culture does matter. However, the real question is: *How* does culture matter? The confining of culture into stark and separated boxes of civilizations or of religious identities...takes too narrow a view of cultural attributes. Other cultural generalizations, for example, about national, ethnic, or racial groups, can also present astonishingly limited and bleak understanding(s) of the characteristics of the human beings involved. When a hazy perception of culture is combined with

> fatalism about the dominant power of culture, we are, in effect, asked to be imaginary slaves of an illusory force.
>
> Given the cultural and intellectual interconnections in world history, the question of what is "Western" and what is not would be hard to decide...Indeed, Europe would have been a lot poorer—had it resisted the globalization of mathematics, science and technology coming from China, India, Iran, and the Arab world, at the beginning of the second millennium. And the same applies, though in the reverse direction, today.[82]

There is a need therefore to decolonize the prevailing clashing geographical imaginations about 'Central Asia' and the Central Asians. The post-Cold War international system is both unipolar (USA being the dominant military power with the entire globe under the surveillance of its global chains of command) and multi-polar or polycentric at the same time with a Germany dominated European Union, China, Russia, Japan and India (with the nuclear and missile tests in 1998, rising foreign exchange reserves, increasing foreign trade and economic growth and the global perception of the political stability of the world's largest democracy) as major players in the contemporary balance of power system. There is every possibility that Eurasian space in particular will continue to be visualized by some strategic-policy think tanks as well as policy makers in terms of Heartland-Rimland, Land Power-Sea Power geopolitical equations and binaries. The Cold War mentalities and structures too will persist in one form or the other, producing in the process what Derek Gregory refers to as "violence of abstraction" and "de-corporealization of place and space."[83] According to Gregory, "it will be necessary to explore other spatializations and other topologies, and to turn our imaginative geographies into geographical imaginations that can enlarge and enhance our sense of the world and enable us to situate ourselves within it with care, concern and humility."[84]

These imaginative geographies of oil, Islam, and terrorism, framed and flagged at various sites in the service of diverse agendas, are increasingly shaping the world-view *of* and *on* Central Eurasia. I have also tried to show how fear is aroused and mobilized in the service of various agendas of political, economic and cultural controls. Our analysis of competing fear-inducing imaginative geographies of the 'New Great Game', 'containment', etc., at various sites, and the manner in which Central Eurasia is being implicated in them, reinforces Gregory's insightful comment that, "...imaginative geographies are spaces of constructed (in) visibility and it is this partiality that implicates them in the play of power."[85] After all,

> Hope and fear are huge swirling compulsions with enormous implications for the lives and deaths of every living thing on the planet. False hopes and groundless fears can be of dreadful, deadly consequence. And yet justified fears when combined with sensible hopes can open new possibilities and thereby help mobilize change for the better, including both better lives and a better world in which to live. How can geographers help examine such consequences and possibilities? And what specifically can our geographical scholarship enable us to contribute to wider negotiations of hope and fear as they continue to shape our world? One of the most useful contributions we can and do make as geographers involves critically exploring the geographical grounds of fear and hope. Our disciplinary calling demands that, among many other things, we map and study the production and extent of such grounds in all their physical, social, economic, cultural, and political complexity.[86]

Again, as pointed out by Gregory "In response [to the manipulation of geopolitics of fear at various sites], *imaginative counter-geographies* are deliberate attempts to displace, subvert and contest the imaginative geographies installed by the dominant regimes of power, practice and representation."[87] Usually these are produced from within the objects of representation. "They seek to give voice and vision to their subjects and to undo the separations between 'our space' and 'their space'."[88] Given its geographic situation in the heart of Eurasia and its landlocked status, its multi-ethnic, multi-lingual societies, its rich and unique cultures, the Central Eurasian region is uniquely placed to facilitate the dialogue between Europe and Asia, provided there is a deliberate and diligent return to human-cultural geographies of the region in all its diversity.

Notes

1. D. Gregory, *The Colonial Present: Afghanistan, Palestine, Iraq* (Oxford: Blackwell, 2004), 17.
2. H. Kissinger, *Diplomacy* (New York: Simon & Schuster, 1994), 813.
3. Z. Brezezinski, *The Grand Chessboard: American Primacy and its Geostrategic Imperatives* (New York: Basic Books, 1997).
4. Gregory, *The Colonial Present.*

5. See E. Kavalski, "Coming to terms with complexity of external agency in Central Asia," *Journal of Eurasian Studies*, 2010 (in press); W.R. Kunzweiler, "The New Central Eurasian Great Game," *Strategic Review* 22, no. 3 (1998).
6. Gregory, *The Colonial Present*, 19.
7. F. Fesharaki, "Energy and the Asian Security Nexus," *Journal of International Affairs* 53, no. 1 (1999).
8. G. Bhagat, "Central Asia and Energy Security," *Asian Affairs* 37, no. 1 (2006).
9. E.V.W. Davis and R. Azizian (eds), *Islam, Oil and Geopolitics: Central Asia after September 11* (Lanham: Rowman and Littlefield Publishers, 2007).
10. S. Chaturvedi and J. Painter, "Whose World? Whose Order? Spatiality, Geopolitics and the Limits of World Order Concept," *Cooperation and Conflict* 42, no. 4 (2007).
11. Neumann, "Regionalization and Democratic Consolidation," in *Democratic Consolidation in Eastern Europe*, J. Zielonka and A. Pravda (eds) (Oxford: Oxford University Press, 2001), 60.
12. Kavalski, "Coming to terms with complexity of external agency in Central Asia," 3.
13. V.D. Mamadouh, "Geopolitics in the Nineties: One Flag Many Meanings," *Geo Journal* 46(1998): 246.
14. Y. Lacoste, "Rivalries for Territory," *Geopolitics* 5, no. 2 (2000): 121-22.
15. Ladis K.D. Kristof, "The Image and the Vision of the Fatherland: The Case of Poland in Comparative Perspective," in *Geography and National Identity*, D. Hooson, (ed.) (Oxford: Blackwell, 1994), 222.
16. K.J. Dodds, *Geopolitics in a Changing World* (Harlow and New York: Prentice Hall, 2000), 33.
17. G.O. Tuathail, "The Bush administration and the 'End' of the Cold War: a critical geopolitics of US foreign policy in 1989," *Geoforum*, 23(1992): 439.
18. D. Gregory, "Imaginative Geographies," in *The Dictionary of Human Geography*, D. Gregory, R. Johnston, G. Pratt, M.J. Watts and S. Whatmore (eds) (Chichester: Wiley-Blackwell, 2009), 369-70.
19. S.B. Cohen, *Geopolitics: The Geography of International Relations* (Lanham: Rowman & Littlefield, 2009), 13.
20. Cohen, *Geopolitics*, 19.
21. G. O Tuathail, *Critical Geopolitics: The Politics of Writing Global Space* (London: Routledge, 1996), 27.
22. See B.W. Blouet (ed.), *Global Geostrategy: Mackinder and the Defence of the West* (London, New York: Frank Cass, 2005).
23. See Gray, "In defence of the Heartland: Sir Halford Mackinder and his critics a hundred years on," in *Global Geostrategy*, Blouet (ed.).
24. Gray, "In defence of the Heartland," 30.

25. N. Takmil-Homayon, "A Glance at Asia: Understanding Central Asia," *Central Eurasia and Caucasus Review* 1, no. 3 (1993): 21-47; G.R. Capisani, *The Handbook of Central Asia: A Comprehensive Survey of the New Republics* (London: I.B. Tauris Publisher, 2000).
26. Shams-ud-Din, "The New Great Game in Central Asia," *International Studies* 34, no. 3 (July-September1997): 329.
27. B.Z. Rumer (ed.), *Central Eurasia in Transition: Dilemmas of Political and Economic Development* (Armonk: M.E. Sharpe, 1996).
28. M. Mesbahi, "Regional and Global Powers and the International Relations of Central Asia," in *The Making of Foreign Policy of Russia and New States of Eurasia*, A. Dawisha and K. Dawisha (eds), (Armonk: M.E Sharpe, 1995), 215.
29. See Kavalski, "Coming to terms with complexity of external agency in Central Asia."
30. J. Agnew *et al.*, "Reading Gerry Kearns' Geopolitics and Empire: The Legacy of Halford Mackinder," *Political Geography* (2010), doi: 10.1016/j. polgeo.2010.09.007.
31. A. Mahmood, "Central Asia's Great Game," *Current Affairs* (2000). http://defencejournal.com/globe/2000/june-july/contents-june-july2000.htm.
32. H.A. Rizvi, "Domestic Politics, External Linkages, and Security," *Sworn & Plough Shares* 10 (1996): 17-23.
33. Rizvi, "Domestic Politics."
34. Ministry of Foreign Affairs, Tehran (2010), Weekly briefing of the Foreign Ministry Spokesman, http://www.mfa.gov.ir/cms/cms/Tehran/en/NEW/258891.html. Accessed on 15 November 2010.
35. S. Hunter, "Iran, Turkey and Central Asia: The Islamic Connection," in *Islam, Oil and Geopolitics*, Davis and Azizian (eds.), 192; see also S. Hunter, *Central Eurasia since Independence*, Washington Papers 168 (Washington DC: Centre for Strategic and International Studies, 1996).
36. Hunter, "Iran, Turkey and Central Asia," 195.
37. Christos Kassimeris, "Turkey's foreign policy options: Europe, the USA or Central Asia?" *Contemporary Politics* 16 (2010): 3, 321-36.
38. R. Israeli, "Return to Source: The Republics of Central Eurasia and Middle East," *Central Eurasian Survey* 13, no. 1 (1994): 19-31.
39. D. Banerjee, "Central Eurasian Republics Today," *Strategic Analysis* (August1994): 537.
40. Hunter, "Iran, Turkey and Central Asia," 196.
41. Shams-ud-Din, "The New Great Game in Central Asia."
42. J. Bakshi, "Shanghai Co-operation Organisation (SCO): Before and After September 11," *Strategic Analysis* 26 no. 2 (2002): 265-76.
43. J. Bakshi, "India and Central Asia: Policy Review and Projecting into Future (2005-2025)," in *Emerging India: Security and Foreign Policy Perspectives*, N.S. Sisodia and C.U. Bhaskar (eds) (New Delhi and Chicago: IDSA, Promilla & Company in association with Bibliophile South Asia, 2005), 245.

44. R. Allison, "Strategic Reassertion in Russia's Central Asia Policy," *International Affairs* 80, no. 2 (2004): 277-93.
45. H. Peimani, Regional Security and the Future of Central Asia (Westport: Praeger, 1998), 54.
46. I. Berman, "The New Battleground: Central Asia and the Caucasus," *The Washington Quarterly* 28, no. 1 (2004): 67.
47. R.G. Suny, "The Pawn of Great Powers: The East-West Competition for Caucasia," *Journal of Eurasian Studies* 1 (2010): 10.
48. Suny, "The Pawn of Great Powers," 11.
49. Suny, "The Pawn of Great Powers."
50. Suny, "The Pawn of Great Powers."
51. Mesbahi, "Regional and Global Powers and the International Relations of Central Asia," 227.
52. A. Hyman, "Central Asia's Relations with Afghanistan and South Asia," in *The New Central Eurasia and its Neighbours*, P. Ferdinannd (ed.) (London: The Royal Institutional Affairs; Pinter Publisher, 1994), 75-94.
53. L.C. Harris, "Xinjiang, Central Asia and the Implications for China's Policy in the Islamic World," *The China Quarterly* 133 (1993): 111.
54. A. Sengupta, *Russia, China and Multilateralism in Central Asia* (Delhi: Shipra, 2005).
55. F. Shaolei, "Chinese-Russian Strategic Relations: The Central Asian Angle," in *Islam, Oil and Geopolitics*, Davis and Azizian (eds), 207.
56. Yu Jincheng, "Emerging Strategic Triangle," *China Daily*, 17 November 2010. http://www.chinadaily.com.cn/opinion/2010-11/17/content_11560684.htm. Accessed on 18 November 2010.
57. M. Mohsenin, "Iran's relation with Central Asia and the Caucasus," *The Iranian Journal of International Affairs* 2(1995): 217-32.
58. Michael Rywkin, "Central Asia in the Forefront of Attention," *American Foreign Policy Interests*, 24 (2002), 41.
59. Kunzweiler, "The New Central Eurasian Great Game."
60. Kunzweiler, "The New Central Eurasian Great Game."
61. M. Klare, "The New Geography of Conflict, " *Foreign Affairs* (May-June 2001): 46-61.
62. Klare, "The New Geography of Conflict."
63. R.D. Kaplan, *Monsoon: The Indian Ocean and the Future of American Power* (New York: Random House, 2010).
64. Klare, "The New Geography of Conflict."
65. K.R. Singh, "Geo-strategy of Commercial Energy," *International* Studies 39, no. 3(2002): 288.
66. Brezezinski, *The Grand Chessboard*.
67. Brezezinski, *The Grand Chessboard*, 123-24.
68. R. Harkavy, "Strategic Geography and the Greater Middle East," *Naval War College Review* 54, no. 4 (2001): 37.
69. Harkavy, "Strategic Geography."

70. G.J. Ilkenberry and A.M. Slaughter, "Forging a World of Liberty under Law: U.S. Security in the 21st Century," Final Report of the Princeton Project on National Security, The Woodrow Wilson School of Public and International Affairs, Princeton University (2007), 48. http://www.princeton.edu/~ppns/report/FinalReport.pdf 2006. Accessed on 15 November 2010.
71. T.P.M. Barnett, "The Pentagon's New Map," *Esquire* (March 2003). http://www.nwc.navy.mil/newrulesets/ThePentagonsNewMap.htm. Last accessed 29 June 2003.
72. Barnett, "The Pentagon's New Map."
73. T.P.M. Barnett, *The Pentagon's New Map: War and Peace in the Twenty-First Century* (New York: Berkley Books, 2004), 179.
74. Roberts, S., A. Secor and M. Sparke, "Neoliberal Geopolitics," *Antipode* 35, no. 5 (2003): 886.
75. Roberts, Secor and Sparke, "Neoliberal Geopolitics."
76. Roberts, Secor and Sparke, "Neoliberal Geopolitics," 888.
77. Anita Sengupta, *Heartlands of Eurasia: The Geopolitics of Political Space* (Lanham: Lexington Books, 2009), 2.
78. M. Bassin and K. Aksenov, "Mackinder and the Heartland Theory in Past-Soviet Geopolitical Discourse," *Geopolitics* 11 (2006): 99-118.
79. Agnew, "Reading Gerry Kearns' Geopolitics and Empire."
80. G. Gleason, "Foreign Policy and Domestic Reform in Central Asia," *Central Asian Survey* 20, no. 2 (2001): 179.
81. A. Sen, *The Argumentative Indian: Writings on Indian History, Culture and Identity* (New York: Picador Publishers, 2006), 103.
82. Sen, *The Argumentative Indian*, 129-30
83. Gregory, *The Colonial Present.*
84. Gregory, *The Colonial Present.*
85. Gregory, "Imaginative Geographies," 371.
86. M. Sparke, "Geopolitical fears, geoeconomic hopes, and the responsibilities of geography," *Annals of the Association of American Geographers* 97, no. 2 (2007): 338.
87. Gregory, "Imaginative Geographies," 371.
88. Gregory, "Imaginative Geographies," 371.

4

Geostrategic Perspectives on Eurasia: Towards Multilateralism in Central Asia

Anita Sengupta

The debate on multilateralism, defined in the broadest sense as international cooperation among more than two states in the international arena, has reemerged in the light of a pervading unilateralist impulse emanating from the Bush administration in recent years.[1] While a debate on the reform of the United Nations, as the principal global multilateral forum, had been an ongoing process, prior to recent US actions, multilateral approach towards regional issues, particularly security issues, with emphasis on confidence building, preventive diplomacy and conflict resolution, was being increasingly accepted as significant to the maintenance of regional security and promotion of regional development. Multilateral confidence building measures reflected the belief that through regularized dialogue and consultation existing and potential conflicts could be effectively managed without the necessity of recourse to coercion. It was pointed out that multilateralism is distinctive, not merely because it coordinates national policies in groups of three or more states, which is something that other organizational forms also do, but additionally because it does so on the basis of certain principles of ordering relations among states.[2]

Questions about the viability of multilateralism were revived in the background of US actions in Iraq that bypassed the United Nations.[3] However, the United Nations was not the only multilateral forum under review. An emphasis on bilateral arrangements with the US also brought into question the viability of regional multilateral forums particularly in the immediate neighbourhood of Afghanistan. This was noted as being particularly significant and projected as a reversal of the post Cold War scenario. The end of the Cold War had been seen as presenting an opportunity to move towards a system of "collective security" that would create conditions for greater international stability and reduce the risk of war. It also envisioned the United Nations as "returning" to the vision and intentions of its founders in becoming an effective instrument for maintaining international peace and security. With the end of the Cold War it was therefore assumed that a more independent stance in terms of regional security forums was in sight since there remained no overarching global dynamic over regional initiatives. Writings on Asian Security Practice, for instance, noted

> Local and regional dynamics are becoming more salient, and states appear to have greater latitude in shaping their immediate environments. Unlike the economic domain, where the Asian economies and their regional activities are becoming integrated into the global economy, the security domain seems to be witnessing the development of a much more independent regional system.[4]

In the post-September 11 scenario, it was noted, this independent stance, at least as far as regional security arrangements was concerned, would change particularly in the region in the immediate neighbourhood of Afghanistan. Here, once again, it was noted that the 'war against terrorism' would demonstrate the significance of either bilateral or global security alignments, particularly where the Central Asian region was concerned. In fact, analysts argued that in the future all campaigns would be 'a coalition of the willing' completely dominated by the US, and with contribution on a bilateral basis.[5] Yet, the 'war against terrorism' itself has proven the importance of multilateral cooperation. Although the decisive battles in Iraq and Afghanistan were largely the product of unilateral US military power, much of the success that has been achieved was through broad multilateral cooperation on a number of lower profile fronts, such as intelligence sharing, border security, economic sanctions and law enforcement.

The debate that followed the US actions, however, was less about strategic choice but more a matter of disagreement about the very meaning and purpose of multilateralism.[6] The debate has since moved in numerous directions.[7] While most of it has been a critique of a process that is still largely defined by states according to convenience, a significant part of the debate also focuses on it as an ideal to be aspired for in a global system that is now being identified as unipolar.[8] As against this unipolar and unilateralist tendency, multilateral options are being advocated by a significant part of the global community.[9] In recent times, Russia and China have advocated global multilateralism and have emphasized the necessity of strengthening the role of the United Nations.[10] They have also sought multilateral solutions to conflicts in their immediate neighbourhood. They share similar views with regard to opposing unilateralist actions by a US led NATO extending beyond Europe into Central and South Asia. The extent to which such common concerns can lead to the development of multilateral cooperation in particular regions remains to be seen, particularly in the light of the fact that multilateralism is often variously defined by them, and commitment to multilateral options have varied particularly in cases which are identified as significant in terms of national interest. For instance, analysts have noted that while China's thinking on multilateralism and regional security cooperation has evolved over the last decade, it is yet to demonstrate that it accepts the principles of multilateralism unequivocally. It is pointed out that China follows *conditional multilateralism*, which is characterized by a low degree of institutionalization of the multilateral forum.[11]

However, there are certain areas where there is broad agreement on the requirement of multilateral action. For instance, there have been attempts to explore multilateral options in terms of security and confidence building in the Central Asian region by Russia and China. The Central Asian states are part of the Commonwealth of Independent States (CIS) and as such most of them are signatories to the Collective Security Treaty (CST) now renamed the Collective Security Treaty Organization (CSTO).[12] In addition they are also part of the Shanghai Cooperation Organization (SCO), which includes Russia and China. Russia and China along with a number of other Asian states are part of the Conference on Confidence Building and Interaction in Asia (CICA), a Central Asian initiative at confidence building in the region.

A significant part of strategic writing emanating from western scholarship brought into question their role in the post 9/11 scenario, and assumed that Sino-Russian arrangements for multilateral regional security would no longer play any significant role in the efforts to deal with terrorism in the region.[13] In fact, it was suggested that regional multilateral forums would no longer be significant and once again, most security agreements would be bilateral. It was also argued that to the limited extent that multilateral options would be considered as viable, transregional institutions would tend to be favoured at the expense of regional collectivities.[14] In the Central Asian case the assumption was that the NATO, sponsored

Partnership for Peace (PfP) would emerge as the most significant security organization in the region as the transition from regional to global security became the guiding norm. This assumption was, however, not a recent one. As early as 1997, Zbigniew Brzezinski had talked about a "new cooperative trans-Eurasian security system" and NATO had expanded its presence in the region since the mid-1990s. The most common comment about regional security arrangements in the post 9/11 scenario was that, given the US presence in the region, multilateral processes initiated by Russia and China would take a back seat. All of these positions were subject to critical assessment in the course of the events that followed the Andijan events and the subsequent Uzbek demand for the evacuation of US forces from their bases in Karshi-Khanabad.[15] In fact in the post-September 11 period there has been an attempt to institutionalize multilateral forums like the CSTO and the SCO. In July 2005, an assertive SCO called for a timetable for the eventual departure of US forces from all Central Asian bases.[16]

The principle contention of the paper is that contrary to the opinion that there is today a revival of the Great Game, principally between three major players, Russia, China and the US in the Central Asian region, cooperation and multilateralism seem to be the watchwords of diplomacy for Eurasian powers. This brings into question the continuing interpretation of the history of the region in terms of an intense rivalry for control over the so-called 'heartland of the world.' In fact, no major geopolitical conflict now divides the powers of the Eurasian heartland and there is a new rapprochement over the region. While, on the one hand, this calls for a reinterpretation of the viability of the great game theories, on the other, it calls for a new look at the emerging multilateralism in the region. In this light a number of issues assume significance. The first and foremost is the question of the viability of multilateralism in the Central Asian region and the extent to which the states themselves are willing to be part of the multilateral process. A second issue is the attitude of Russia and China towards multilateralism in general and about the viability of Russian and Chinese led multilateral processes in the Central Asian region, given the reality of US presence. A debate on these two issues leads towards an understanding of how the concept and practices of security in the multilateral arena itself might be changing and the desirable scope of multilateral action on a broader Eurasian level.

Multilateralism in Central Asia

It is generally accepted that the purpose for any regional organization is twofold: the acceleration of economic development and the reinforcement of regional stability and security. The role of multilateral regional initiatives on a Central Asian level as primary providers of security has not been rated very high. It has been observed that such initiatives have been unable to convey hard defence guarantees, create joint military units, negotiate arms reductions or enforce the end of overt conflicts. However, a correct assessment of these initiatives would have to begin with noting their existential significance as groups of states that recognize themselves as sharing some elements of community and can define their national identity as complementary rather than adversial to their neighbours. Regular meetings and the creation of personal ties encourage *esprit de corps* and may help to defuse crisis. In fact non-traditional security issues like environment, defence against pollution, water management, drug smuggling, organized crime, migration and refugees have provided more useful areas for regional discourse. In addition there have been attempts at economic cooperation with an understanding that economic development is conducive to the security of the region.[17]

It is undeniable that compared to the more successful of regional multilateral efforts, a great deal remains to be achieved.[18] However, prior to any critical evaluation of these efforts it is crucial to keep in mind that in a number of indirect ways both development and stability have been contributed to by these regional processes. Representative of this are the numerous agreements that have been made regarding environmental degradation. This is a case that in the Central Asian region could lead to regional instability and also affect economic development. This is particularly so since the ecological crisis in the Central Asian region overlays and aggravates a structural, economic and social crisis. Central Asia is a developing region, characterized by a high share in agricultural production, low industrialization, mass unemployment and a high population growth. With the standard of living considerably below the Soviet average it was very dependent on the subsidies from the centre. The disintegration of the Soviet Union meant the beginning of a new process of nation building in the region and a redefinition of political and cultural identities. It also saw the emergence of a new international water basin, the Aral, with all consequent consequences for the political, ethnic and economic relations between the states. The entire political geography changed and once shared natural resources that were controlled by central directions became the 'national wealth' of the newly independent states. Rivers became national borders and the division into upstream and downstream riparians became politically relevant. While it is accepted that environmental issues are unlikely to be the primary cause of conflict, it is also argued that they play a complex role in shaping relations among states. And here the success of regional initiatives in the Central Asian region cannot be denied. Speaking to the Carnegie Endowment for International Peace, Dr. Kadir Gulomov, Minister of Defence in Uzbekistan noted that security has many aspects. Efforts to promote regional cooperation through the use of water and energy resources are an important way to reduce tensions in the area.[19]

A very significant multilateral effort initiated by the Kazakh President Nursultan Nazarbayev is the Conference on Interaction and Confidence Building in Asia (CICA). The CICA vision for security in Asia elaborates on multilateral approaches towards promoting peace and security and visualizes itself as the forum for dialogue, consultation and adoption of decisions and measures on the basis of consensus on security issues in Asia. CICA originated with the idea that there was necessity for a pan-Asiatic system of security which while addressing problems of security and confidence building would also keep in mind cultural origins, national peculiarities and also the complicated history of relationship among them. The purpose behind the initiative was the creation of a system of security in Asia where safety would be guaranteed by the whole complex of measures. CICA has been involved in dialogue over three groups of issues—military-political affairs, socio-economic development and humanitarian concerns. CICA identifies certain elements as challenges to security and seeks to find ways to eliminate them. In this context it resolves to support efforts for the elimination of weapons of mass destruction, to ensure the establishment of nuclear free zones, to curb excessive accumulation of conventional armaments, condemn terrorism, not to render any assistance to separatist movements in other states, reject the use of religion as a pretext for terrorists and separatists, emphasize the significance of curbing the movement of illicit drugs and corruption. In the context of achieving these objectives the CICA will take necessary steps for the elaboration and implementation of measures aimed at enhancing cooperation and creating an atmosphere of peace, confidence and friendship. All states are encouraged to resolve their disputes peacefully through negotiations in accordance with the principles enshrined in the UN Charter and International law.[20]

The most significant aspect of CICA is its membership which includes not just the Central Asian states and the two Eurasian powers, Russia and China but also major South and South East Asian powers. In addition it includes the US as an observer. This is significant as the reality of US presence and interest in the region cannot be wished away. Members include Afghanistan, Azerbaijan, China, Egypt, India, Iran, Israel, Kazakhstan, Kyrgyzstan, Mongolia, Pakistan, the Palestinian National Administration, Russia, Tajikistan, Thailand, Turkey and Uzbekistan. Thailand was accepted as the 17th member in 2004, and Republic of Korea as the 18th member in 2006. Observers of CICA are Vietnam, Indonesia, Korea, Malaysia, USA, Ukraine, and Japan; international organizations like the United Nations, Organization of Security and Cooperation in Europe and the League of Arab States.

The multilateral basis of the CICA is evident in the first principle enshrined in the Declaration at the Second Summit of the CICA in Almaty, in 2006. It notes:

> We are convinced that multilateral cooperation based on the principles enshrined in the Charter as well as the Principles Guiding Relations among States and in the Almaty Act is more necessary today than ever for maintaining international peace and security. To this end we will intensify our efforts to develop a forum for political dialogue through elaborating common approaches to security on the basis of consensus.

While the above is a brief account of multilateral initiatives on a regional level it was a debate on the significance of the international coalition in dealing with issues of regional security which has been the dominant focus of literature on the region, in the year following the events of September11. Here, contrary to the general perception of a movement towards bilateral arrangements with the US, there has been an increasing movement by the Central Asian states to accommodate both the US and Russia within their security arrangement. This meant that while bilateral arrangements with the US remained in place there was no attempt to move away from multilateral arrangements within the CIS or the SCO either, at least as far as some of the states were concerned. The former Kyrgyz President Askar Akaev, while explaining the existence of both American and Russian bases in his country, had an interesting explanation. He pointed out that the two parties perform different functions. While the American forces are focused on Operation Enduring Freedom in Afghanistan the Russian forces have peacekeeping objectives and are part of the CSTO commitments in combating terrorism and other regional security threats. Such agreements with multiple states and participation in multiple organizations are the common norm in the region today.

Strategic writings from Kazakhstan, for instance, clearly indicate that this is the preferred *multivector* policy that the state pursues.[21] Concluding the study on the post-September 11 scenario in Central Asia it is pointed out

> The multivector approach of foreign policy of RK has once again confirmed its expediency in complex conditions of international anti-terrorist campaign. It is necessary to pay attention to the following aspect of the foreign policy of RK in this period: inspite of the fact that Kazakhstan promoted active cooperation on the bilateral level, the importance of the regional factor and multilateral level of cooperation has greatly increased in our policy for the last year.[22]

There are interesting examples of the Central Asian states participating in different interstate organizations and in plans involving states outside the region simultaneously. For example, with the exception of Turkmenistan, the Central Asian states are participants of both the SCO and various NATO programmes. Kyrgyzstan joined the World Trade Organization in 1998, although this contradicted with the principles and interests of the customs union of various post Soviet states and of the Eurasian Economic Community, headed by Russia, which was set up on the basis of the customs union and in October 2000, and of which Kyrgyzstan is also a member. Kazakstan has been involved both with the Tengiz-Novorossiisk and the Baku-Ceyhan oil pipeline projects, the main lobbyists for which are respectively, the Russian Federation and the USA. Of course this policy has had its share of critics within the region. Talgat Ismagambetov notes that while this allows the Central Asian states to maneuver between the interests of the three world powers and where possible to extract for themselves certain short term advantages it does so without solving any problems related to the entire area of their national security.[23]

It is not surprising therefore that alternatives to the multivector policy have emerged. It has been argued for instance that Central Asia should be considered as an independent "security system."[24] As such participation of the Central Asian states in a single anti-terrorist coalition should be supplemented by their independent cooperation in this sphere. It has been argued that a "market" for security and anti-terrorist activities has taken shape in Central Asia where a number of international organizations offer their "professional assistance" in the field of regional security including UN agencies, EU, OSCE, CSTO, NATO and SCO. In addition there are a number of bilateral security agreements like the Uzbek-US strategic partnership and the Uzbek-Russia strategic partnership, the CSTO joint military exercises and the Kazakhstan-China strategic cooperation established in July 2005. As such, it has been argued that Central Asian find themselves deeply entangled in this "market."[25] In order to avoid entanglement, arguments have been put forward for the states in the region to manage their security on their own in order to escape the effects of "geo-politics and reliance on extra-regional powers."[26] In any case, it has been emphasized that the Central Asian states need to reject the "zero-sum game" and adopt a "win-win" strategy. Criticizing "inadequate old-fashioned zero-sum game geopolitics," it has been argued that instead of regarding the states of the geopolitical triangle—US, Russia, China—as permanent rivals and worse still regarding themselves as victims of geopolitical rivalry, the states should take measures towards inviting all sides of the triangle to constructive cooperation in Central Asia. As for the powers involved, geopolitical pluralism rather than geopolitical antagonism will be based on the economic incentive of energy security.

Such statements call for a reevaluation of the significance of multilateral regional forums, particularly in the light of statements that predicted their demise in dealing with problems of regional security. They also call for a more detailed analysis of evolving multilateral processes in the region like the Shanghai process.

'Constructive Strategic Partnership' as a Multilateral Form

In 1996, Russia announced the establishment of a strategic cooperation partnership with China. The rationale for evolving such a mechanism of cooperation was based on a number of factors. First, both sides recognized the dividends of a strategic partnership and Beijing has been consistent in nurturing it with good results. The Moscow-Beijing bipartisan consensus was in favour of evolving a multilateral strategy to combat threats to regional security. This was the outcome of a strong and increasingly stable bilateral entente between the two states.[27] Second, as part of a growing convergence of interests, Moscow and Beijing have pledged not to interfere in each other's domestic affairs. China has defended Russia's use of military force in the Caucasus and Moscow now defends Beijing's policy towards Taiwan, Tibet and Xinjiang. To craft issues of national interest around regional security appears to be the Sino-Russian agenda. Third, and most important, the two share resentment against a unipolar system dominated by the United States. Anxiety about the expansion of US military and economic intervention in Central Asia and the inevitable clash of interests has helped in forging a Sino-Russian entente in the Central Asian region through the creation of the Shanghai mechanism.

The process of the formation of the SCO was deeply connected with the creation of the 'strategic partnership' between Russia and China. The signing of the Shanghai Agreement in 1996, came just after a declaration of Sino-Russian 'strategic partnership' in Moscow. In the Russian foreign policy context the idea of a 'partnership' had first been used vis-à-vis NATO as the 'partnership for peace' in 1994. This phrase, proposed by the Clinton administration, was meant to denote a "peaceful buffer" between Russia and the NATO.[28] As Russian foreign policy shifted in the mid-1990s President Yeltsin first talked about a "constructive partnership" and then a "strategic partnership" with Zhang Zemin in 1996. The two parties declared their partnership as non-union and non-bloc.[29] The SCO, whose core is based on Russo-Chinese partnership turned into a multilateral partnership coping with a new threat in the SCO border areas. In 1996 Russian diplomacy had appealed for this 'strategic partnership' as a model, which in the twenty-first century could overcome the historic antagonism between countries with a long, shared border and suggested its desire for the enlargement of the partnership between China and India which share a long border.[30] China however was more cautious about the use of the term 'partnership' and expansion of Shanghai organization.

Chinese strategic writings identified the constructive strategic partnership between China, Russia and the Central Asian Republics as a stabilizing multilateral institution that will help define stability and cooperation in the region.[31] The effectiveness of the SCO in dealing with a number of issues and particularly border problems has also been noted as significant in recent Central Asian strategic writings.[32] In common with their Chinese counterparts these also point out that the continuing significance of the mechanism would depend on the relationship between Russia and China as the two main axis of the organization. While there has been cooperation within the SCO, the Chinese policy of developing the western regions and the Russian policy of strengthening the collective security mechanism, underscores the fact that there are continuing attempts at consolidating their respective positions within the region. There is also a clear recognition that this today is dependent on a number of factors the most significant of which is the development of Russo-American and Sino-American relations.

The Shanghai Forum has been identified as a new type of constructive diplomacy, which would provide Russia and China with a forum to keep in check their nascent rivalry in the region and to coordinate positions on major regional and international issues. Prior to the terrorist attacks on the US, China had become vociferous in its opposition to NATO expansion and Moscow had toughened its attitude to the US military presence on its southern borders and the US-Japan military alliance. During Russian Defense Minister Igor Sergeev's visit to China in October 1998, Moscow and Beijing stressed their common approach to three international issues: they categorically objected to NATO expansion in the east, denounced the use of force in Kosovo and disapproved of the US-Japan plans of establishing an anti-missile defense system.

The question that begs an answer is whether there can be a common strategic framework within which these issues may be addressed, given the fact that interests and perspectives of divergent states need to be taken into account. One issue on which there is common agreement is the need to develop a multilateral response to the threat of terrorism. The regional initiatives that are involved here are the SCO, CSTO and NATO. These share a number of overlapping multilateral antiterrorist activities in the Central Asian region. To reduce redundancies and exploit potential synergies the development of dialogue among them is essential.[33] It has been suggested that dialogue between the SCO, CSTO and NATO is most crucial since the United States, China and Russia are the most significant non-regional powers involved in the region. Here an ambitious idea would be to establish an overarching coordination mechanism for the region's major anti-terrorist institutions. In mid December 2005, CSTO General Director Toktasyn Buzubayev said that the CSTO favoured creating a Eurasian Advisory Council that could include representatives from the CSTO, the SCO, NATO, the EU and the Eurasian Economic Community (which includes Belarus, Kazakhstan, Kyrgyzstan, Russia and Tajikistan). It has been suggested that at a minimum such a body would allow representatives from the various institutions to meet periodically to exchange ideas and explore possible collaborative projects.[34]

Alternatively, a mechanism could be devised whereby individual SCO hosts could invite NATO observers to its sessions. At the July 2005 summit in Astana, the then SCO Chairman and host Kazakh President Nursultan Nazarbayev established a precedent by inviting senior officials from India, Iran and Pakistan to participate as 'guests of the Chairman'. Although these countries obtained formal observer status at the summit, Afghan representatives have attended several SCO meetings without receiving or requiring such status. Commenting on the inclusion of the three states with observer status Pan Guang notes that this is a big step based on a number of factors.[35] First, it exhibits to the international community the promise of openness and cooperation on regional and global issues that was made at the launch of the initiative. Secondly, it demonstrates that the SCO is concerned not just with Central Asia but also with the Middle East and South Asia as regions with close inter-connections with Central Asia. Third the recent expansion makes up a new platform for multilateral and bilateral cooperation between SCO members and SCO observers.

The SCO has also been very active in developing contacts and cooperative relations with other regional organizations and states. At the SCO Tashkent Summit the group adopted "The Regulations on the Observer Status of the Shanghai Cooperation Organization." Since then the SCO has established working relationships with some other regional organizations. In April 2004, the SCO Secretariat and the CIS Executive Committee signed a Memorandum of Understanding expressing their willingness to cooperate in the areas of trade anti-terrorism and social contacts. A similar memorandum was signed between the SCO Secretariat and the ASEAN Secretariat. These two organizations intend to cooperate in a wide range of areas including economics, finances, tourism, environmental protection, use of natural resources, social development, energy, fight against transnational crime and others.[36]

Additionally, NATO governments could seek to become a partner of specific SCO organs such as RATS (Regional Anti-terrorism Structure). Similarly in the field of narcotics trafficking there have been proposals for cooperation between the CSTO and the NATO. Strengthening security along the Tajik-Afghan border is another area where there could be collaboration between the SCO, CSTO and the NATO. The Tajik-Afghan border provides an optimal locale for multi institutional collaboration since the zone of interest of all three overlap here. The CSTO has established a special contact group with Afghanistan and the SCO has invited Afghan delegations to several of its meetings. The NATO enjoys overflight rights over Tajikistan in support of its operations in Afghanistan and provides technical assistance to Tajik border guards. The members of the three institutions have been especially concerned with the transit of Afghan heroin through Tajikistan to Russian and European markets.

Central Asian analysts have generally commented favourably on the achievements of the SCO.[37] However, there is also the recognition that the process is far from complete.

> The potential abilities of the organization have not been fully exhausted. Upto this day, the main goal of the organization was the problem of security in the region. However, the leaders of

> the six states have pointed out the necessity of intensifying the development of the programme of economic cooperation. This sphere of activity has a very promising future. A combined market of the SCO states will be the largest in the world.[38]

Here, while Beijing has been pressing for the SCO to move towards establishing a free trade area Russia has not been an enthusiastic partner as it fears Chinese advantage in the establishment of any such free trade zone. Of the two fundamental areas of SCO activity, security and development, Moscow has been emphasizing the former. Questions have also been raised about whether the SCO will be able to deal with the challenges of geopolitics and democracy that the region faces today. Here it will be faced with a dilemma; should the Organization maintain the status quo or should the Organization move towards changing the status quo and towards a new democratic regional order?[39] The extent to which the organization is able to satisfy the shared strategic objectives of Russia and China also remains to be seen.

Conclusions

Most writings on geo-strategic transformations in the Central Asian region in the post 9/11 period stressed on an undermining of multilateral security structures. The transition back to the bilateral in terms of security arrangements was in fact predicted as the most significant aspect of the transition. Moving away from arguments that identify the post—September 11 scenario as a major watershed, this paper has argued for the recognition of a reality where a multiplicity of security arrangements dealing with multiple security issues is the norm rather than agreements under one global system. While older security arrangements remain in place, newer ones are being forged to deal with emerging security issues. This is not just a reflection of the presence of Russia, China and the United States as parts of various security structures that exist in the region but also a professed policy that the states themselves follow. This becomes crucial in any understanding of geo-strategic transitions in the recent past and in examining questions that the "war against terror" has thrown up in the region.

The Central Asian region forms a significant part of the interaction between Eurasian powers today. This became more particularly so in the aftermath of September 11 with the recognition of the significance of the region in any 'war against terror'. As American presence increased and the US was offered basing rights by the Central Asian states an entirely new set of geopolitical relations was seen to be emerging where traditional areas of interest were projected to have been transformed. Along with this was the realization that the United States has developed important stakes in the region and its periphery, which would demand, continued American presence. The region is now a significant part of the strategic concerns that lies at the core of the US's interests.[40]

Yet, it is equally significant that the US perception of the region has moved beyond that of the region as an arena for a new Great Game. Strobe Talbot, Former American Deputy Secretary of State, reflected this sentiment when he pointed out, "We want all responsible players in the Caucasus and Central Asia to be winners."[41] The US focus is therefore to construct cooperative instruments in the region. In order to do so it will seek to secure Russian support and Chinese acquiescence. There is clear recognition that this is a pragmatic necessity. A confrontationist US policy will require material and manpower commitment that the US will find very difficult to commit in the region. On the other hand there is also recognition within Russia and China that the US presence is a reality, which cannot be ignored. Chinese analysts point out that while being aware of geopolitical factors China does not necessarily regard Sino–US relations as one of confrontation.[42] Sino–Russian relations did not change with the improvement of Russo–US relations and China's position in the Central Asian region was not undermined in the post 9/11 period. The SCO in fact institutionalized itself in this period. It is also a reality that none of the three want to undermine their bilateral relations and their coexistence in the region restrains open confrontation as well. None intends to ally with one against the other and none is pleased to see a united front formed by two against one. At the same time none want to see the region monopolized by one power. Counter-terrorism and the need for stability and development in the Central Asian region remain the common interest pursued by all three.

However, a number of analysts have pointed out that since 2003, there seems to be the revival of geopolitical rivalry in the region centred round Uzbekistan and the SCO. This would be unfortunate. A more realistic move would be towards cooperation on issues where all three share common positions. Here the lack of a road map on where this cooperation could begin is a major obstacle. Similarly questions have been raised about the sustainability of such institutions. It has been suggested that deep multilateral cooperation is unrealistic at the present stage. There is also no strong necessity for the setting up of a trilateral cooperation framework in Central Asia separate from those that already exist. Beside any cooperation framework that excludes the Central Asian states will be problematic. A multilateral cooperation mechanism on a larger scale would be more effective option for dialogue. In this connection suggestions have been put forward that the US be accepted as an observer in the SCO process since it cannot be completely excluded from the region.[43] Similarly, in the long run NATO's expansion towards the Chinese border is equally inevitable. The inclusion of China within the PfP could be another option though it carries with it its own problems.[44] Another option would be to consider the CICA as an effective multilateral forum for dialogue.

This article has sought to set out the parameters of a more comprehensive and informed debate on the pros and cons of the multilateral system in the Central Asian region. This is challenged today by the competitive interests and demands of a number of state as well as alternative non-governmental institutions. What has been argued for in this article is for the recognition of the fact that these tend to complement rather than undermine the necessity of these multilateral institutions. What remain significant is to develop these institutions as more effective in terms of decision making and operational mechanisms.

Notes

1. See for instance, Stephen Schlesinger, "The United States and the World: Is a Return to Multilateralism Possible?" in *United Nations: Multilateralism and International Security*, C. Uday Bhaskar and others (eds) (Delhi: Shipra Publications, 2005).
2. John Gerard Ruggie (ed.), *Multilateralism Matters, the Theory and Praxis of an Institutional Form* (New York: Columbia University Press, 1993).
3. Collective security as a distinct multilateral approach towards global security was the centrepiece of the United Nations Charter. The lack of institutionalized sanction against states that deliberately defied the principle, however, proved to be its major impediment.
4. Muthiah Alagappa, *Asian Security Practice: Material and Ideational Influences* (Stanford: Stanford University Press, 1998), 4.
5. See for instance, Anatol Lieven, "The End of NATO," *Prospect*, December 2001, cited from Anar Khamzayeva, "Novaya Strategiya NATO? Ee Posledstviya Dliya Tsentralnoi Azii," *Kazakstan i Sovremennie Mir* 1 (2), 2002.
6. It has been argued that the US is not a principled multilateralist but an instrumental multilateralist whose core is pragmatism. For a detailed

analysis of the various visions about multilateralism see, Joachim Krause, "Multilateralism: Behind European Views," *The Washington Quarterly* 27(2), Spring 2004.

7. John Van Oudenaren, "What is Multilateral?" *Policy Review* 117 and "Unipolar Versus Unilateral," *Policy Review* 124.
8. This idea is represented in this quote from a Chinese scholar Huang Zhengji who notes, "multipolarity just refers to the multiple forces in the international community that are possessed of certain strengths and are representative of certain interests." See, Hung Zhengji, "The Irresistible Multipolarity Trend of the World," *International Strategic Studies* no. 4, 1997.
9. In the Central Asian region the emergence of "new" threats has led to calls for reform of the UN and creation of effective multilateral forums to curb terrorism. See for instance the speech by the State Secretary-Minister of Foreign Affairs of the Republic of Kazakhstan, "Vestupleniye Kasymzhomarta Tokayeva na Transaziatskom Parlamentskom Forume PA OSCE vorba protiv terrorizma: ucpekhi, noviye ugrozi," *Kazakhstan i Sovremennie Mir* 2 (5), 2003, where he clearly notes that "there is no alternative to global multilateral cooperation of nations."
10. In recent times Russia has stressed the significance of multilateralism. See for instance *Speech by Minister of Foreign Affairs of the Russian Federation Igor Ivanov at the Joint Session of Federation Council and State Duma Foreign Affairs Committees*, 12 February, 2004 which points to "assertion of multilateralism in international relations, the strengthening of the role of the UN and International law." Russian Ministry of Foreign Affairs, http://www.russianembassy.org. Similarly the Ministry of Foreign Affairs, China elaborating on foreign policy clearly points to the necessity of multilateral options. www.fmprc.gov.cn/eng
11. For a detailed analysis of this conditional multilateralism see, Jing-dong Yuan, *Asia-Pacific Security: China's Conditional Multilateralism and Great Power Entente* (Carlisle, Pennsylvania: Strategic Studies Institute Publication, 2000). This, however, seems to be changing with regard to at least some multilateral organizations. The SCO for instance is now attempting to institutionalize its activities with the establishment of a Secretariat and the regional anti-terrorist centre at Tashkent.
12. Uzbekistan is the most recent entrant in the CSTO process. This means that Uzbekistan is now committed to maintaining security in all CSTO member states.
13. For writings that stress on the inevitability of change in geopolitical alignments around Central Asia and the image of the region as "liberated" from the Russo-Chinese condominium institutionalized in the SCO, see Svante E. Cornell, "Introduction," *Nordic Newsletter of Asian Studies* 3, 2002. See also Stephen Blank, "The Shanghai Cooperative Organization: A Post Mortem," *Nordic Newsletter of Asian Studies* 3, 2002.
14. See for instance, S Neil MacFarlane, "The United States and Regionalism

in Central Asia," *International Affairs* 80(3), May 2004, who argues that the US has actively promoted the establishment of the NATO's PfP, rather than seeking to establish a free standing regional security structures and similarly in the economic sphere has promoted accession to the WTO far more consistently than any regional trading structures.

15. In May 2005 there were demonstrations in Andijan when thousands of protestors took to the streets attacking a prison to protest the detention of 23 prominent businessmen. The men were charged with anti-constitutional activity and forming a criminal and extremist organization, *Akramia*, accused by the Uzbek Government of having links with the outlawed radical Islamic party *Hizb-ut-Tahrir*. The arrested men formed the backbone of Andijan's small business community giving employment to thousands of people in the impoverished and densely populated Ferghana Valley. Armed demonstrators then went to a prison and freed nearly 2000 inmates, including men accused by the Uzbek Government of criminal activities. The severity with which the demonstration was put down by government forces was criticized by the US Government subsequently leading to a downswing in Uzbek-US relations.
16. At the July 2005 Summit of the SCO a statement was issued to the effect "As the active military phase in the anti-terror operation in Afghanistan is nearing completion, the SCO would like the coalition's members to decide on the deadline for the use of temporary infrastructure and for their military contingents' presence in those countries." This was remarkable in that it indicated a possible rebalancing of foreign policy priorities and interests for SCO members. However, assigning the SCO statement its proper significance is a complicated task. The US maintains important ties with individual members of the SCO and all the observers, except Iran. It is unlikely that this relationship will be sacrificed over Central Asia or that Central Asia provides a compelling base of support from which to challenge US leadership.
17. Mashan Meiirzhan elaborates on the role of the Central Asian Economic Union in this regard in his article, "Regional Security as a System Factor in Central Asian Integration," in *Peace and Security in Central Asia*, Jasjit Singh (ed.) (New Delhi: IDSA, 2000).
18. For a detailed discussion see, Anita Sengupta, "Region, Regionalization, Regionalism: The 'Myth' of Tsentralnaya Aziia Revisted," in *Central Asia since Independence*, K. Warikoo and Mahavir Singh (eds) (New Delhi: Shipra Publications, 2004).
19. Cited from *Carnegie Endowment for International Peace, Meeting Report* 2(8), 3 November 2000, www.ceip.org/files/events/gulomov.asp?EventID==218
20. For a detailed analysis of CICA see, Murat Laumulin, *The Security, Foreign Policy, and International Relationship of Kazakhstan After Independence, 1991-2001* (Almaty: Kazakhstan Institute of Strategic Studies and Freidrich Ebert Shiftung, 2002) and Ashimbaev *et al* (eds), *New*

Challenges and New Geopolitics in Central Asia After September 11 (Almaty: Kazakhstan Institute for Strategic Studies, 2003).

21. *Multivector* refers to a policy where choices were kept open for both bilateral and multilateral agreements on particular issues according to specific security perceptions of individual states. In the Central Asian case options for bilateral agreements were kept open with all the major powers, Russia, China and the United States.
22. M. Ashimbaev et al (eds), *New Challenges and New Geopolitics in Central Asia After September 11.*
23. Talgat Ismagambetov, "Some Geopolitical Peculiarities of Central Asia, Past and Present," in *Oil, Transition and Security in Central Asia*, Sally N. Cummings (ed.) (London and New York: Routledge-Curzon, 2003).
24. A security system, as defined by Barry Buzan, is a group of states whose security interests bind them sufficiently closely so that their national security cannot be realistically considered separate from each other.
25. Farkhod Tolipov, "East Vs West? Some Geopolitical Questions and Observations for the SCO," *CEF Quarterly,* July 2005.
26. Farkhod Tolipov, "Multilateralism, Bilateralism and Unilateralism in Fighting Terrorism in the SCO Area," *China and Eurasia Forum Quarterly* 4 (2), 2006.
27. Stephen Blank, "Which Way for Sino-Russian Relations?" *Orbis*, Summer 1998.
28. This however did not work since the US changed its cautious policy towards the NATO and Poland, the Czech Republic and Hungary became a part of it. For details see, V Zhurkin, "Russia and the Enlargement of NATO," in *The Emerging New Regional Order in Central and Eastern Europe*, T. Hayashi (ed.) (Sapporo: Slavic Research Centre, 1997).
29. See the text of the Russo-Chinese Joint Declaration in *Sbornik: Rossiisko-Kitaiskikh Dogovorov*, 1999 cited from Akihiro Iwashita, "The Shanghai Cooperation Organization and Its Implications for Eurasian Security: A New Dimension of 'Partnership' after the Post Cold War Period," in *Slavic Eurasia's Integration into the World Economy and Community*, S. Tabata and A. Iwashita (eds) (Sapporo: Slavic Research Centre, 2004).
30. *Krasnaia Zvezda*, 30 April 1996, cited from Iwashita, "The Shanghai Cooperation Organization and Its Implications for Eurasian Security."
31. Pan Guang, "China-Central Asia-Russia Relations and the Role of the SCO in the War against Terrorism," *SIIS Journal* 9(2), May 2002.
32. Ashimbaev *et al* (eds), *New Challenges and New Geopolitics in Central Asia After September 11.*
33. In fact the idea has been present within strategic think tanks in the region as well. In the course of a meeting that the author had with members of the Centre for Foreign Policy and Analysis in Almaty, in December 2003 (an organization under the Ministry of External Affairs, Kazakhstan), the idea of developing a cooperative mechanism between NATO, CICA and

SCO was referred to. It was emphasized that since the three share common concerns coordination among them would prevent unnecessary overlap

34. For a detailed discussion see Richard Weitz, "Terrorism in Eurasia: Enhancing the Multilateral Response," *China and Eurasian Forum Quarterly* 4(2), 2006.
35. See Pan Guang, "The New SCO Observers: Making a Leap Forward in Cautious Augmentation," *CEF Quarterly*, July 2005.
36. For details see, Zhou Huasheng, "The SCO in the Last Year," *CEF Quarterly*, July 2005.
37. Bondarez, "Formirovaniye Systemi Collectivnoi Bezopasnosti v Tsentralnoi Azii—osobennosti, itogi, perspectivi." However, there remains opinion to the contrary. In the course of a conversation with the author, on November 26, 2003 at the *Institut Vostokovedennia* in Moscow, Professor Shaken Nadirov, an ethnic Kazakh associated with the *Institut Vostokovedeniia*, pointed out that the SCO was a Chinese creation aimed at dealing with separatism in Xinjiang. As such it has nothing to do with the Kazakh people.
38. Assylbek Tauasarov, "SHOS Priobretaet Realnie Ochertaniya," *Kazakhstan i Sovremennie Mir* 2(5), 2003.
39. Tolipov, "East Vs West? Some Geopolitical Questions and Observations for the SCO."
40. For details see Amitabh Mattoo, "United States of America and Central Asia: Beginning of the Great Game," in *Central Asia the Great Game Replayed, an Indian Perspective*, Nirmala Joshi (ed.) (Delhi: New Century Publications, 2003).
41. Strobe Talbott, "A Farewell to Flashman: American Policy in the Caucasus and Central Asia," Speech at the Central Asia Institute, School of Advanced International Studies, The John Hopkins University, 21 July, 1997.
42. Zhou Huasheng, "China, Russia and the United States: Prospects for Cooperation in Central Asia," *CEF Quarterly*, February 2005.
43. Dmitri Trenin, "Russia and the Shanghai Cooperation Organization: A Difficult Match," *CEF Quarterly*, July 2005.
44. See for instance, Huasheng, "China, Russia and the United States: Prospects for Cooperation in Central Asia." Huasheng is Director of the Centre for Russian and Central Asian Studies at the Fudan University in Shanghai.

5

Turkey's Search for Identity: A Eurasian and Islamic Country

Ayla Göl

The revival of Islam since 9/11 has often been identified as a failure of modernization and the inexorable emergence of fundamentalism and terrorism in the western media and in political discourses. The role of Islam in Turkish politics cannot be directly related to the rise of Islamism in regional and global contexts after 9/11 and the US-led occupation of Iraq. Turkey is usually described as a bridge—according to the so-called bridge theory—between Europe and Asia, the West and the (Middle) East or the western and the Islamic civilizations.[1] This identification seems logical given the fact that Turkey is geographically located in between Europe and the Middle East. Historically, Turkey was the first example of the transferring of an Islamic empire to a secular nation-state outside Europe, in the 1920s. It is also the first Muslim country that achieved candidature for the European Union (EU) membership in the twenty-first century. However, the ongoing debates about Turkey's membership in the EU have put, not only its role as a bridge, but also the Turkish identity, its history and culture in question, in the context of European collective history and identity.

While the so-called 'bridge theory' suggests that Turkey acts as a mediator between the West and the East the counter argument emphasizes Turkey's role as a geographical barrier between Europe and the conflict zones in the Middle East and the Caucasus. According to Huntington, rather than a bridge Turkey had become a 'torn' country that "has a single predominant culture which places it in one civilization but its leaders want to shift to another civilization."[2] Huntington argues that "a bridge ...is an artificial creation connecting two solid entities but is part of neither. When Turkey's leaders term their country a bridge, they euphemistically confirm that it is torn."[3] He also identified Australia, Mexico and Russia as other torn countries, which are identified by two phenomena. "Their leaders refer to them as a 'bridge' between two cultures, and observers describe them as Janus-faced. 'Russia look West—and East'; 'Turkey: East, West, which is best?'; 'Australian nationalism: Divided loyalties'; are typical headlines highlighting *torn country identity problems*."[4] (Emphasis mine) In Huntington's opinion, among these states Turkey is "the classic torn country which since the 1920s has been trying to modernize, to westernize, and to become part of the West."[5] However, the Muslim character of Turkish society and the Islamic legacy of the country are not compatible with westernization and modernization. Despite the secular character of the Turkish state, Huntington places it in the Islamic civilizational realm when categorizing civilizations of the world.[6]

This chapter challenges Huntington's 'torn' country and 'clash of civilizations' thesis by arguing that the Turkish historical experience is based on a *synthesis* rather than a clash of competing Islamic and western civilizations. Turkey is neither a torn country nor a bridge between Europe and the Middle East, but a 'Eurasian' country that historically combines the fundamental characteristics of both the East and the West, geographically connecting Europe to Asia. There is no doubt that Turkey's engagements with the western model—characterized by modernization, democratization and secularization—pose a matrix of political, religious, cultural and social questions but this should not be interpreted as Islam's incompatibility with the western civilization.

There is a general tendency—mainly influenced by Gellner and Huntington's arguments—to claim that wherever Islam is a powerful societal force, as it is in the case of Turkey, there is little success in building a modern democratic and secular state based on the western model. This chapter disagrees with the essentialist understanding of Islam in the context of Turkey. It argues that western modernity does not clash with the Islamic character of Turkish society. However, the universal character of modernity does not imply that Turkey's unique historical and societal factors are unimportant. On the contrary, these socio-historical dimensions are important to explain the complexity of a Muslim society's engagement with the West in the context of democratization and secularization, which are two sides of the same coin. On the one hand, the Turkish experience in secularism with its 'authoritarian' character essentially differs from any other western society. On the other, Turkey is not a fully-fledged democracy due to the interference of the military in politics and the lack of minority rights. These obstacles cannot be attributed to the strength of religion but to the existence of a strong state and a weak civil society in Turkey. Thus, this chapter aims to explain how Turkey has produced its own *synthesis* by combining its Islamic and European characteristics.

The first part of the chapter will put the alleged clash of civilization thesis into question in relation to Turkey's torn country status and related identity problems. In the second section, I explore what secularism means in Turkey. The main assumption is that the claim about a binary opposition between the secularism of the Turkish state and the Muslim identity of Turkish society is misleading in understanding the current political developments and protest meetings of 2007. The third part of the chapter will explain the possibility of a Muslim democracy in Turkey by refuting Huntington's claims. Turkey's experience in democratization will be analysed in relation to its specific social and historical conditions as well as international and regional dynamics. The chapter concludes by suggesting that Turkey is neither a bridge nor a torn country between the two civilizations but a unique country, which produced its own endogenous 'Eurasianism' between two geo-cultural and socio-political systems. Such an analysis recognizes the possibility of interacting civilizational dynamics and '*multiple modernities*' in the world.[7]

Turkey as a Torn Country

Based on his essentialist understanding of Islam and unitary conception of civilizational identity, Huntington claims that "[a]t some point, Turkey could be ready to give up its frustrating and humiliating role as a beggar pledging for membership in the West and to resume its much more impressive and elevated historical role as the principal Islamic interlocutor and antagonist of the West."[8] According to his thesis, Turkey is more likely to turn back to its Islamic identity after "having experienced the bad and good of the West in secularism and democracy."[9] As Casanova suggests, "Huntington would apparently welcome such a transformation of Turkey from a secular to a Muslim state, if only to fulfil his own prophecy of the inevitable clash of civilisations."[10] However, Huntington's claims in the context of Turkey's relations with the West are historically and geopolitically inaccurate. It seems that Huntington is referring to the golden age of the Ottoman Empire as the antagonist of the West. He fails to acknowledge that the Sublime Porte—*Bab-i Ali*—was geopolitically part of the Concert of

Europe and developed close relations with the West through war, trade and diplomacy, since the fifteenth century.

Unlike other post-colonial countries in Asia, Africa, Latin America and the Middle East, there is no evidence of strong anti-western feelings in Turkish politics. On the contrary, Turkey has always had a pro-western orientation not only with the establishment of the Turkish Republic under the leadership of Mustafa Kemal Ataturk in 1923, but also since the Ottoman modernization policies of the nineteenth century. The modern Turkish state became the 13th member state of the Council of Europe in 1949, and then a member of the North Atlantic Treaty Organization (NATO) in 1952.[11] Therefore, Turkey has already secured its membership in two key military and cultural organizations of the West. Huntington's claim about Turkey's "humiliating role as a beggar pledging for membership in the West," is incorrect, unless he is referring to Turkey's problematic candidacy for the economic organization of European states, the EU.[12] Turkey's unsettled membership within the EU reflects the political divisions among European states in reference to what the European project and identity means. More importantly, the European states have to reach an agreement whether they recognise Turkey's place in Europe or not.

According to Huntington's thesis, there are at least three requirements of redefining a torn country's civilizational identity: "First, the political and economic elite of the country has to be generally supportive of and enthusiastic about this move. Second, the public has to be at least willing to acquiesce in the redefinition of its identity. Third the dominant elements in the host civilization, in most cases the West, have to be willing to embrace the convert."[13] If we apply these conditions to current identity politics in Turkey there are contradictory aspects, which refute Huntington's claims, as manifested in the current protest meetings in the name of republicanism and secularism, in April and May 2007.

In relation to his first requirement, the AKP (*Adalet ve Kalkinma Partisi*—Justice and Development Party—JDP) Government, despite its Islamic roots, has not been challenging Turkey's pro-western direction and policies since it took power in November 2002. If Huntington was right the AKP would have given up the previous Turkish Government's aim to become a member of the EU and redefine Turkey's identity as an Islamic state and thus, acclaim its Islamic civilization. In Huntington's thesis, it is not very clear how Turkey under the AKP Government must redefine its civilizational identity: is it regarded as part of European or Islamic civilization? Huntington argues that only the Kemalist oriented elite wants to be a part of the West, while the society itself has a different orientation. But a democratically elected government clearly represents the political will of a society and the AKP's victory is not an exception.

When the AKP came to power many claimed that Islam was on the rise in Turkey. The AKP's victory demonstrated that political Islam was a reaction to Turkey's failed modernisation based on Kemalist secularism.[14] The AKP's domestic and foreign policies have, after almost five years in government, not yet shown anti-modernization and anti-western orientations. In fact, the AKP is determined more than any previous government to achieve Turkey's EU membership. It is usually an overlooked fact that the AKP used a populist and nationalist discourse in order to win the elections in 2002.[15] Moreover, the AKP is not the first party to play the 'Islamic card' in Turkish politics. Since 1950, both right wing and religious parties have used the religious factor to their own ends. The AKP learnt from the mistakes of its predecessors: the National Salvation Party (*Milli Selamet Partisi MSP*) under the leadership of Necmeddin Erbakan in the 1970s, the Welfare Party (*Refah Partisi, RP*) again under Erbakan's leadership in the 1980s and 1990s; the Virtue Party (*Fazilet Partisi*) and the Felicity Party (*Saadet Partisi*) which were established after the 1997 post-modern coup. The Virtue Party was closed down by the Constitutional Court in 2001, for anti-secular activities.[16] All these parties clearly played the 'Islamic card' during the election campaigns but they knew that voters cared more about economic issues than religious issues.[17]

The former mayor of Istanbul, Recep Tayyip Erdogan, led the reformist group of the Welfare/Felicity Party to leave the traditionalists and establish a new party—the AKP.[18] Its leaders emphasized the idea of a new and clean (*ak* literally means both white and clean in Turkish) leadership that was determined to eradicate corruption from the state system. Many voters wanted to get rid of the old leadership and two-thirds of them had never voted for Islamist parties before. The crucial factor was the economic crisis of 2001, which led the voters to try out a new party and its promising leadership. While the AKP introduced new blood into politics, the majority of its voters were enticed by economic and social problems rather than the party's views on religion. For instance, the most controversial headscarf issue was in 8th place—way below more significant concerns about the economy, corruption and joining the EU. The AKP leaders not only used a very clever mix of modernity and tradition but also aimed to attract different sections of the society. The AKP continued to operate within the structure of the existing political system and to use an even stronger nationalist discourse for the early election campaigns in the summer of 2007.

According to the second requirement of Huntington's torn country claim, the redefinition of a civilizational identity takes place reluctantly without protests. The political tension between Kemalist secularists and the AK Party government has been highlighted by the presidential candidacy of the foreign minister Abdullah Gül, who is accused of having a hidden Islamist agenda. The protest meetings of secularists—described as the Republic Protests (*Cumhuriyet Mitingleri*)—which took place in Ankara, Istanbul and Izmir, between 14 April and 20 May 2007, was the first example of its kind in Turkish history which challenges Huntington's claims. He argued that "Turkey may be equally qualified to lead Islam. But to do so it would have to reject Ataturk's legacy more thoroughly than Russia has rejected Lenin's."[19] The protest meetings prove him wrong: many demonstrators carried pictures of Mustafa Kemal Ataturk and Turkish flags while chanting slogans to express their determination to protect secularism and republicanism as the main principles of Kemalism.[20] These peaceful mass rallies clearly demonstrated the determination of the people to protect Ataturk's legacy and support the country's secular system against any Islamic agenda.

These events had been the strongest manifestation of the acceptance of secular identity by a broad spectrum of the Turkish society. Although there are controversial debates about which groups—in particular the army or retired members of the Turkish military forces—were involved in organizing these meetings, there is no doubt that millions of people were mobilized and they were strongly supported by NGOs, in particular women's civil society organizations.[21]

It is also important to note that the secularist demonstrators criticized the role of the army in Turkish politics as well as the hidden Islamic agenda of the AKP Government. For these people, neither a military coup nor an Islamic state—*Shari'a*—is desirable for Turkish democracy.[22] The problem is not Islam itself but the use of religion and religious identity, demonstrated by the presidential candidacy in state affairs. It is not easy to decide to what extent these claims are valid. If we accept that modernity is inherently creative then it is consequently, never a completed process. As such, the AKP's tenure in power is clearly not aimed to Islamize the state institutions but to create a sense of identity to remove attention away from state and high politics which disguise the agency of the public sphere. The fears of Islam and the alleged hidden agenda of the AKP seem to be exaggerated.

Consequently, the AKP's use of the state power with support of the Muslim bourgeoisie, media and the discourse of nationalism, for its own ends, created a new cycle within which the secularists are politically *constructed as the new reactionaries*. This group perceives that their secular identity and daily lifestyle, such as the freedom of drinking alcohol, wearing non-religious clothing—from mini skirts to bikinis and not wearing head scarves as well as being able to hold a driving licence for women—is threatened by the AKP's envisaged Islamic identity. In this case, one can argue that secularism in Turkey has moved beyond a state project and become a social phenomenon. This challenges not only Huntington's claims but also the classic textbook explanations about Turkish secularism: there is a tension between the secular character of the state and the Islamic identity of the society. On the contrary, recent developments prove that there is a tension between the Islamic agenda of the AKP Government and the secular character of the Turkish society.

Huntington's third requirement of the redefinition of a civilizational identity is probably the most acceptable and relevant claim. Turkey with its secularized state institutions and society represents a convergence, not a clash between eastern and western civilizations. Nevertheless, the acid test is whether the host civilization—the West—will recognize such a convergence. As Huntington puts it, "The West has to be willing to embrace the convert."[23] Although Huntington is right to identify the West—i.e. member states of the EU—as representative of the host civilization his description of Turkey as a 'convert' is misleading. Moreover, "the view from inside Turkey attests that Huntington's picture is a mere caricature of Turkey's political realities. Certainly, there is—as in all EU member-states—a broad coalition of EU sceptics."[24] Even if Turkey does not become a member of the EU in the near future, the possibility of turning itself into an Islamic state seems to be a preposterous suggestion. Huntington does not recognize that the historical processes of secularization and democratization have also begun in Turkey, evidenced by the pro-western choices of its leaders.

The Turkish experience proves that democratic institutions can take hold in a Muslim society where religion and politics are separated. Whether European states will acknowledge the diversity of Turkey with its five-times-a-day praying calls and Eurasian identity depends on how they define 'Western civilization'. Most probably, Turkey is not European enough to be accepted as part of the West. Similarly, due to its secular character Turkey is not Islamic enough to be regarded as part of the Muslim world. Therefore, the next section explores what secularism means in Turkish politics.

Secularism as a Social Phenomenon

It is a historical fact that Turkey is the first secular state in the Muslim world. Gellner and Huntington's claims can be identified as the most influential theses of secularization and modernization. According to Gellner, Muslim societies cannot be secularized since Islam as a religion displays unique characteristics which are resistant to modernity and secularization.[25] Furthermore, "secularisation and democratisation have been often considered mutually reinforcing processes" in modernisation theories.[26] If we focus on the secularization thesis first, the separation between religion and politics takes place in societies through the development of modernization, industrialization and rationalization.

Many views on the incompatibility of Islam, secularism and democracy are generally based on an essentialist as well as Orientalist view of Islam.[27] In this view, Islam is portrayed as a unified homogenous phenomenon, which is incompatible with European modernity and its essential characteristics of secularism and democracy. This view does not acknowledge that there are different interpretations and political trajectories of Islam, that are wide ranging from Algeria, Morocco via Turkey to Indonesia and Malaysia. More importantly, the lack of democracy in many developing countries in Latin America, Africa and Asia, cannot be attributed to the strength of Islam when there are different belief systems in these countries.

In reference to secularization and Islam, it is important to make a differentiation between a separation of religion and state (*din wa dawla*) and that of religion and politics (*din wa siyasa*). Turkey's experience in secularisation is described as laical (*laiklik*),[28] "based on the principles of positivist secularism that was modelled after French republican laicity, Jacobin statism, and vanguard elitism."[29] In its classic definition, "secularisation refers to the divorce of public affairs, including law and education, from religion."[30] Therefore, there is a clear separation between religion and state institutions, but not necessarily between religion and politics.

It is usually claimed that the founders of the Turkish Republic achieved the separation between religion and state in an 'authoritarian' way.[31] However, religion was placed under the control of the state rather than create a distinct separation between the two. The abolition of the Caliphate in 1924 instigated the institutionalization of cutting ties with Islam, which represented tradition, the irrationality and backwardness of the Ottoman Empire. In the same year, the closure of Holy Places, banning of Dervish orders and the establishment of the Directorate for Religious Affairs were followed as part of this revolutionary transition. Islamic authority, practice and knowledge, was tightly *included* rather than *excluded* under the strict control of the secular state which controlled the public visibility of Islam. The banning of the veil and the *fez* (the latter was banned in the Hat Law of 1925) was an attempt to project an image of civilization during the founding years of the Republic. Indeed, a raft of other measures such as the imposition of the Gregorian calendar, the introduction of a Western Penal Code as well as the replacement of Arabic script with a Latin alphabet in 1928 and a Turkish translation of the Koran from Arabic (with the call to prayer—*ezan*—sung in Turkish), were all implemented to reinforce the visibility and symbolic omnipotence of a secular way of life.[32] These reforms, to a certain extent, reflected the competing representations of tradition and modernity, Islam and secularism.

Consequently, Turkey's particularly unique experience in secularism was criticized for putting religious affairs under the direct control of state institutions rather than the common pattern in the West where all religious affairs are separated from formal political affairs. This process has two important repercussions. First, the Turkish secularism produced "a ruling administrative military-civilian bureaucratic elite with a distinct identity as 'laik Turks,' separate from ordinary backward Muslim subjects." Second, Islam is perceived as a threat to the secular character of the state, which produced "the ideology of a national security state with an exclusionary code of violence."[33]

However, the main problem with this analysis is that it assumes a strong tension between the above-implemented secularism of the state and the repressed Islam of the Turkish society. For this understanding, it is the very nature of the secularization project as an imposition from above that contributed towards the politicization of Islam. The control of religion by state led to the repression of Islam that has been regarded as 'reactionary' for its subversive potential by the Republicans. Not only the binary oppositions of state and society, public and private are inherently problematic but also the assumption that secularism remains as a state *project* is deeply problematic. Such an understanding does not acknowledge the possibility of turning a secular project into a social phenomenon and historical process that penetrates into the different layers of the Turkish society.

In particular, the sheer support of the civilians to the Republican mass rallies in 2007 and 2008, can be interpreted as a sign of the Turkish people's acceptance of secularism. To be more specific, a counter model of the Turkish secular state would be an Islamic state where the legal system is based on the Islamic law (Shari'a). According to the Gallup's World Poll Special Report on the Muslim World in 2006, Turkey is the only country, "where 57 per cent say Shari'a should not be a source of legislation, not surprising for a country whose constitution explicitly limits the role of religion in the governmental sphere."[34] Interestingly, Lebanon is the second as 33 per cent and Indonesia is the third as 18 per cent concur with this view. Iran is the fourth with 14 per cent while 66 per cent supports the idea that "S*hari'a* must be a source of legislation but not the only source." This percentage is 23 in Turkey.[35] Only 12 per cent of Turkish people support the idea of an Islamic state by accepting Shari'a as the only source of legislation.[36]

Two polar opposite trends—the militant secularist *v* the radical Islamists—do not represent the majority of Turkish society's views on secularism. One can argue that *laicity* (*laiklik*) has established itself in important areas of state and society, "largely due to the power resources available to the secular state apparatus"—in particular legal and educational systems—as well as its international connections.[37] The AKP's electoral victory has been wrongly interpreted as the rise of Islamism in Turkish public affairs. Many observers interpreted it as the previous bastion of secularism in the Muslim world was endangered.[38] The secularist demonstrations of 2007 and 2008 proved that these observers were wrong. Similarly, the secularist demonstrators criticised the army's interference in state affairs, which is also an important indication of current political developments.

The Turkish experience demonstrates that secularism and democratization are the two sides of the same coin. They mutually constitute and reinforce each other. However, the recent developments in Turkey reveal the contested nature of a paradoxical relationship between secularization and democratization. On the one hand, secularization is seen as an essential prerequisite of democratization and on the other, Turkey's relative progress in democratization is also associated with its authoritarian state secularism. There is a *paradoxical partnership* between secularism and democratization in Turkey due to the role of the army in this relationship, which raises the question: Can there be a Muslim democracy?

Turkey as a Muslim Democracy

Despite the fact that Turkey has sustained democracy since 1946, it is the only democratic Muslim country, not only in the Middle East but also the Muslim world, yet it is not recognized as a democratic state by Freedom House.[39] According to this US-based international think tank, Israel stands out as the only democracy in the Middle East, despite also being classified as the least democratic region in the world. Based on these assumptions, the essentialist view of Islam concludes that the 'democracy deficit' in the Middle East is a consequence of religious or cultural obstacles.[40] It is either Islam or Arab culture or both, which obstruct democratization in the region.

According to research by Alfred Stephan, in the 47 countries with an Islamic majority, 11 (23 per cent) countries have democratically elected governments.[41] This situation deserves very careful consideration of the underlying historical, socio-economic and international factors—such as colonialism, underdevelopment, illiteracy and poverty—rather than explaining it as an 'Arab exceptionalism.'

The Turkish engagement in the establishment and consolidation of democracy in spite of its own "fault lines" has differed from those of both developing western states, most developing countries, as well as Arab states of the Middle East.[42] Many scholars argue that democracy took root in Turkey only after Islam was excluded from the public realm in the early years of the Republic.[43] However, the recent history of Turkey demonstrates that democracy has been consolidated by the gradual inclusion of Islam into politics, even "while constitutional and legal secularism have been kept intact."[44] This is the key to understanding the causes of the recent public demonstrations: to protect constitutional and legal secularism via democratic mechanisms, in Turkey.

There had been a strong state tradition in Ottoman/Turkish history, and this tradition remains to be the main obstacle of the Turkish transition to democracy. The rigid control of the public sphere by the state was the dominant character of Turkish politics between 1923 and 1946 under the single-party rule (*Cumhuriyet Halk Partisi*—Ataturk's Republican Peoples Party). A multi-party system began after the first victory of an opposition party (Democrat Party) in 1950. State power softened gradually throughout the 1950s and the 1960s while the global liberalization policies of the 1980s and the 1990s introduced new conditions for democratization. Meanwhile, Turkish democracy was interrupted by three direct and two indirect military interventions in politics: three direct military coups in 1960, 1971, and 1980, and then a post-modern/soft coup in 1997, followed by the indirect interference into the presidential candidacy in April 2007.[45] The Turkish Armed Forces act as the self-appointed guardians of the secular state system. "In its self-appointed role as the 'guardian' of the unitary, secular state, the military occupies the paradoxical position of 'safeguarding' democracy while at the same time posing a major challenge to further democratisation."[46] Well-trained Turkish generals must be well aware of the fact that there is no place for a strong army in a fully democratic Turkey.

One can argue that it is almost a tradition to experience a military intervention in every decade since Turkey's advance to a multi-party system. However, direct military rule has been an exception rather than a constant rule in Turkish politics since 1960. There is a paradox here: the army interferes as the guardians of secularism and each military intervention seriously harms democratization processes by pushing the country's democratic advancement at least 10 years back. It sounds like the famous Turkish march—two steps forward and one step backwards. Furthermore, military interferences also produced a unique military-state elite and mentality which utilized religion, when necessary, according to their own understandings and needs.

As Feroz Ahmad argues, the paradoxical role of the military particularly contributed to the politicization of Islam after the 1980 coup and religion has become an instrument of social control.[47] Within the Cold War mentality, the atheist communist threat from the Soviet block was framed as the main threat to Turkish security. The generals of the 1980 coup blamed this communist threat for the ideological and violent street struggles between left and the right wing youngsters. The solution was found in the so-called "Turkish-Islamic synthesis," which was originally theorized by intellectuals (*Aydinlar Ocagi*—Intellectuals' House) of the right. It "became the quasi-official ideology of the military regime. Based on the typical fascist tripod of 'barracks, mosque and family,' the Turkish-Islamic synthesis was geared to bring the rebellious youth back into the folds of the establishment through emphasising obedience to authority and fear of God."[48] Although this semi-religious, semi-military nationalism did not function as the generals expected, this mentality led the state elite and the establishment to turn a blind eye to growing religious organizations and sentiments during the 1980s and 1990s. The increasing visibility of Islam in the public sphere in the 2000s only makes sense within these socio-historical conditions.

The AKP won the elections in 2002 and 2007, because it had embraced the rules of the only game in town—democracy and recognized the legitimacy of the army as the guardian of secularism. Although the relationship between secularism and democratization appears to be paradoxical in the Turkish context it still proves that "Muslim democracy is as possible and viable today in Turkey as Christian democracy was half a century ago in Western Europe."[49] If Turkey is less advanced than Europe it is also relatively more advanced in democratization than other Middle Eastern countries. The following historical, socio-economic and international explanations will help us to understand Turkey's exceptionalism:

i. *Historical explanation*: Turkey, of all the Muslim countries has had the longest engagement with democracy. In accordance with the modernization policies of the Ottoman Empire, Turks were introduced to the idea of a constitutional parliamentary regime first between December 1876 and February 1878, and second, between July 1908, and January 1913. Therefore, the Turkish experiment in parliamentary democracy was not commenced by the establishment of the Republic in the 1920s but it has been going on for more than a century, the longest experience in the Muslim world. "In Turkey, democratic institutions were neither imposed by the victors, as happened in the defeated Axis countries, nor bequeathed by departing imperialists, as happened in the former British and French dependencies, but were introduced by the free choice of the Turks themselves. This surely gave these institutions a much better chance of survival."[50] Turks under the Ottoman Empire were part of the ruling elite and had never been directly colonized. It was an endogenous movement not an exogenous one, as experienced in many post-colonial contexts. Nevertheless, this cannot be the only explanation, given the fact that Afghanistan, Saudi Arabia, and Iran, like Turkey, never experienced direct colonial rule except for some interruptions of foreign rule in their histories. Moreover, in comparison to these countries, Turkey is also more advanced in nation-state building, which leads us to other socio-economic factors.
ii. *Socio-economic explanation*: The Ottoman Empire's close relations with the European states triggered a specific form of socio-economic and political changes since the mid-nineteenth century. Its progress in democratization in the twentieth and twenty-first centuries undoubtedly rests on this socio-historical experience. The empire's modernization policies also contributed to economic changes, which produced a professional, technical, managerial and entrepreneurial middle class. The establishment of the Turkish Republic not only established a secular nation-

state but also consolidated a national market economy. Many observers have attached great importance to Turkey's economic development, which was not related to its natural revenues, unlike other oil-rich Muslim countries.[51] Turkey is not a *rentier* state. Turkey's economic growth was a consequence of its participation in the capitalist market economy. As described by Lipset, the proverb, 'No taxation, no representation,' makes clear sense in understanding the relationship between economic development and democratization in Muslim societies.[52] In oil-rich countries of the Middle East, citizens of a state usually do not have a voice in decision-making as long as the state provides the basic services and satisfies public needs, such as jobs, health care and housing, etc. In return, the oil-rich states do not need taxes to finance these services. In the Turkish context, the state cannot depend on its oil revenues and therefore, taxation and representation mutually reinforce each other on the path to democratization.

iii. *International dimension*: Turkey has had the longest geopolitical and closest diplomatic relations with the West, dating back almost to the fifteenth century. The Ottoman Empire's problematic existence within the Concert of Europe was resolved with modern Turkey's firm commitment to the pro-western alignment through its NATO and European Council membership as well as its EU candidacy. Thus, as stated earlier, there is no strong sense of 'anti-Westernism' in Turkish politics. Turkey has become one of the closest allies of the USA and Israel in the Middle East, which reflects the secular character of its foreign policies. Neither American nor Israeli governments have criticized the role of a strong army in Turkish politics while establishing close security and defence relations. It is through Turkey's EU membership that the role of the army has been criticized. As Ilter Turan identifies, "The EU has been critical of Turkey in three broad areas: the restricted nature of civil liberties, the insufficient protection of minorities and the unusual political influence of the Turkish military."[53] Therefore, it is difficult to decide whether the army usually returns to barracks because of their dedication to democracy or the 'international factor' indirectly forces them to hand power to civilians. Clearly, the key obstacle in front of Turkey's consolidation of democracy is not the strength of Islam but the existence of a *strong state* tradition and the paradoxical role of the army as the guardians of secularism. The answer lies in the rise of civil society to balance the state power and resolving its poor record of human and minority rights.

All these historical, socio-economic and international factors created a specific political culture, within which democratic values and institutions have been *synthesized* gradually in the social context of Turkey. The current AKP Government, despite its Islamic roots, is identified as the most democratic government and the example of Muslim democracy. Ironically, the AKP leaders never described themselves as 'Muslim democrats' but 'conservative democrats'.[54] The rise of AKP as the continuity of its predecessors can only make sense within the specific historical and socio-economic conditions of Turkish domestic and international policies. The rise of Islam in the Turkish public sphere cannot be interpreted "as a deviation from the country's modernization process," but a product of modernity.[55] The AKP leaders have not changed Turkey's pro-western policies but achieved the greatest political reforms in order to gain Turkey's EU membership.

Turkish leaders must cease reducing its European credentials to membership and identity issues. The political discourses of the current AKP Government as well as the previous governments give the impression that EU membership is regarded as "the ultimate mark of being European."[56] In the twenty-first century, it is time to change this mentality and it is not Turkey, which has an identity crisis but Europe, which suffers from such a crisis.

The public debates in Europe over Turkey's admission have shown that Europe is actually the torn country, deeply divided over its cultural identity, unable to answer the question whether European identity, and, therefore, its external and internal boundaries, should be defined by the common heritage of Christianity and western civilization or by its modern secular values of liberalism, universal human rights, political democracy, and tolerant and inclusive multiculturalism. Publicly, of course, European liberal secular elites cannot share the Pope's definition of European civilization as essentially Christian. But they also cannot verbalize the unspoken 'cultural' requirements that make the integration of Turkey into Europe such a difficult issue.[57]

It will be easier for both sides if Turkey's Eurasian identity is recognized geo-culturally. As a former foreign minister (1997-2002), Ismail Cem argued, successive Turkish governments have failed to define Turkey's identity in reference to '*Avrasya*' (Eurasia) by presenting Turkey as if sharing a European collective identity.[58] Turkey's insistence on its

European-ness has been counter-productive on two accounts: it creates a false consciousness about its identity as 'non-European'-'Islamic' and leads to a futile resistance to its 'Asian-ness'. Turkey culturally shares more characteristics with Central Asia than the Arab Middle East and also it has historical relations with European countries.

For European states, it will be relatively easier to accommodate Turks in a multi-cultural EU when Turkey's Eurasian identity is promoted. Economically, the EU can also benefit from Turkey's energy corridors via the Baku-Tbilisi-Ceyhan oil pipeline and the Baku-Erzurum gas pipeline. Turkey's EU membership will open Central Asian markets to Europe, which has a vested interest in expanding its commercial relations and influencing their socio-political developments towards plural democracy. Within the Cold War mentality, Turkish policy makers refrained from formulating policies that would reflect Turkey's 'Eurasian-ness'. In the post-Cold War and post-9/11 era, Turkey is perhaps the best candidate to realise the need for 'Euro-Asian' dialogue. Such a dialogue challenges not only Huntington's thesis, but also the existing American hegemony in regional and global contexts.

Conclusion

Turkey is the first historical example of a 'secular'–'Muslim democracy' in the Islamic World. Turkey's unique experience shows that it is neither a bridge nor a torn country. Twenty-first century Turkey must geopolitically and geo-culturally redefine its endogenous Eurasian identity. Its spatial existence in Europe and Asia is enhanced by combining its temporal experience between the western and Islamic civilizations. As Casanova suggests, "The contemporary transformation of Muslim politics in Turkey offers perhaps the best illustration of Muslim democratisation and the most compelling refutation of Huntington's thesis."[59] The demonstration movements exhibit that Ataturk's legacy and secularism remain to be part of the Turkish political culture. It is a historical fact that Turkey has *created* its own modernity by synthesizing Islam with contemporary western secularism and liberal democracy. The Turkish experience also proves the possibility of turning secularism from an above-imposed state project into an evolving *social phenomenon.* However, it is now the West's turn to recognize Turkey's western credentials and Eurasian identity with its unique historical and cultural experience. Eurocrats in Brussels must realize that Turkey's EU membership will promote the idea of 'unity in diversity' rather than a clash of civilizations.

Notes

1. Mumtaz Soysal, "The Future of Turkish Foreign Policy," in *The Future of Turkish Foreign Policy*, Lenore G. Martin and Dimitris Keridis (eds) (Cambridge: The MIT Press, 2004), 38; Ismail Cem, *Turkiye, Avrupa, Avrasya*, vol. 1 (Istanbul: Bilgi Universitesi Yayinlari, 2004), 69-70.
2. Samuel Huntington, *The Clash of Civilizations and the Remaking of World Order* (New York: Simon and Schuster Inc., 1996), 138.
3. Huntington, *The Clash of Civilizations*, 149.
4. Huntington, *The Clash of Civilizations*, 139.
5. Huntington, *The Clash of Civilizations*, 138.
6. Huntington, *The Clash of Civilizations*, see Map 1.3, 27.
7. S.E. Eisenstadt, "Multiple Modernities," *Daedalus* 129, no. 1 (Winter 2000): 1-29; Goran Therborn, "Entangled Modernities," *European Journal of Social Theory* 6, no. 3 (2003): 293-305; Peter J. Katzenstein, "Multiple Modernities as Limits to Secular Europeanization?" in *Religion in an Expanding Europe*, Timothy A. Byrnes and Peter J. Katzenstein (eds) (Cambridge: Cambridge University Press, 2006).
8. Huntington, *The Clash of Civilizations,* 178.
9. Huntington, *The Clash of Civilizations*, 179.
10. Jose Casanova, "Catholic and Muslim Politics in Comparative Perspective," *Taiwan Journal of Democracy* 1, no. 2 (December 2005): 102.
11. Oliver Roy, "Turkey: a World Apart, Or Europe's New Frontier?" in *Turkey Today: A European Country?* Olivier Roy (ed.) (London: Anthem Press, 2005): 11.
12. Huntington, *The Clash of Civilizations*, 178.
13. Huntington, *The Clash of Civilizations*, 139; Casanova, "Catholic and Muslim Politics," 102.
14. Mustafa Kemal Ataturk (Father of Turks) is considered the founder of the modern Turkish Republic in 1923. The followers of his ideas are described as Kemalist while the state ideology is described as Kemalism—based on the six principles of republicanism (*cumhuriyetcilik)*, nationalism (*milliyetcilik*), secularism (*laiklik*), statism (*devletcilik*), populism (*halkcilik*) and reformism (*devrimcilik*), which were first identified as the main principles Ataturkism (*Ataturkculuk*) and then codified in the Fourth Congress of the People's Republican Party (*Cumhuriyet Halk Partisi*) in 1935.
15. It is a point worth emphasizing: the AKP had 35 per cent of votes but 65 per cent of the parliament due to the current political system, which has a 10 per cent electoral threshold for representation in the Turkish Parliament.
16. *Dunden Bugune Anayasa Mahkemesi: 1962-2007, 45. Yil Albumu, 2007,* p. 177-178, <http://www.anayasa.gov.tr/images/loaded/pdf_dosyalari/mahkeme/dundenbuguneaym.pdf> Accessed on 07.07.2007.

17. Binnaz Toprak, "Islam and Democracy in Turkey," *Turkish Studies* 6, no. 2 (June 2005): 171-3.
18. Senem Aydin and Rusen Cakir, *Political Islam in Turkey*, Centre for European Policy Studies Working Document No. 265, April 2007, 1.
19. Huntington, *The Clash of Civilizations*, 179.
20. "*Ankara'da Tarihi Cumhuriyet Mitingi*," NtvMsnbc News, 16 Nisan 2007, http://www.ntvmsnbc.com/news/405418.asp; '*Cumhuriyet Mitingleri Izmir, Manisa ve Canakkale'de*,' Radikal, 2 Mayis 2007, http://www.radikal.com.tr/haber.php?haberno=220043; '*29 Nisan Cumhuriyet Mitingi*,' YouTube Video, See http://www.youtube.com/watch?v=EdKlIl pnR9o, accessed on 9.07.2007.
21. *Samsun'da Cumhuriyet Mitingi*, BBC Turkish Service, 20 Mayis 2007; http://www.bbc.co.uk/turkish/news/story/2007/05/070520_turkey_update.shtml, accessed on 10. 06.2007.
22. *Samsun'da Miting Coskusu*, CCN Turk, 20 Mayis 2007; http://www.cnnturk.com/TURKIYE/haber_detay.asp?PID= 318&haberID= 349478, accessed on 10. 06.2007.
23. Huntington, *The Clash of Civilizations*, 139.
24. Dietrich Jung, *Turkey's Future: EU Member of 'Islamist Rouge State'?* Danish Institute for International Studies Brief (DIIS: Copenhagen, January 2007), 3.
25. Ernest Gellner, *Muslim Society* (Cambridge: Cambridge University Press, 1981).
26. Majid Tehranian, "Disenchanted Worlds: Secularisation and Democratisation in the Middle East," in *Democratisation in the Middle East: Experiences, Struggles, Challenges*, Amin Saikal and Albrecth Schnabel (eds) (Tokyo: United Nations University Press, 2003), 81.
27. Abdou Filali-Ansary, "Muslims and Democracy," in *Islam and Democracy in the Middle East*, Larry Diamond, Marc F. Plattner and Daniel Brumberg (eds) (Baltimore: The John Hopkins University Press, 2003), 193-207.
28. There is no equivalent word in either Arabic or Turkish to describe the separation between religion and politics. *Laiklik* in Turkish is clearly derived from the French word *laicite*.
29. Casanova, "Catholic and Muslim Politics," 102-3.
30. Binnaz Toprak, "Islam and Democracy in Turkey," *Turkish Studies* 6, no. 2 (June 2005): 168.
31. Nilufer Gole, "Authoritarian Secularism and Islamist Politics: the Case of Turkey," in *Civil Society in the Middle East*, A.G. Richard (ed.), vol. 2 (Leiden, Netherlands: Brill, 1996).
32. Toktamış Ateş, *Dünyada ve Türkiye'de Laiklik* [*Laicite* in Turkey and the World], 10th edition (Ankara: Ümit Yayıncılık, 2000), 120-5.
33. Casanova, "Catholic and Muslim Politics," 103.
34. Gallup World Poll, *Special Report: Muslim World, Islam and Democracy* (Princeton: Gallup Organisation, 2006), 2.http://media.gallup.com/

WorldPoll/PDF/GALLUPMUSLIMSTUDIE SIslamandDemocracy030 607.pdf, accessed on 07.07.2007.

35. Gallup, 2.
36. Gallup, 2.
37. P.W. Sutton and S. Vertigans, "The Established and Challenging Outsiders: Resurgent Islam in Secular Turkey," *Totalitarian Movements and Political Religions* 3, no. 1 (Summer 2002): 64.
38. Jung, Turkey's Future, 5.
39. Daniel Brumberg and Larry Diamond, Introduction, in *Islam and Democracy in the Middle East*, Larry Diamond, Marc F. Plattner and Daniel Brumberg, (eds) (Baltimore: The John Hopkins University Press, 2003), x-xii; *Freedom in the World*, http://www.freedomhouse.org, accessed on 15.05. 2007.
40. Manus I Midlarsky, "Democracy and Islam: Implications for Civilisational Conflict and Democratic Peace," *International Studies Quarterly* 42, no. 3 (September 1998): 485-511; Alfred C. Stepan, "Arab, not Muslim, Exceptionalism," *Journal of Democracy* 15, no. 4 (2004): pp. 140-6.
41. Alfred C. Stepan, "An Arab More than a Muslim Electoral Gap," *Journal of Democracy* 14, no. 3 (2003): 30-44.
42. Toprak, "Islam and Democracy in Turkey," 171.
43. See Serif Mardin, "Religion in Modern Turkey," *International Social Sciences Journal* 19, no. 2 (1977): 279; Bernard Lewis, "Islamic Revival in Turkey," *International Affairs* 28, no. 1 (January 1952): 46; E. Shakman Hurd, "Negotiating Europe: The Politics of Religion and the Prospects for Turkish Accession," *Review of International Studies* 32 (2006): 401-18.
44. Metin Heper, "Islam and Democracy in Turkey: Toward Reconciliation?" *Middle East Journal* 51, no. 1 (Winter 1997): 33.
45. Göle, "Authoritarian Secularism," 49.
46. Toprak, "Islam and Democracy in Turkey," 179.
47. Feroz Ahmad, "Islamic Reassertion in Turkey," *Third World Quarterly* 10, no. 2 (April 1988): 757.
48. Toprak, "Islam and Democracy in Turkey," 179.
49. Casanova, "Catholic and Muslim Politics," 103.
50. Bernard Lewis, "Why Turkey is the Only Muslim Democracy?" *Middle East Quarterly*, March 1994, p. 5; Also available at http://www.meforum.org/article/216, accessed on 31.05. 2007.
51. Hootan Shambayati, "The Rentier State, Interest Groups, and the Paradox of Autonomy: State and Business in Turkey and Iran," *Comparative Politics* 26, no. 3 (April, 1994): 307-31.
52. Seymour Martin Lipset, "Some Social Requisites of Democracy: Economic Development and Political Legitimacy," *The American Political Science Review* 53 (March 1959): 69-105.
53. Ilter Turan, "Unstable Stability: Turkish Politics at the Crossroads?" *International Affairs* 83, no. 2 (2007): 328.

54. Cuneyt Ulsever, "An Analysis of the AKP," *Turkish Daily News,* 26 May 2007, http://www.turkishdailynews.com.tr/article.php?enewsid=74056, accessed on 30.05.2007; see A.K Party Official Web Site at http://eng.akparti.org.tr/english/chairman.html, accessed on 10.07. 2007.
55. Jung, Turkey's Future, 5.
56. John Redmond, "Turkey and the European Union: Troubled European or European Trouble?" *International Affairs* 83, no. 2 (2007): 315.
57. Jose Casanova, "The Long, Difficult, and Tortuous Journey of Turkey into Europe and the Dilemmas of European Civilisation," *Constellations* 13, no. 2 (2006): 241.
58. Cem, *Turkiye, Avrupa, Avrasya,* 7; Ismail Cem, "Turkey and Europe: Looking to the Future from a Historical Perspective," http://www.mfa.gov.tr, accessed on 23.06. 2007.
59. Casanova, "Catholic and Muslim Politics,"102.

6

September 11, the Colour Revolutions and the Birth of Sovereign Democracy

The Role of Norms and Values in Creating a Eurasian Identity

Daragh McDowell

The relationship between Russia and Kazakhstan is perhaps one of the most important factors in the evolution of the politics of Central Asia and Eurasia as a whole. The study of this relationship in western literature has been dominated by largely materialist paradigms, focusing on Russia's economic and security links with Kazakhstan and the other Central Asian Republics (CARs). Lena Jonson, in particular, has articulated through her work what has become the dominant paradigm for western analyses of Russo-Central Asian relations. In her view, Russia's continued influence over the Central Asian space is largely a result of its continued economic domination of the region, primarily through its control over the extensive Soviet-era pipeline network, and thus over Central Asian access to world energy markets critical for their continued development.

Jonson depicts these economic links as existing in a state of inexorable entropy due to increased competition from outside actors in the Central Asian energy market. Jonson predicts that due to the superior resources available to western economic actors Russia is being incrementally forced out of the region as Central Asian economic and political relations reorient themselves towards the West. This is a process she refers to as "involuntary disengagement."

In my opinion, Jonson has failed to sufficiently account for the normative factors underpinning Russia's relations in Central Asia. Particularly with regard to Russia's relationship with Kazakhstan the historical experience of unified statehood under the Russian and Soviet empires has had a profound impact on the development of their relationship as independent states. Normative, rather than purely pragmatic factors, have had a significant effect on the formation of policy. In particular, Russian and Kazakh attempts to articulate a 'Eurasian' identity in order to provide an anchor for their respective foreign policies and to placate potentially restless domestic minorities, have formed a greatly underappreciated aspect of Russo-Kazakh relations.

The September 11 terrorist attacks heralded a major increase in western engagement in Central Asia and seemed to accelerate the process of "involuntary disengagement" described by Jonson. However, as will be further explored below, the cultural differences between the West and its new 'Eurasian' partners in Central Asia served to ultimately undercut western engagement in the region. This 'culture clash' took the form of differing western and 'Eurasian' reactions to the 'Colour Revolutions' in the former Soviet space as well as the Andizhan massacre.

This essay will begin with an exploration of the effect of historical and cultural links on the relationship between Russia and Kazakhstan. It will then move onto the effects of September 11, the 'Colour Revolutions' and the Andizhan massacre on their relationship and the development of a 'Eurasian' identity complete with its own norms and values which affect the conduct of foreign policy throughout the region.

Historical-Cultural Links

One of the most under-appreciated yet critical problems facing Russian and Kazakh elites in the initial formulation of policy for their respective states has been the lack of historically rooted archetypes to return to in order to legitimize the state and provide a guide for the formulation and conduct of foreign policy.

Sally Cummings[1] has provided an excellent account of the intimate link between the search for an appropriate identity for the new Kazakh state and the making of its foreign policy. The initial question was not simply what policy should be, but why it should be in a certain form, what the interests of the Kazakh state and its people actually were. This was further complicated by the lack of substantial trained foreign policy cadres in Kazakhstan because at the time of the collapse, Soviet foreign policy was the exclusive domain of Moscow.[2] For the other CARs with their relatively ethnically homogenous populations, the creation of 'ethnocratic' nation-states, legitimized by representing the titular and dominant nationality and pursuing policies based on advancing the said nationality's interests, was a relatively painless process (the exception being Tajikistan). Russia, particularly with regards to its formation policy towards what it terms the 'near abroad', faced similar problems. The Russian Federation represents an incarnation of the Russian state with no historical analogue. Forced to jettison the politics of imperialism, Russia has been challenged to forge a new identity for its large, multi-ethnic population to underpin the direction of its foreign policy.

At the time of the Soviet dissolution, the ethnic Kazakh and Russian populations within the borders of Kazakhstan were roughly equal, and while present-day Kazakhstan geographically roughly conforms to the traditional lands covered by pre-imperial Kazakh nomads, the borders of the Kazakh state today are largely the product of Soviet administrative fiat. The development of Kazakhstan as a sedentary and industrialized state occurred entirely under the aegis of the Russian and Soviet empires. The Russian dominated northern regions are geographically and economically intimately linked to southern Siberia, rather than the rest of Kazakhstan, and represented a serious threat to the integrity of the new Kazakh state. Separatist agitators could plausibly argue that the northern steppe was in fact "Russian" (as Aleksandr Solzhenitsyn famously did in 1996[3]).

Martha Brill Olcott has also commented on the effect of cultural links on the Russo-Kazakh relationship, especially highlighting the contrasts between 'traditional' decolonization processes: the Soviet Union operated more as a unitary state than as an empire, and while its imperial nature left legacies of mutual antagonisms between colonizers and colonized a shared history, including the unifying experiences of the second world war has also served to bind Russia and Kazakhstan together.[4] In less abstract terms, Russia and Kazakhstan's bureaucratic governance structures and elite culture are both in large part held over from the Soviet Union, which along with the shared use of Russian as the language of officialdom, has helped preserve ties. Cummings[5] has confirmed this by highlighting the high degree of nomenklatura retention in the creation of the new Kazakh elite, and how the contact networks the Kazakh nomenklatura made in Russia during the Soviet period have survived to the present day. In political systems where personal contacts and patronage have assumed such an important role, the effect of these contacts on regional and foreign policy-making should not be underestimated.

Conversely, Naumkin[6] and Alexandrov[7] have both pointed out the adverse effects that close cultural links have had on the development of the political relationship. The issue of dual citizenship for ethnic Russians in Kazakhstan, and the Russian affirmation of its 'right' to defend its ethnic kin in the near abroad in particular introduced tensions into the relationship, as did early support for the creation of a 'Greater Russia' by nationalist politicians. More interestingly Naumkin has illustrated the importance of a "learning process" in Russo-Kazakh relations on Moscow's behalf, on how it has learned to treat the states it still refers to as the 'near-abroad' as fully independent and sovereign entities, and adjusted its relations with them accordingly. But while there have been 'pushing' and 'pulling' aspects of Russo-Kazakh cultural links, the overall effect has been one of drawing the two states politically much closer together.

Language has also played an important role in the construction of Kazakhstan's identity. While the Kazakh elite have emphasized the need for the general adoption of the Kazakh language in order to enhance national identity and coherence, Russian has been maintained as a 'state' if not 'official' language, due mainly to its widespread use. As the African experience of decolonization has demonstrated, former imperial powers which 'grant' their own language as the broader administrative tongue within colonies tend to continue to exercise what Joseph Nye has termed "soft power" over these colonies.[8] Periodic attempts have been made by the Kazakh elite to restrict the use of Russian in the mass media as part of a general strategy of 'Kazakhisation', but such attempts have generally made little progress beyond provoking nationalist reaction in Moscow. The continued use of Russian in Kazakhstan is both a valuable component for the construction of a 'Eurasian' identity and a continued source of Russian power over its development.

Under the Putin presidency, Russia has made considerable efforts to emphasize the continued existence of close cultural ties between the two states. This has been most noticeable by the re-appearance of the old Soviet term "fraternal nations," and its frequent use by Putin and Nazarbaev in describing the links between Russia and Kazakhstan. Putin has even gone so far as to declare that steps towards greater Russo-Kazakh integration have "been pre-determined by history itself and, I would say by the very *genetic memory* and closeness of our peoples."[9] (Emphasis added) Nazarbaev has echoed this statement claiming that Russia and Kazakhstan's "shared history" has pre-determined their "eternal friendship."[10] Putin and Nazarbaev desire to portray the relationship as more than simply a very healthy and friendly one between two states, but rather as an organic and pre-destined partnership. Further issues relating to the terminology employed by the Russian and Kazakh elite will be covered in the next section.

As part of this process Moscow and Astana have also staged a number of reasonably high profile cultural initiatives, including alternating "Years of Kazakhstan in Russia" and "Years of Russia in Kazakhstan." In President Putin's words, the impetus behind these events is "to open the road to public and business initiative, and to fling the doors wide for direct human contacts, and for extensive information and cultural exchanges. And, what is particularly important, to create in the changed historical conditions effective stimuli for deepening bilateral contacts and bringing our countries and nations closer together."[11] Academic exchanges and deepening educational ties[12] have also continued apace, with around 16,000 Kazakh students studying at Russian universities in 2003.[13] One effort to promote cross-cultural links involved the celebration of the Russian poet Pushkin in Astana and the Kazakh poet Abai in Moscow.[14]

This is all indicative of a relatively intentional policy of promoting a 'Eurasian' identity, within which the Kazakh elite can successfully co-opt its population in all its religious and ethnic diversity, and the Russian elite can extend its 'soft power' over the post-Soviet space, through Russia's status as the dominant nation within what has been termed a "Eurasian super-ethnos"[15] as well as aiding the process of co-opting its own domestic minorities.[16]

September 11 and After

The September 11 terrorist attacks in New York and Washington DC immediately made Central Asia an area of vital strategic interest in American and western security calculations. This resulted in Central Asia becoming a major field of competition for influence between Russia and the West, but also opened up policy windows to the then relatively fresh Putin administration. In Moscow's considerations, the perceived danger of NATO bases in Central Asia, and the possible loss of Russian influence in the region were outweighed by the potential benefits: an improvement in Russo-US relations, still at a low ebb after the 1999 NATO campaign in Kosovo, a chance to diminish western criticism of alleged human rights abuses in Chechnya by recasting Russia's campaign in the north Caucasus as part of the larger 'War on Terror', and the potential removal of a common foe and source of Central Asian instability, the Taliban regime in Afghanistan. Moreover the political costs of being seen to seriously obstruct NATO's campaign against Al Qaida after the magnitude of the September 11 attacks would have been enormous.

For the CARs western cooperation with NATO cannot have been a difficult decision to make. NATO military bases were followed by generous amounts of economic, military and humanitarian aid, in greater amounts than Russia could afford. "Involuntary disengagement" seemed to be occurring at a rapidly accelerated pace as the western engagement in the region increased massively almost overnight, while Russia remained constrained by its chronic shortage of resources to commit to the region. Uzbekistan, which had already been actively courting the West, in particular benefited greatly from western engagement. Its substantial pre-September 11 military-to-military contacts with the US allowed NATO to rapidly establish a presence in the country and made it the natural strategic fulcrum for the NATO engagement to pivot upon.[17] At the time, it seemed clear that the decade-long struggle between Astana and Tashkent for regional leadership had been decided decisively in the latter's favour.

Finally it should be noted that NATO's engagement has also served as what Sergei Morozov terms "the weighty argument"[18] in the debate over energy policy. While it has already been noted that the lifting of Russia's security burdens in Central Asia could potentially be of great benefit to Moscow, the disintegration of its oil transport monopoly would remove the last of its major levers of influence over the region. The potential stabilization of Afghanistan in and of itself would open up a major land-transport route for Central Asian oil and gas, bypassing both Russia and Iran on its way to refineries and harbours in the Persian Gulf. Tellingly, the long-delayed Baku-Tbilisi-Ceyhan pipeline finally began construction in September 2002, one year after the attacks.

The post-September 11 development of Central Asia seemed to have justified predictions of eventual Russian displacement. However, as will be demonstrated further on in this essay, ideational and normative factors have played a greater role in the formation of policy in Central Asia than has generally been acknowledged.

The Colour Revolutions and Andizhan

Beginning with the ouster of Eduard Shevardnadze in the Georgian Rose Revolution of 2003, the western position in Central Asia, based around the Uzbek fulcrum began to seriously deteriorate. While the extent of western involvement in the 'Colour Revolutions' cannot be completely determined due to its clandestine nature a definite pattern emerges out of the events in Serbia in 2000, Georgia in 2003, Ukraine in 2004-05, and to a lesser extent in Kyrgyzstan in 2005, of grassroots opposition groups staging massive public protests in the face of fraudulent election results. Substantial evidence has emerged that both western NGOs and US governmental organizations, from the State Department to Freedom House, funded and trained many of these 'grassroots' movements in the tactics of non-violent civil resistance.[19] Russia almost immediately regarded these revolutions as an active western plot to undermine its position in the post-Soviet space, and its relations with Georgia and Ukraine have deteriorated significantly in their wake, to the point of near armed conflict with Georgia in mid-2006.

The events in the previously obscure Uzbek town of Andizhan in May 2005, presented a serious dilemma for the West and a major opportunity for Russia with regard to their respective positions in Central Asia. While the US response to what has now been termed the 'Andizhan Massacre' was initially muted due to Washington's unwillingness to deliberately antagonize Tashkent, media coverage of the events and the resultant public outcry quickly made this position untenable. Public opinion in Europe and the US would not countenance the continuation of military and economic support to the repressive Uzbek regime, especially during the Iraq War, the ostensible mission of which was to begin democratizing the Middle East. The EU quickly implemented an arms embargo, and the US demanded an independent enquiry into the Andizhan events.[20] The Uzbek reaction was equally swift. President Islam Karimov ordered all NATO forces to evacuate their bases in Uzbekistan within 180 days, in July 2005. Karimov has subsequently been very outspoken on his version of the Andizhan events, strongly hinting he believes them to have been instigated by the US.[21]

The speed with which the West lost its strategic fulcrum in Central Asia is reflected by the speed with which Russia was able to reassert its position in the region through its fulcrum, Kazakhstan. While the mercurial nature of Karimov's foreign policy means that any 'realignment' in Central Asia dependant on Uzbekistan must be considered subject to future reversal, the lessons of Andizhan have not been lost on the leaders of the CARs. Authoritarian and autocratic regimes ultimately rely on a certain amount of political repression. While the western powers have in the past not been above supporting anti-democratic and repressive states the centrality of 'democratisation' to NATO's post-Cold War mission and the Bush administration's wider foreign policy, coupled with the scale of violence necessary to prevent a 'Colour Revolution' has made it politically impossible for the West to continue to so overtly support the CARs. While the West has, of course, remained engaged in the region and with

Kazakhstan at a relatively deep level, it cannot be the unqualified political and economic support that Russia and China can. Russia, as well as China and Uzbekistan's other neighbours have shown themselves willing to regard internal repression as outside their sphere of concern, and provided a multi-lateral framework to defend Uzbek actions in the form of SCO, preventing it from potential diplomatic isolation.

Uzbekistan's return to CSTO and joining of the Eurasian Economic Community (EurAsEC) have greatly enhanced the credibility of both of these organizations as military-political blocs, and the dominance of Russian and Kazakh influence in both of these organizations should leave us with little doubt about the primary shapers of security policy in the region. US withdrawal from all but the Manas airbase in Kyrgyzstan (which looks increasingly less tenable as the Bakaev Government grows less stable) in addition to the revival of CSTO and EurAsEC has also greatly raised the profile of SCO in the region. Famously, the SCO was the forum used to issue a demand that NATO withdraw from Central Asia in the summer of 2005[22] and has increasingly been looked to (rhetorically at least) as the primary body for combating "terrorism, separatism and extremism" in the region. For example during the aforementioned meeting Nazarbaev "called upon [SCO] to become a shield that will protect us from the terrorist threat"[23] as the organization simultaneously called for NATO, the previous shield, to exit the region.

The story of western security engagement in Central Asia illustrates the prominent role of politics, in particular the maintenance of the authoritarian Central Asian regimes, and how it has been underestimated in the development of Central Asian security cooperation. Most pre-Andizhan commentary on the state of Central Asia and Kazakhstan treated as inevitable Russia's final and largely total withdrawal from the region in the face of superior western financial and security resources on offer to the CARs. However, the inability of western democratic states to be seen as propping up what are frequently highly repressive regimes in Central Asia, compared with Russia's willingness to defend the stable status quo has proved to be a more decisive factor. The security organizations that have taken over in the face of Western withdrawal, have been largely shaped and guided by Russo-Kazakh cooperation, and will probably shape security policy in the region for the foreseeable future. In short, the NATO engagement that was seen by proponents of the 'Jonsonian' perspective as the culmination of the process of Russian 'involuntary disengagement' has turned out to be largely a transitory phase. On 26 March 2007, Nursultan Nazarbaev categorically stated that there would 'never' be US bases in Kazakhstan.[24] The relationship between Russia, Kazakhstan, and the West in the security sphere has thus come full circle.

The Birth of 'Sovereign Democracy'

The onset of the 'Colour Revolutions' led Kazakhstan, as well as its Central Asian neighbours to question the advantages of closer alignment with the West. After all, the EU and USA were firm supporters of the 'revolutionaries'. It has also reinforced the importance to Moscow of the domestic politics of the former Soviet states for its policy in the post-Soviet space. Part of the appeal of Viktor Yushchenko and Mikheil Saakashvili to their supporters was their rejection of Russian dominance, and support for a more western oriented foreign policy.

By adopting a policy of support for existing friendly governments against revolutionary movements, and a willingness to support (or possibly even to facilitate through CSTO) repression of dissent, Russia has discovered a source of soft power in the "Orange Menace." One of the main manifestations of this "soft power" influence has been the spread of Ediniya Rossiya's (the pro-Kremlin Russian "party of power") concept of "Sovereign Democracy"[25] into the lexicon of the Kazakh elite. While something of a loose term, "sovereign democracy" has been expressed as a rejection of external (primarily western) interference in the internal political development of the state and is primarily a normative concept intended to guide the foreign policy of the state. Darigha Nazarbaeva has defined sovereign democracy as being a rejection of "a path to democracy guided by maps prepared in the West."[26] Vladimir Surkov, the Russian architect of the concept has also explicitly painted it as a rejection of recent western notions about the 'post-sovereignty' international system.[27] The fact that the phrase first started being widely used by Russian figures in 2005, after the "Orange Wave" reached its crest is further indication that its development is a reaction to the onset of the 'Colour Revolutions', and that it is part of Russia's strategy for combating them.

However "sovereign democracy" as adopted by Moscow and Astana is not simply a reactionary slogan to revolutionary developments, even if it does not contain a substantial ideological platform beyond a rejection of external interference in internal affairs. It is the political side of the 'Eurasian' identity, an attempt to form a common ideology to provide 'Eurasianism' with a normative basis. Importantly, it is an ideology defined by Russia and adopted by Kazakhstan, a strong indicator of Russian soft-power. Sovereign democracy in this way plays a role similar to that of communism during the Soviet period, though obviously a greatly reduced one. As I mentioned earlier both Russia and Kazakhstan have struggled to find and articulate a concrete ideological basis for the conduct of their respective foreign policies. Sovereign democracy, though still a relatively young concept may fill that gap.

Conclusion

The course of Russo-Kazakh relations during the Putin presidency has had to weather the turbulence of September 11, the 'Colour Revolutions' and the Andizhan massacre. The result has been two realignments in Central Asian foreign policy remarkable in their suddenness as well as their apparent depth. This process has underlined the importance that identity-formation and norm-sharing have had in the politics of the post-Soviet space, despite the predictions of many writers on the topic.

Western engagement in Central Asia post-September 11 highlighted the degree to which the western mission of "democracy promotion" has made significant engagement in Central Asia troublesome. Russia, through its articulation of the concept of sovereign democracy as the ideology of the Eurasian space has provided an intellectual framework for the formulation of its own foreign policy in opposition to the western 'post-sovereignty' consensus. Its adoption by Kazakhstan has helped make it a Eurasian 'value' and given a certain ballast to the ideological identity of the multi-ethnic Kazakh state.

While it is too early to fully gauge whether or not sovereign democracy will prove to be an enduring concept, it is clear that it has already made a substantial contribution to the formation of a Eurasian identity, or super-ethnos. Furthermore, it has highlighted the continued importance of this identity in the formation of political identities, and thus policy goals.

Notes

1. S.N. Cummings, *Kazakhstan: Power and the Elite* (London: I.B. Tauris, 2002), vi, 202.
2. I.S. Ivanov, *Novaìa rossiiskaìa diplomatiìa: deciat' let vneshnei politiki strany* (Moskva: Olma-Press, 2002), 381.
3. A. Solzhenitsyn, "Conversations with Aleksandr Solzhenitsyn," *Komsomolskaya Pravda,* 1996.
4. G.I. Chufrin and Stockholm International Peace Research Institute, *Russia and Asia: the Emerging Security Agenda* (Oxford: Oxford University Press, 1999), xvi, 534.

5. Cummings, *Kazakhstan.*
6. R. Legvold and American Academy of Arts and Sciences, *Thinking Strategically: the Major Powers, Kazakhstan, and the Central Asian Nexus*, American Academy Studies in Global Security (Cambridge: American Academy of Arts and Sciences, MIT Press, 2003), xii, 243.
7. M. Alexandrov, "Uneasy Alliance: Relations between Russia and Kazakhstan in the Post-Soviet era, 1992-1997," *Contributions to the Study of World History*, no. 66 (1999): xiv, 327.
8. J.S. Nye, *Soft Power: the Means to Success in World Politics* (New York: PublicAffairs, 2004), xvi, 191.
9. *Vladimir Putin: Vystuplenie na tseremonii otkrytiya Goda Rossiya v Kazakhstane*, 9 January 2004. www.kremlin.ru
10. D. Kimmage, "Kazakh President Touts 'friendship' with Russia, rejects talk of Union," *RFE/RL Newsline*, 2006.
11. *Vladimir Putin: Vystuplenie na tseremonii.*
12. N. Isingarin, *Kazakhstan i Sodruzhestvo: problemy ekonomicheskoi integratsii: uchebnoe posobie* (Almaty: BIS, 2000), 213.
13. *Vladimir Putin: Vystuplenie na vstreche s sekratryami sovetov bezopasnosti gosudarstv-uchastnikov Organisatsii Dogovora o kollektivnoi bezopasnosti*, 21 March 2003. www.kremlin.ru.
14. *Vladimir Putin and Nursultan Nazarbaev: Nachalo vstrechi s Presidentom Kazakhstana Nursaltanom Nazarbaevym.* 5 July 2005. www.kremlin.ru.
15. A. Terent'ev, *Vybory v Kazakhstane: Ukroshenie "Oranzhevoy" Volny*, Mirovaya Ekonomika i Mezhdunarodnaya Otnoshenniya, 2006.
16. D.D. Shlapentokh, "Putin's Neo-Eurasianism, or Models of the Construction of a New Russian Identity and Their Implications," *Prague Watchdog*, 2007.
17. S.E. Cornell, "America in Eurasia: One Year After," *Current History* (October 2002).
18. S. Morozov, *Diplomatiya V.V. Putina: vneshnreaeia politika Rossii, 1999-2004* (Sankt-Peterburg: Izmaæilovskiæi, 2004), 250.
19. I. Traynor, "US Campaign behind Turmoil in Kiev," *The Guardian*, 2004.
20. A. Tully, *Uzbekistan: US Sharpens Call for Independent Probe of Andijon Bloodshed, while Russia objects*, 2005. www.eurasianet.org.
21. A. Kolesnikov, "Upheaval of All Liberties—Russia Prods Asia to Give America an Ultimatum," *Kommersant* (translated and reprinted in *the Current Digest of the Post-Soviet Press*), 2005.
22. Kolesnikov, *Upheaval of All Liberties.*
23. Kolesnikov, *Upheaval of All Liberties.*
24. "Russia needs friend, long-term partner," *ITAR-TASS*, 2007.
25. P. Moore, "Kremlin Theoretician Develops Ideas on Democracy," *RFE/RL Newsline*, 2006.
26. D. Kimmage, "'Sovereign Democracy' in Almaty and Moscow," *RFE/RL Newsline*, 2006.
27. M. Zygar, "Beer without Friendship is a Waste of Money," *Kommersant*, 2005.

7

Region as a Space of Interacting Autonomies

Ranabir Samaddar

In discussions on Eurasia, which are often heavy with geopolitical tinges, it is natural that we speak of the emergence of a region, new regions, interface of two regions, etc. However, I am not very sure as to how we want to define a region. It is possibly a geopolitical term, whose variables are flexible. It may be defined by history, administrative decisions, linguistic and cultural affinities, geo-economic commonness, or by a common colonial past, by sharing borders, or possibly by some other factors, or by some or all of these combined elements. To someone from India and South Asia, the term region, connotes many meanings—for instance, South Asia as a whole is a region, while in India there are several regions. In that case, in inter-state relations, the first question will be: whose region is it? This is the traditional way of looking at things; it asks us to take into account the perspective of power, although we have to admit that this approach does not view the question of region from the point of view of popular politics, and views politics only from the top. It is a state-centric view, a governmental view. The interesting question rather will be: do people of this 'region' take it as a common political space, so that we can say that the same dynamics of popular politics marks this space? I suggest that the answer to this question, as to what makes a region a region, be searched in its non-definability, its middle-ness, its position between the globe and the state (or the state and the locality), the simultaneous existence of and non-state character in it. This is an increasingly discernible phenomenon of our time.

Several consequences follow from this. Till date democracy has been defined in the compelling presence of power, flag, identity, and laws. Democracy needs the state to be legitimized, a government to be operational, a nation to be vindicated, and laws in order to be defined, arbitrated, and strengthened. Thus democracy and the nation state's conjugal existence has been taken as natural. Since we assume, and it is correct, that democracy calls for a shared recognition of the democratic claims, it implies a shared recognition of a set of standards, institutions, and agencies. Democracy—we take it as natural—will operate under flags; flags would proclaim rights. Globalization has had a double impact on this scene. On the one hand, it has reduced democracy's capacity to retain its commitment to citizens. Its negotiating capacity vis-à-vis world trade rules and military might of the Great Powers is limited and diminishing, On the other hand, democracy is thought to be a certain 'national' virtue, which some nations supposedly historically-culturally possess, and others do not. Thus globalization is not weakening the discourse of the national form of democracy, but accentuating it. In the process it is making democracy aggressive, expansionist, racist, and exclusive. Under the flag of democracy, imperial nations will hereafter fight wars. How do we escape the bind? The way France and Germany are conducting their relations towards Iran shows the intrinsic difficulties in conceptualizing a new region (call it Eurasia or anything else) based on old ideas and old realities.

I do not know what the reader's answer will be here, but to this great question of our time, namely how do we escape the bind, certainly there is a strong post-colonial response, which produces two interlinked answers to the question, and all the responses are deeply political, and all of which reinforce the figure of the *region.* I am drawing attention to the necessity of post-colonial reasoning, because we must realize that only in the background of a centralist state built on the colonial model and colonial history, that the issue of region has become prominent in modern times (in Spain, France, Italy, United Kingdom, etc., or in Asia, or elsewhere). Now these two answers or routes if you like are: (a) the two distinct discourses of politics and claims—global and the local—are being negotiated under specific post-colonial conditions, which make the region the site of negotiation of these conflicting claims; (b) in the post-colonial context where substantive citizenship and rights often face the paradigm of government and sovereignty, the question of autonomy needs to be considered in the new light of popular politics. But it needs to be told at the outset that I am referring to the principle of autonomy here not as a banal issue of administrative or legislative devolution of power, or even as a part of the principle of subsidiarity. I mean by the principle of autonomy the autonomy of middle-ness, autonomy of the site of dialogue. It not only means autonomy of the political society over the politics of the state and of governmentalism, it means also autonomy of political common sense, autonomy of the site where different trends interact (global, local, etc.). It means further that the principle of autonomy has to be a building pillar of democracy, and not a palliative for some marginal or recalcitrant community or region, like the Basque, or Kashmir, or Tibet. It has to be an integral part of democracy, which has to be now re-envisioned as a federal unity of autonomies. In this federal conception of politics, *region is the figure—region is not as a state in disguise, but as that unbounded site of dialogue, negotiation, and interaction.*

In this emerging politics of region as the site of interacting autonomies, we can also notice the globalization of the politics of autonomy. The latter means the increasing strength of politics—its autonomy—to cope with the global fallout of new discourses, new global political economy, and the emerging issues of rights and justice.

We can recall here the key issues of an autonomous arrangement to realize how these can constitute the middle-ness of certain geopolitical realities, constituted by cultural affairs, education, official language, (national) symbols, health and social services, economy, taxation, resources, environmental policy, transportation, post and communication, law and order, administration of justice, currency and monetary policy, determination of citizenship, foreign policy, defence, customs, border control, and immigration. Yet we have to remember, as classical political philosophy had sought to impress upon us, that while these issues mentioned above relate to collective autonomy, autonomy as a principle begins with personal autonomy. To be autonomous is to be a law to oneself; autonomous agents are self-governing agents. Most of us want to be autonomous because we want to be accountable for what we do, and because it seems that if we are not the ones with power to do what we like, then we cannot be accountable. More importantly, perhaps, the value of autonomy is tied to the value of self-integration. Here too region plays an important part, for quite often our identities are not bound by the borders and are created by the state or by our disciplinary social structures. I may like to be South Asian besides being Indian. Similarly, within India I may like to be a part of the East or the North-east besides being a person from West Bengal.

I

The following exposition examines why a region becomes crucial in the realization of political autonomy.

When people living in some region of the world declare that their group has the right to live autonomously, they are saying that they ought to be allowed to govern themselves. In making this claim, they are, in essence, rejecting the political and legal authority of those not in their group. They are insisting that whatever *power* these outsiders may have over them, this power is illegitimate; they and they alone, have the *authority* to determine and enforce the rules and policies that govern their lives. This assertion expresses a rationality that takes us beyond the metaphysics of agency, to politics.

An agent is one who acts. In order to act, one must initiate one's action. And to initiate action, one must have the power to initiate. In short, every agent has an authority over herself that is grounded, not in her social role, nor in any law or custom, but in the simple fact of her political power, which means the power to initiate her actions. However, despite the inalienable nature of the authority, which the political subject has over herself, it is possible for her to fail to govern herself. Just as a political leader's official status is compatible with her having no real power to initiate actions, so too the subject can have an authoritative status with respect to her motives without having any real power over what she does. Autonomy is therefore not a matter of formal status in politics, but one of having the capacity of being the effective counterpoint to sovereignty. What distinguishes the autonomy-undermining influences on the political subject's will from those motivating forces that play a positive role in the self-governing process of the political subject? This is the question that all accounts of political autonomy try to answer. And, as the number and variety of these accounts indicate, the distinction is extremely elusive. The puzzle at the heart of this problem is about the relationship between the agent's power and the power of the forces that move her. And it is a puzzle about the relationship between the political subject's authority and the status of these motivating forces. All these take us to the issue of citizenship, closed to us for quite some time and which now needs to be re-opened.

It can be reopened in the following way: can citizenship be enough of a description of the political subject of the new regions in a reconfigured space? In the perspective of immigration and cross-border population movements, do we not need to reconfigure the subject in the corpus of a political society in a new way so as to embrace the migrant, the stateless, frontier workers, and other trans-border subjects, like the divided peoples? In my earlier work on issues such as peace accords as the basis of autonomous arrangements, the public policy of conducting dialogue with rebels to arrive at regulatory arrangements of a quasi-autonomous political nature, and the various success, semi-success, and failure stories of autonomies, I tried to show three things: (a) there is a close relationship, one of link and contest, between governmentality and autonomy; (b) the autonomous space is a dialogic form towards ensuring 'minimal justice'; and (c) there is a consequent re-negotiation of the democratic question in the autonomous spaces.[1] Clearly the form of the modern state is inappropriate for the re-negotiation of relations I am referring to here. We need to work on these three phenomena more rigorously, because in the last few years the environment of governmental relations has clouded the principle of self-determination everywhere, so that we need to study autonomous practices in the light of this reality, and find out how the autonomous spaces are being retrieved and recreated today. In fact we can now say with confidence that autonomous principles are unworkable in the modular form of the modern state, which acts as the inheritor of sovereignty in a centralized deposit. Autonomy can work only in the milieu of 'shared sovereignty', which regions can embody. If we are thinking of Eurasia in any meaningful way, we cannot think of this as an active region with the present nation states in this vast region remaining in their places as they are, yet allowing a politico-economic region called Eurasia to come into play. The emergence of a region, below or above the state, also changes the state in the process. Federalization of politics would mean here the sharing of sovereign power that would inevitably accrue from the emergence of such a vast region. One can easily see how space and scale matter in politics, and our critical-normative preferences must be ready to confront them and come out with solutions in a creative manner.

Autonomy, therefore as a principle, is different from freedom, because freedom is essentially a value, while autonomy is essentially a category of power. It is different from self-government, because while self-government focuses on the ability of the individual or the collective individual to govern itself, autonomy always points towards the supplement that remains after government has been accomplished. Autonomy thus indicates middle-ness as a strategic situation in the landscape of power. Autonomies in the various forms we witness today indicate the way politics in the future may take shape, the new forms of contestations, and the new possibility of disentangling the democratic theory from its close association with the dominant organization of power, which still remain sovereignty—all said and done an imperial form. Autonomous practices in sum indicate the way society can be reorganized among others in a form that can be termed as *region*, the dialogic zone where autonomies may negotiate, the responsibilities that autonomies may have to bear in order to converse among themselves—a situation that can be described as the daily plebiscite of democratic collectives.

The deliberate vagueness and the middle-ness of the figure of the region will be clear when we contrast it with the hard governmental realities of our political lives. Foucault makes the sense of governmentality clear when he stresses the connection between a government and economy in the perspective of the relation between family and economy. He says, "To govern a state will mean, therefore, to apply economy, to set up an economy at the level of the entire state, which means exercising toward its inhabitants, and the wealth and behaviour of each and all, a form of surveillance and control as attentive as that of the head of a family over his household and his goods."[2] Government besides indicating the process of governing—and governing indeed is a process—which its association with economy reveals, also means the right disposition of things. Once again we are being indicated by the term that there is a field of "intervention through a series of complex processes, which are absolutely fundamental to our history," and this field also means a right disposition, that is arrangement, of things and men. And how are these two terms—things and me—equated here? Because, men are governed means men in their relations, their links, their "imbrication with these things that are wealth, resources, means of subsistence, the territory with its specific qualities, climate, irrigation, fertility and so on, men in their relation with those other things that are customs, habits, ways of acting and thinking, and so on; and finally men in their relation to those still other things that might be accidents and misfortunes such as famine, epidemics, death, and so on…government concerns things understood in this way, this imbrication of men and things."[3] To govern means, then, to govern things—and to stretch the point a little, governing men by turning them into things. Yet we have to keep in mind that if one origin of the idea of governmentality is the utilitarian task of governing, the other origin is sovereignty. Sovereignty denotes exceptional power; also the power to lay down rules and institutions to govern. If governmentality keeps power in a capillary shape, sovereignty maintains power bounded, centralized, ready to be used, and foundational.

This dual feature has implications for our discussion on region as a figure of autonomy. First, the ensemble of institutions, procedures, calculations, tactics, etc., known as government is aimed at population; and its basis is the knowledge of political economy; on the other hand the ensemble of democratic collectives known as autonomies as forms of shared sovereignty, aim at turning spaces into regions from their earlier existence as either unities of sovereignties or unities of units of a sovereign power. Second, when governmental rationalities are dominant, they overwhelm the principle and practices of autonomy, and turn autonomy into self-government; self-government is equated with autonomy, and the sovereign meanwhile retains exceptional powers to take care of states of exception and maintain states. Thus we often find regions becoming institutions of self-government, while sovereignty remains in the hands of dominant powers—region becomes only an extension of state, and not another spatial principle of power. As opposed to this, a region (below or above the state) can become the ground of many autonomies working out their continuous coexistences. Region is thus a *space* when we take it as a *void*, whose emptiness can be the site of many significant overlapping existences. Imagine Eurasia as a vast space (of void?)—the imaginary other of the geopolitical arguments we have heard for more than a century that invoke power and armed might, and may bring to us echoes of the sounds of galloping horses of an Alexander or Genghis Khan, but in the context of popular politics today these arguments seem sickeningly banal.

Intersecting autonomies present a picture of a heterogeneous field of politics—we can say negotiation of autonomies. Autonomous movements and political practices for autonomy therefore present a picture of variety. They are infected with these rationalities. Yet movement after movement for self-determination, and more significant new spaces in society claiming autonomy show the limits of governmentality. Peace talks do not end violence, nor do they produce devotion to constitution. Indeed constitution provokes autonomy of the street. Indigenous people demand autonomy. Spaces in society clamour for legal pluralism, which is the other word for autonomy of other forms of legal thinking than the centralised modern legal system, and the sovereignty of the basic law. Women claim autonomy, and increasingly, feminism is used as a resource for generating and enriching autonomy of spaces. Similarly, as the failure of so-called peace accords and autonomy packages demonstrates, either these governmental packages fail to satisfy discontent and rouse more desire for a share of sovereignty (the recurrent Bodo and Tripura accords in India illustrate this), or they incite the imagination for an enriched form of autonomy that would redefine the two principles of justice and democracy. Themes such as the history of the constitutional deliberations on autonomy, the interface of geo-politics and the ethno-politics in the emergence of every autonomous space in society provide us with a solid bunch of historical illustrations of the fact that autonomy represents the element of 'excess' that political imagination represents over and above the politics guided by governmentality.[4] Thus, beyond the boutique variety of multiculturalism, autonomy has become one of the fundamental principles of reorganizing society. Indeed, today's political society stands on two related recognitions—(a) politics has autonomy, and it is not going to listen to economic wisdom always, and (b) that political existences or spaces must have some degree of autonomy in order to coexist with others and make politics meaningful.

Let me now take my argument a little further. Governmental science produces multiplicities, and wants to handle this multiplicity on a homogenous scale, by a homogenous standard, at a homogenous level. Yet, there remain difference, distance, and inequality, from which arises heteronomy. Autonomy is produced from the phenomenon of heteronomy. "Difference, distance, and inequality" are not only signs of multiplicities; they are essentials to this heteronomic world. In other words *difference is autonomous*. Difference is essential, and it owes its fundamental existence to such physical factors existing at the micro-level such as distance, degree, and inequality. Weberian rationality cannot suppress differences that propel autonomy. Distinct physical realities of politics defeat Weberian rationality. Two consequences linked to each other are produced from this: (a) a region by virtue of its middle-ness can allow differences thereby producing a heteronomic world, which is distinct from a nation-centric universe, because it can live without the burden of sovereignty, homogeneity, and sameness; and (b) autonomy springs from this physically uneven nature of the political universe. We can put the same two-fold issue in another way, namely, that governmentality produces difference from the top; autonomy is the mark of negotiating difference from below. Autonomy is therefore not an exceptional principle of democracy conceded to some belligerent section of society or some areas or groups of the population, such as frontier populations insistent on autonomy or a problem-region; autonomy is the organizing principle of the emerging political society, autonomies in perpetual dialogue among themselves, linked by respective responsibilities to retain the autonomous places in a dialogic universe. This is the condition of new democracy, which in its traditional form shows itself to be singularly incapable of coping with what I call the "politics of autonomy". The South Asian experiences of

Sri Lanka, India, Nepal, Pakistan, and Bangladesh, or the European experiences of Basque, Kosovo, Northern Ireland, all point out to the incapacity of democracies to appreciate the paradox and tensions with the politics of autonomy, and imagine new forms of political society. I argue that the emergence of the region as a catalyst in many places in the world today is an indicator of autonomous politics, which means crafting of a strand of politics that is distinct and different from both the modern nation state and the imperial unity in the form of a great power, both being the habitation of sovereignty.

In India as elsewhere the political struggles for autonomy have led to a wide variety of constitutional forms, in the introduction of which the colonial administrative practices too had an equal hand. Indeed, the Indian experience is most instructive because of its diversity and range, the full extent of colonial innovations, multiple forms of autonomy, the complex path of constitutionalism, a wide variety of accords, yet the persistent demands for self-determination in various forms, and an unyielding sovereign determined to keep the destined nation intact while keeping others from gaining nationhood. It is also important to recall in this context the political and constitutional ways in which the minorities have been negotiated by the Indian state—limited form of autonomy in personal laws and cultural autonomy, and that too mainly for religious minorities, a process I had discussed in detail in an earlier work, *A Biography of the Indian Nation, 1947-97*.[5] In short, in the experiments and innovations of democracy, modern law has not proved to be a self-fulfilling prophecy working towards the satisfaction of the political subject. Faced with asymmetries of power it can manage at best the coexistence of various normative orders, and at worst it can become a willing accomplice to the manipulation of the public principles by a particular group. It also shows that beyond the given territorial form of autonomy, we have not been able to engineer other forms of autonomy that will combine both spatial and spiritual dimensions. With the governmentalization of politics and the popular demand for autonomy bound in a deadlock, we are in a situation of closure—dialogue or self-determination? And how to combine both? The aporia, which I term as the 'democratic closure' is clear, and the discovery of the region in recent times is one way out of this closure. To create a region of Eurasia as the playground of various autonomies (culture, economies, local systems, histories, work-patterns, migration systems, etc.) will be one of the most imaginative tasks of this century, reviving possibly the dream of Alexander of uniting the Hellenic world and that of the barbarians. Death met him in his efforts. Who knows which big powers will be upset and violent at such a venture!

II

One great problem in this experimental venture will be race. If a region as I have argued is a work site of democracy by virtue of housing autonomies (even though in an asymmetrical way), the first requirement in this qualification will be that it has to show a new way of constituting popular sovereignty, which will mean above all shared forms of sovereignty cutting across racial boundaries. The return of the race question as we all know has been occasioned by the massive migrations of our time, when cultural differences have been tuned into biological essentialisms. Therefore in a huge space called Eurasia which has to be based on interacting autonomies we shall have to ask, is there any way to share sovereignty among citizens and migrants—without which reconstitution of a people of a region makes no sense? Can we think of a deeper dialogic situation in this respect?

The most salient feature of an atmosphere of civility (which lies at the core of the assumed racial differences today) is that there is a persistent attempt to make the control over the bodies and minds of the dominated as peaceful as possible and as normal as ever through basically two techniques: discipline and normalization. In short, civility as practice is marked by an awesome fear of the body, and as consequence a desperate desire to keep the physicality of contentions and social conflicts underground. We may ask, how could this fear of the body arrive as a factor in the grammar of rule? How could *difference as we see become finally physical, and thus racial*? I shall suggest a brief answer. It relates to the factor of conquest: one way to move away from idealist histories and ground the history of civility and savagery on material grounds will be to look into the impact of the phenomenon of conquest on politics. When we ground this issue in the politics of the Eurasian region, it will mean giving more importance to territory, and space in general, in our understanding of political battles. We can see then how conquest led to racism, and racism became in time the most indelible instance of physicality of differences. Conquest led to annexation; annexation led to reorganization of the conquered territory and the political space in general; this reorganization included imposition of a division of population between the ruling population group and the ruled group, and establishing institutional modes of maintaining differences and divisions. What is striking in this is that, the more conquest became a universal feature of political relation, out of which many social relations grew, the more particular divisions (such as between two groups) became wide, so wide as to claim universal applicability. That is why, as Etienne Balibar shows, racism, an ideology of particularity, is finally universal as ideology. The universality of the civility/barbarity polarity should not therefore astonish us. Who is this invader? What are his traits? What does he eat? Whom does he marry? How does he marry? How does he kill? How does he drink? What are his apparels? All these inquiries are important to establish that the conqueror/conquered is *different*—different as human beings, physically, racially, in colour, in body, in life. Racism long ago began in this way and is now apparent in all forms of security politics, threatened by a beard, a short nose, or a dark colour, or the infamy of a place.

Seen in this perspective, we can see why dialogue across differences (which include firstly cultural differences) is the vision of several new political imaginations today. Let me put very briefly some aspects of the dialogic vision: (a) there is a political dimension here that speaks of the will not to be lost in differences; in other words a discovery of sameness; (b) this is a will as well as a cognitive dimension; (c) set against the centuries-long history of discrimination, racism, colonialism, big power domination, post-colonial ethnocratic regimes, and now the inbuilt superiority of certain forces, classes, countries, and regions in the process of globalization, the will to know the others and not to be lost in differences has the dimension of protest; (d) there is in this, as we all know, massive inter-personal dimensions demonstrating the direct physical elements involved in the will to overcome difference; (e) there is a communicative exercise involved in this, which tells us the steps in a series; (f) the vision puts the need for improvisation and to be creative above rules and rule-bound formations; (g) it argues for a combination of several modes of function; and finally, (h) the dialogic mode continuously de-philosophizes the element of difference and reduces it to the level of practicality. Dialogue in short then, means working on the margins. As we know, modernity not only brings a change in the system of knowledge, we also become *differently knowing*. Chairman Mao spoke of three sources of knowledge—struggle against nature, struggle for truth, and class struggle—and as he saw it, these three activities produced three 'knowledges', namely scientific knowledge, philosophic knowledge, and political knowledge. While each of these influences the other two, broadly we can say that the will to know is not a homogenous trend. The will to knowledge is connected to dialogues in as much as it is connected to power.

Dialogue across differences is the core of the work site, which for the region becomes the moment it starts housing autonomies. This also indicates newer ways of establishing a political community, which while retaining some of the characteristics of the older method exhibits novel features emanating from the combination of the political with community bonds. By community I am not indicating here anything primordial in particular, but those actions or claims by which a population group achieves a community identity cutting across state boundaries (I have in mind all the instances of the divided peoples in the Eurasian region) in the face of the political sovereignty of the state. In the gradual decrease in the importance, if not disappearance, of the national-people and the appearance of autonomies we have an extraordinary displacement in modern political history, whose significance we shall need time to understand fully. At least we can say this, and this is particularly important for a region, if the first generation theory of citizenship talked of citizenship in a political sense, that is to say citizenship as membership of a political community, and the second generation theory talked of social citizenship in terms of acquiring rights and being strengthened by social power through the acquisition of these rights, a process demonstrated by Marshall,[6] these autonomies have produced the third generation theory of citizenship, which we can name as citizenship by virtue of membership of plural sites—a phenomenon that produces a new form of power. Citizenship of a region will require construction of new institutional requirements—administrative, political, and legal—appropriate to such plural memberships.[7] Thus the identity of a region as a field of autonomies generates a new chapter in politics, which can be described like this:

> State expansion → expanding political activity → citizenship → standardized politics → local grievances cutting across boundaries → popular resistance → struggle → autonomy → emergence of autonomous areas and themes in a region → expanding political activity

III

Is it a utopian vision? It may not be so, for the crucial factor here will be the space, the *vastness of the space*. In making Eurasia a reality we are conferring on this world a new space marked, as all vast spaces are, with "frontiers of freedom." Obviously I am changing the Jacksonian idea of the freedom of the frontier, and the idea of conquest of space, which is accomplished by conquest of territory and the people who live there. I am invoking here a sense of Tartar freedom, characteristic of the Eurasian vastness. Space gives rise to new subjects, a new and refreshing sense of autonomy. Therefore freedom of movement across the borders becomes crucial. It is the opposite of the idea of the '*polis*' as the centre of the political universe, and makes politics a product of confederal unity of peoples inhabiting and moving across this vast space. It is again different from the Jacksonian idea of space as freedom, because unlike the American case in the eighteenth and the nineteenth centuries, traversing the space will not be related to founding of private property, appropriation, colonization, and expansion. But space brings in a sense and practice of freedom, which a centralized state cannot easily usurp, and which becomes the core of a new concept of society as distinct from the state. Space produces dynamism, creativity, and a rich imaginary of life. This autonomy is irreducible. It is able to disconnect popular sovereignty and centralized state apparatus, and give rise to a new sociality.

Does this suggest a Jeffersonian accommodation, which would mean always "towards the frontier, beyond the frontier, towards freedom that will consolidate democracy"? My answer is no, for here democracy is not linked with creating a constitution and founding a system of rule, or annexing property, or conquering space. In this neo-liberal milieu of globalization, we have to be cautious. However, this does not mean that we stop enjoying space as the common asset of peoples inhabiting the space. I still think that the weakening of the nation states in this vast region, coupled with the dissolution of the old vast state machinery straddling the old Eurasian space gives new opportunities to use the space a new imaginative way. But this will demand moving away from the British model of politics (liberalism, centralized state marked by separation of powers, parliamentary sovereignty, etc.) and the American model of democracy (marked by freedom of private property and capital as the essential requirement of democratic space), and imagining a much more nomadic or mobile sense of politics, representation, sociality, and inter-subjectivity. The power of capital creates space, but this space is marked by disconnections of all kinds—disconnect between the location of consumption and location of production, between location of control and location of war and other engagements, between the city and the inner city with waste sites and redundant population, location of imperial power and the location of its subjects, and finally between location of location of means of rule and location of politics. These disconnections mark a vast space created by capital. As against this or at least as distinct from this, I suggest that the concept of Eurasia offers us a sense of vast space with connections of different locations, and thus a more free sense of sociality.[8]

Notes

1. Ranabir Samaddar, "Autonomy and the Requirements of Minimal Justice" and "Governing Through Peace Accords," in *The Politics of Dialogue* (Aldershot: Ashgate Publishing, 2004), ch. 5 and 6.
2. Michel Foucault, *Essential Works of Michel Foucault, 1954-1984*, vol. 3 (New York: New Press, 2001), 207.
3. Foucault, *Essential Works*, 208-09.
4. See the essays published in R. Samaddar (ed.), *The Politics of Autonomy* (New Delhi: Sage, 2006). Each of these essays is a commentary on autonomy's other, namely governmentality.
5. Ranabir Samaddar, *A Biography of the Indian Nation, 1947-97* (Delhi: Sage, 2001); also see, Samaddar, *The Politics of Dialogue*, chs 5 and 7.
6. T.H. Marshall, "Citizenship and Social Class," in *Class, Citizenship and Social Development—Essays by T.H. Marshall* (Garden City, New York: Anchor Books, 1965), 65-122.
7. To my mind, in this context women's demands for autonomy are more significant than any territorial demand for autonomy, for the former shows in a clearer way as to how the occupation of multiple sites produces power in a new way, and transforms the concept of citizenship. See in this context, Paula Banerjee, "Debates over Women's Autonomy," *Policies and Practices* 3, Calcutta Research Group, Calcutta (2005); see also, Anupama Roy, *Gendered Citizenship—Historical and Conceptual Explorations* (Hyderabad: Orient Longman, 2005).
8. On this, a careful reading of the origins of the American Revolution will help us to grasp better the idea of space as freedom; see for instance, Roderick Nash, *Wilderness and the American Mind* (New Haven, CT: Yale University Press, 1982); Dick Howard, *The Birth of American Political Thought, 1763-1787*, Davis Amis Curtis (trans.) (Minneapolis: University of Minnesota Press, 1989). I am also suggesting a reverse reading of Turner; see Frederick Jackson Turner, *The Frontier in American History* (New York: Holt, 1947), and William Henry McNeill, *The Great Frontier—Freedom and Hierarchy in Modern Times* (Princeton, N.J.: Princeton University Press, 1983).

8

The Paradox of Cosmopolitan—Eurocentrism in the Rise of the West

The Dialectical—Dialogues of Civilizations

John M. Hobson

Since 1978, and the publication of Edward Said's *Orientalism* it has become commonplace to characterise European identity as Eurocentric and imperialist. Recently, the critique of Eurocentrism has emerged within studies of the rise of the West.[1] *Inter alia*, these scholars emphasize the role of the imperial exploitation of non-western peoples and resources. However, in recent years a literature is emerging, wherein Europe's identity is presented not as Eurocentric but as cosmopolitan.[2] At first sight, these literatures would appear to be diametrically opposed; one pointing up the claim that Europe exploited and oppressed the non-West through imperialism, with the other insisting that Europe's identity was far less certain and self-assured such that positive interaction and learning from the non-West is viewed as having been integral to Europe's development.[3] Thus for Said, the possibility of cosmopolitan interaction between the West and East seemingly becomes ruled out given that the former's identity has been defined negatively against the latter, through the construction of Orientalism. And, moreover, the possibility of cosmopolitan interaction would seem to be denied insofar as Eurocentrism/Orientalism entails imperial confrontation and the subjugation of the non-western Other.

But it is worth citing the more recent words of Edward Said in the Preface to the recent reprint of *Orientalism*:

> Rather than the manufactured clash of civilizations we need to concentrate on the slow working together of cultures that overlap,

> borrow from each other, and live together....But for [this] kind of wider perception we need time and patient and skeptical enquiry supported by faith in communities of interpretation that are difficult to sustain in a world demanding instant action and reaction.[4]

Moreover, there are all manner of similar quotes that are contained within his 2004 book, *Power, Politics and Culture*.[5] Two notable examples are worth citing here.

> The worst thing ethically and politically is to let [Eurocentric] separatism simply go on, without understanding the opposite of separatism, which is connectedness.... What I am interested in is how all these things work together. That seems to me to be the great task—to connect them all together—to understand wholes rather than bits of wholes.[6]

> In a wonderful phrase, Disraeli asks, "Arabs, what are they?" and answers: "They're just Jews on horseback." So underlying this separation is also an amalgamation of some kind.[7]

Indeed, I believe that this emphasis on symbiotic connections between civilizations is something that is central to Said's 2004 book. Does this mean, therefore, that Said effectively abandoned his emphasis on Europe's Orientalist identity only to side with a more cosmopolitan reading on the eve of his untimely death?

In this essay I want to argue that in so doing, not only was Said true to his original emphasis on Europe's Orientalist identity, but that Eurocentrism and cosmopolitanism have constituted the two sides of Europe's identity. That is, these are complementary rather than opposing forms of identity. Of course, thus far the two literatures have tended to exist side by side, with no reconciliation seemingly in sight. The problem here, though, is that the 'debate' has rested on a problematic 'either/or' framework. In this piece I want to replace this 'either/or' with a 'both/and' framework by arguing that the "cosmopolitan dialogues" and "Orientalist/imperial dialectics" of civilizations in the rise of the West are not separate or mutually exclusive but were co-constitutive in the rise of the West—hence the "paradox of cosmopolitan-Eurocentrism." Here I shall focus on the two sides of Europe's seemingly schizophrenic identity by examining the interlinked forms of civilizational interactions that Europe undertook with respect to various eastern civilizations in the specific context of the rise of the West.

More specifically, I refer to the "cosmopolitan dialogues of civilisations," which refers to the manifold ways in which each civilization develops through the borrowing and assimilation of resource portfolios (ideas, technologies and institutions) that emanate from other civilizations. This process has been going on since at least 500 CE.[8] Here I suggest that in the dialogue, the meeting point of civilizations is a two-way "dialogical zone" that generates *poly-civilizational hybridity* through what Mary Louise Pratt[9] calls "transculturation," in what amounts to a form of "dialogical negotiation" (as opposed to a monologic one-way passive receptivity). In turn, this of course, forms an alternative conception to that offered by Samuel Huntington in his famous treatise, *The Clash of Civilizations and the Remaking of World Order*.[10] Alongside the dialogue we can trace the Eurocentric/imperial "dialectic of civilisations," where Eurocentric western identity has fuelled an imperial and exploitative relationship with the East. In Jan Nederveen Pieterse's conception this refers to the process wherein the bottom-up logic of emancipation/ resistance entwines with the top-down logic of imperial domination.[11] Here I shall focus only on the entwined connections between the cosmopolitan dialogues of civilizations and the Eurocentric dialectics of civilizations in the making of the West. The first part of the chapter examines these linkages through foregrounding the dialogues while part 2 foregrounds the imperial-Eurocentric dialectics.

Cosmopolitan Civilizational Dialogues in the Rise of the West

The image of Europe clashing with other civilizations is one that is conventionally thought to mark Europe's history, past and present. Naturally this image has been cemented by the popularity of Huntington's "clash of civilizations" thesis. The popular imaginary reaches back to the Crusades and the clash between Christian Europe and Islamic West Asia. And in this conception the idea of a Manichean clash of two great antithetical civilizations leaves no room for any kind of symbiosis or mutual learning. But the paradox here lies in the point that at the very time when the Europeans were engaged in military confrontation with Islam, they not only continued trading with the Muslims but were avidly borrowing a wealth of Islamic ideas, technologies and institutions that in turn propelled Europe forward. Indeed, at all times, the Venetian hub of European commerce gained its vitality through its constant links with the trading world of Islam in West Asia and North Africa. In other words, focussing only on the European clash with Islam serves to obscure the many symbiotic cosmopolitan dialogical interactions that have occurred between the two.

It is also important to emphasize the point, *contra* Eurocentric world history, that Islamic West Asia did *not* constitute a threat to 'Western Europe'. It is certainly true that the Muslims took over certain places such as Sicily in 902, Spain after 711/756 and, of course, the Ottomans penetrated the Balkans later on. But Eurocentric world historians almost invariably emphasize the "attempted conquest" of France by an invading Islamic army in 733. In the first instance, though, this does not square with the point that in the Muslim histories of the period, the battle of Tours, Poitiers and the figure of Charles Martel go largely unmentioned. Far greater emphasis is accorded to the Arab defeat at Constantinople (718). Of course, the Eurocentric response to this might be that this was only to be expected given that Muslims' histories would naturally seek to downplay their historic losses and defeats (the Arab defeat at Constantinople in 718 notwithstanding!). However, it was not the power of Martel's shock cavalry that defeated the Muslims, but the fact that he managed to lure the so-called invaders to a fort from where his army showered the attackers with a barrage of arrows and javelins. Most significantly though, this was no "Islamic invasion," but was rather a small band of raiders embarking on a minor raiding mission (the target of which was the wealthy shrine of St. Martin). Indeed, even such an authority as Bernard Lewis concedes that:

> There can be little doubt that in disregarding Poitiers [and Tours] and stressing Constantinople, the Muslim historians saw events in a truer perspective than the later Western historians. The Frankish victors at Poitiers encountered little more than a band of [Islamic] raiders operating beyond their most distant frontiers, thousands of miles from home.... It was the failure of the Arab army to conquer Constantinople, not the defeat of the Arab raiding party at Tours and Poitiers, which enabled both Eastern and Western Christendom to survive.[12]

Thus while the Muslims had taken various parts of 'Western Europe', the reality was that they were not interested in going any further than this. And the reason for this was simple: the western part of Europe was backward and of little interest to them. Byzantium was both more powerful and more attractive. As Marc Bloch originally noted, of all the "enemies of Western Europe, Islam was certainly the least dangerous.... For a long period neither Gaul nor Italy, among their poor cities, had anything to offer which approached the splendour of Baghdad or Cordova."[13] In fact the many waves of migrations that had flooded into Europe since the fourth century CE had wreaked far more havoc than had the sporadic Islamic raiding parties. On top of all this the Muslims living in 'Western Europe', especially in Spain, constituted a kind of conveyor belt along which Islamic and non-Islamic eastern resource portfolios were carried from West Asia and North Africa into Europe, where they in turn stimulated European development in all manner of ways. Moreover, in Islamic Spain, Jews, Christians and Muslims all lived peaceably and harmoniously side by side.[14]

The profundity of these manifold symbiotic links necessarily raises the question as to why they have been largely ignored in world history in favour of an emphasis on a monological clash between Europe and Islam. Certainly the Christian prelates sought to define Europe negatively against Islam. Thus by exaggerating the "universal threat" of Islam so they sought to cement a new European identity as "Defender of the One True Faith" (i.e. Christianity). And so while Europeans drew on all manner of ideas that were invented or developed in Islamic West Asia/North Africa, nevertheless they did not want to be seen to be relying on Islamic knowledge, particularly at the time when they were waging war with the Muslims. Thus the various monarchs who sought to have Muslim scientific texts translated into Latin often employed Jewish translators (as did the Spanish and Portuguese kings), in order to obscure the Islamic linkages. Notable too is that at the very time when Dante was consigning Muhammad to the eighth circle of Hell in his book *Inferno*—one step removed from Satan—he was simultaneously borrowing many of his ideas from Islamic philosophers (which was why he consigned them to Purgatory rather than to Hell in his book).

But there is another factor which is important to emphasize here: namely that the Europeans placed a high priority in terms of promoting an image of European inventive originality. And this tendency is evident throughout the period of the rise of the West from c.800-1900, when Europe borrowed all manner of eastern "resource portfolios" (ideas, technologies, institution, all of which is to suggest that the cosmopolitan side of Europe was nestled or embedded within a more exclusionary identity-formation process; and to bracket or separate the two out is to miss a good deal of that which was going on.

This is particularly evident when we examine two of the major dialogues that Europeans undertook with non-western civilizations. The first comprises the Islamic-European dialogues that underpinned the emergence of the Renaissance and the scientific revolution, and the second constitutes the Sino-European dialogues in the rise of the West. Note, however, that these are two (albeit major) examples of the multi-civilizational dialogues that Europe undertook with various non-western civilizations.

Islamic-European dialogues in the Renaissance and Scientific Revolution

Italy is famous, of course, for the Renaissance, which in turn set Europe off into the post-feudal era. This epistemic revolution is typically thought to have been in effect a recalling of the scientific and rational ideas that had been pioneered by the ancient Greeks (hence the importance of fabricating Greece as purely European[15]). The immediate problem here, though, is that many of the ideas that were 'invented' in Greece were actually derived from ancient Egypt.[16] But more important is the point that the Renaissance owes a huge debt to the contemporary Muslims, as did the Scientific Revolution.[17] It is not possible to give a full account of the dialogue here, but it is worth noting a few pertinent examples to illustrate the point.

It is generally assumed that one of the vital aspects of the Renaissance was a key development in art: the invention of single-point perspective. Previously artists painted an object or person from a variety of different angles rather than from a singular point perspective. Moreover, the size or scale of the subject was based on the social importance of the person being depicted, rather than being a reflection of his or her actual size. Generally, the inventor of this perspective is thought to be the Italian Renaissance painter, Filippo Bruneschelli, around 1425. But this approach was already developed some 400 years earlier by the famous Muslim scholar, Ibn al-Haytham (Alhazen), in his optical theory. Indeed "to represent the world as it is or as it appeared to the eye of the observer—without the interposition of idealizations or spiritual projections—became a real possibility and excited Renaissance artists… the world now could be considered to have become transparent to the human visual gaze."[18] In addition, al-Haytham's other major contribution was in helping promote the turn to mathematical realism—a formulation that broke fundamentally with Greek thinking.[19] And, no less significantly, the Baconian idea that science should be based on the experimental method was one that had been pioneered by the Muslims in general (and *not* the Greeks), and the likes of al-Haytham in particular.

Islamic breakthroughs in mathematics including algebra and trigonometry were vital. The former term was taken from the title of one of al-Khwārizmī's mathematical texts (as a result of the translation made by the Englishman, Robert of Ketton, in 1145). By the beginning of the tenth century all six of the classical trigonometric functions had been defined and tabulated by Muslim mathematicians. Developments in public health, hygiene and medicine were also notable. Al-Rāzī's medical works were translated and reprinted in Europe some forty times between 1498 and 1866. And Ibn Sīnā's (or Avicenna's) *Canon of Medicine* became the founding text for European medical schools between the twelfth and fifteenth centuries. The Muslims developed numerous medicines and anaesthetics and pioneered the study of anatomy. Notable here is that the Egyptian physician, Ibn al-Nafis (d. 1288), whose work on the human body, which contradicted the traditional position of the Greek physician, Galen, fully pre-empted the much heralded work of William Harvey by 350 years. The Muslims were also keen cartographers, astrologers and astronomers and their ideas were avidly borrowed by the Europeans (see below). Notably, Ibn al-Shātir's mathematical models bore an uncanny resemblance to those used by Copernicus 150 years later. Indeed, Noel Swerdlow has suggested that it "seems too remarkable a series of coincidences to admit the possibility of independent discovery [on the part of Copernicus]."[20] Also of note is that as early as the ninth century, al-Khwārizmī calculated the circumference of the Earth to within 41 metres.

Finally, ancient Egyptian hermetic texts also featured in the Italian Renaissance, given that they were translated after 1460 by Marsilio Ficino at the Court of Cosimo de Medici. Accordingly, the very term European 'Renaissance' is problematic, since it exaggerates its ancient Greek foundations and denies its substantial eastern heritage.

If there was a series of eastern ideas that underpinned the so-called European Renaissance then we need ask two interrelated questions. First, why have these non-western roots been either ignored or forgotten? And second, do such dialogues point up an unambiguous cosmopolitan interaction between Europe and Islamic civilization? As we have already noted, at the very same time that the Muslims were supplying the Europeans with new and more advanced ideas, the Christians were demonizing Islam and waging war on them through the Crusades. This meant that the Europeans were loathe to admit that they were learning from the infidel. Second, the East furnished many of the ideas of the western Renaissance, only to find that the Europeans subsequently turned around and disingenuously claimed that they had independently come up with the ideas in the first place. Of course, this tendency is by no means unique to the Europeans. But it does seem fair to say that no other civilization has been so reliant on the ideas and inventions of others as has Europe. It is indeed true that Europe put all these multi-civilizational contributions together to make the final breakthrough to modernity. But the problem is that Europeans, past and present, insist that it was Europe that single-handedly made the breakthrough all by itself. And notably, rather than play up the dialogical nature of the West's achievement, Europeans and westerners more generally came to pronounce the West as the embodiment of advanced rational civilization while the East was dismissed as an inferior civilization that was but an irrational intellectual wasteland. Moreover, it was this conception that formed the discursive basis for the idea of the western imperial civilizing mission that would emerge gradually after 1492, but take off in the nineteenth century. Thus what began as complementary civilizational-learning and civilizational dialogues morphed later into a Eurocentric conception of western identity that entailed the imperial subjection of the Other. In this way, then, the dialogues and dialectics of civilizations became entwined in Europe's interactions and relations with other civilizations.

Sino-European Dialogues in the Rise of the West, C. 1500–1800

After about 1500 Chinese influence was vital in retracking the still relatively backward West onto a catch-up phase with the East that culminated in the breakthrough to capitalist-industrial modernity. How then did this occur?

Let us begin by returning to the European Age of Rediscovery. China's contribution here was at least as important as that of Islam's. In particular, the Chinese passed on the all-important inventions of the square hull and stern-post rudder, the triple mast system, and the compass, in the absence of which oceanic sailing would have been stymied. The other feature of the European voyages that is usually mentioned is the deployment of cannon on their ships. But this misses the point that the cannon was invented in China around 1288. The first European cannon is dated to 1326 in Florence, and 1327 in England (the earliest illustration of an English cannon is found in Walter de Millemete's manuscript). This particular illustration is significant because it reveals that the English cannon was in fact identical to the earlier Chinese version, implying that the former was unlikely to have been an independent invention. Also of note here is that gunpowder was invented in China around 850 (and the first metal-barrelled gun firing a metal bullet was invented in China no later than 1275), and there are various possible transmission paths for these resource portfolios.[21]

But perhaps the most significant contribution that the Chinese made was to the pivotal British industrial and agricultural revolutions.[22] The British agricultural revolution was spurred on by a series of inventions, including the iron mouldboard plough, Jethro Tull's seed drill and horse-drawn hoe, the horse-powered threshing machine and the rotary winnowing machine. Added to this were breakthroughs in crop rotations. But in each case, these inventions had been accomplished in China as early as the sixth century. In the case of the plough and rotary winnowing machine, Chinese models were directly brought across (either by the Jesuits, European scientists or Dutch sailors). And the remainder were most likely copied from Chinese manuals that flooded Europe after 1650. Finally, while Eurocentrism equates Turnip Townshend with the breakthrough in crop rotations, these were already in place in sixth century Chinese agriculture.

Much the same story applies to the British industrial revolution. Thus while Eurocentrism celebrates James Watt for his pioneering skills in inventing the steam-engine, it is likely that he owed much to the Chinese. The essentials of the steam-engine go back to Wang Chên's *Treatise on Agriculture* (1313), which in turn goes back to the Chinese invention of the water-powered bellows (31 CE). While it is usually acknowledged that Watt's engine stems back to Wilkinson's, nevertheless the latter's engine shared many similarities with Wang's. Moreover, the Chinese box-bellows was a double-acting force and suction pump, which at each stroke expelled the air from one side of the piston while drawing in an equal amount of air on the other side. Not only did it share a "close formal resemblance" to Watt's engine but, by the late seveneteenth century, the Chinese had developed a steam turbine.[23] Moreover, Chinese breakthroughs in gun manufacturing were also important in enabling the later invention of the steam-engine (given that the cannon or gun is in effect a one-cylinder combustion engine and all of our modern motors are descended from it). Interestingly, a further link here is that one of the major challenges confronting James Watt was the need to bore an airtight cylinder. This is interesting because Watt turned to John Wilkinson for help in this matter, given that Wilkinson owned a boring mill that was designed for cannon production.

Given China's substantial lead in iron and steel production, it was not surprising that British producers (including the famous Benjamin Huntsman of Sheffield) undertook detailed studies of Chinese production methods as late as the eighteenth century in order to develop their own steel manufacturing techniques. Noteworthy too is that the European invention of the Bessemer converter (1852) was significantly derived from the breakthroughs made by the American, William Kelly, in 1845. But what is not usually pointed out is that Kelly himself had brought over four Chinese steel experts to Kentucky from whom he learned the principles of steel production.

The other great pillar of the British Industrial Revolution was the development of cotton manufacturing. But while Eurocentrism celebrates pioneering British inventors such as John Lombe, this misses the point that some of their inventions had been pioneered in China many centuries earlier. John Lombe's silk machines became the model for the Derby cotton machines. But while Lombe's 'invention' was a copy of the Italian machines, they in turn were a direct copy of the earlier Chinese inventions from the thirteenth century. Notable too is that in textiles, the Chinese had long developed machines which differed in only one detail to that of James Hargreaves' famous 'spinning jenny' and John Kay's equally famous 'flying shuttle'.

However, once again, it might be objected that even if China had bequeathed much to Europe this was, however, only economic or technological, thereby enabling Eurocentric historians to uphold their point that the Europeans maintained their pioneering edge with respect to cultural innovations, most notably the European Enlightenment. But this obscures the point that between 1700 and 1780, much of Europe formed a virtual love affair with the world of Rococo and sought to emulate many aspects of Chinese civilization. This was fuelled by the wealth of translated Chinese pamphlets and books that flooded Europe after about 1650, many of which were transmitted by the Jesuits.

The link between the European Enlightenment and Chinese thought was ultimately bridged by the shared faith in reason as the centre of all things. Reason enabled the discovery of the autonomous 'laws of motion' that were allegedly inscribed within all areas of social, political and 'natural' life. While many Enlightenment thinkers positively associated with China and its ideas, Voltaire was undoubtedly the major Sinophile. He drew on Chinese conceptions of politics, religion and philosophy—all of which were based on rational principles—in order to attack the European preference for hereditary aristocracy. Indeed, many of the major Enlightenment thinkers derived their preference for the 'rational method' from China. Chinese ideas also played a very important part in influencing British culture and political economy.[24]

In the Anglo-Saxon canon *the* central European political economist was the Scotsman, Adam Smith. But while Anglo-Saxons parochially think of Smith as the first political economist the fact is that behind Smith lay François Quesnay, the French 'Physiocrat'. And crucially, behind Quesnay lay China. Indeed in his day Quesnay was generally known as the 'European Confucius'. And Quesnay, not Smith, was the first European to critique the ideas of mercantilism. The term 'physiocracy' means the 'rule of nature'. The significance of his ideas, derived from China, was at least two-fold: first, Quesnay saw in agriculture a crucial source of wealth (which became an important idea that lay behind the British agricultural revolution). Second, and more importantly, he believed that agriculture could only be fully exploited when producers were freed from the arbitrary interventions of the state. Only then could the 'natural laws' of the market prevail (as the Chinese had long realized). Quesnay's debt to Chinese conceptions of political economy was found in many ideas, the most important being that of *wu-wei*, which is translated into French as *laissez-faire*. Indeed around 300 CE Kuo Hsiang described *wu-wei* as that which lets "everything be allowed to do what it naturally does, so that its nature will be satisfied" (although it should be noted that the concept pre-dates the start of the Common Era). And once this had entered the mind of Adam Smith, as they say, "the rest was history."

None of this is to say that the European Enlightenment was the *pure* product of Chinese ideas, for clearly there were some Enlightenment thinkers who rejected China as a model for Europe, most notably Montesquieu and Fénelon. But it would be entirely remiss to ignore the Chinese input in this major epistemic turning point of western civilization. And to sum up this section more generally: none of this is to say that the rise of western civilization is the pure product of eastern influences. But it is to say that without all this eastern influence, western leaders would not be able to strut the world stage today and denounce as barbaric the very peoples who helped it rise to where it now somewhat fortuitously finds itself.

We have noted how the Europeans sought to cover their tracks by obscuring their indebtedness to the inventive thinkers in Islamic civilization. This was partly because the Renaissance thinkers themselves were anxious to forge a new European identity that was independent of the Islamic world. Indeed "the return to the classical [Greek] world was seen as the answer to the [perceived] threat from Islam to European culture."[25] The paradox of the Renaissance, then, was that it was in part created to differentiate Europe from Islam and yet it was from Islam that the Renaissance scholars drew so many of their new ideas. Clearly the religious antipathy towards Islam was *a* factor here, given that in the eighteenth century many (though by no means all) European Enlightenment scholars associated positively with China. No less clearly, the Europeans found Confucianism far less threatening than they did Islam and were, therefore, more open to positively associating themselves with China. That said, though, it would be wrong to assume that European inventors and Enlightenment thinkers openly conceded that many of their ideas came from China. Interestingly, Jonas Norberg, speaking of the invention of the rotary winnowing machine, broke with European convention when he admitted that, "I got the initial idea... from three separate models brought here from China."[26] But his admittance was very much the exception that proved the rule.

Moreover, just as the Europeans had borrowed all manner of ideas from Islamic civilization only to then proclaim a uniquely European originality, so after about 1780 the Europeans turned similarly to denounce China. For now China, like Islamic West Asia, found its place in the Eurocentric construction of the world, which depicted Europe at the top, with the Blacks at the bottom and the 'Yellows'—Chinese, East Asians and Muslims—in the middle.[27] And, of course, this Eurocentric construction in turn played a vital part in stimulating European imperialism. In this way, Europe's cosmopolitan dialogues and imperial dialectics vis-à-vis eastern civilizations are neither antithetical nor contradictory. They formed, as it were, both sides of the same schizophrenic European identity. The next section reveals the Eurocentric-imperialist face of Europe's identity. But for the moment I want to conclude thus far by emphasizing the point that while Europe was heavily dependent on the inventions and contributions of other civilizations, it stood out insofar as it proclaimed a monopoly of inventive and progressive economic capacity. Thus Europe's dialogical cosmopolitanism went hand-in-hand with a desire to appear monologically separate, uniquely inventive and, above all, exceptional—the very essence of Europe's Eurocentric identity.

The (Imperial) Dialectics of Civilization in the Rise of the West: Eurocentric Identity and the Exploitation of the East

Thus far we have noted how the rise of the West was significantly fuelled by the assimilation of eastern resource portfolios as Europe engaged in an often hidden series of dialogues with the East. But if we left it here we would first of all exaggerate the potential degree of harmony and cosmopolitan linkages that have existed between East and West, while simultaneously eliciting the impression that the West was a passive beneficiary of Eastern largesse (as in inverted Orientalism or Occidentalism). This section seeks to dispense with such conclusions by revealing the Eurocentric origins of the drive that underpinned the rise of the West. This 'drive' or 'restlessness' had an internal and an external (dialectical-imperialist) dimension. And here I shall also emphasize the important point that this Eurocentric restlessness, which fuelled Europe's catch-up and eventual overtaking of the East, also fed directly into the escalating dialogues between East and West after 1500 (some of which I examined in the previous section), thereby qualifying the assumption that the dialogues were representative of a purely harmonious cosmopolitanism.

Most non-Eurocentric world historians produce arguments that emphasize a materialist epistemology. The assumption is that all civilizations are driven by the same desire to develop, with cultural or identity-based factors being dismissed altogether.[28] In their analyses, European imperialism plays an important part of their account, but it is conceptualized in standard materialist terms. Europe colonized large parts of the East because it *could*: that is, it had the material means to do so and thus it was axiomatic that it *would*. In what follows I want to argue that an adequate account would focus on both materialist and identity-based factors. In essence I argue that civilizations are motivated to act in different ways depending upon their own identities. This emphasis on identity is certainly charted in considerable detail in my book but it was done in the context of specifically explaining Europe's drive to imperialism after 1492.[29] Here I deploy it to explain two key aspects of the rise of the West. First I apply it to explaining Europe's adaptive capacity to assimilate eastern resource portfolios that it had received through civilizational dialogues before eventually refining and deploying them to higher economic ends in order to promote its industrial breakthrough. And second, I note that this identity fuelled European imperialism, which in turn played a vital role in stimulating the rise of the West through the exploitation of the East.

The culturalist-based identity argument of relevance here begins principally in the year 1453, when the perception of an Ottoman 'identity threat' confronted Christendom, leading the Papacy to issue a series of papal bulls. These effectively ordered the Iberians to undertake another round of Crusades by expanding outwards to make links with the Catholic priest-king, Prester John, in the 'Indies' with whom they were to forge a

Christian alliance and attack the Muslims from the rear. Columbus, of course, dutifully sailed westward in search of the (East) Indies.[30] But in literally "stumbling" across the Americas, the Europeans soon came to believe—for the first time in a millennium—that they were superior to another civilization. And this emergent sense of superiority was exacerbated through their encounter with, and subsequent exploitation of, Black African labour. The sixteenth century in European history saw not the rise of Europe to the top, since Europe was still way behind China, India, Islamic West Asia and an emergent Japan under the Tokugawa (after 1600), but the rapid rise of a new aggressive and acquisitive Eurocentric identity.

Echoing Frank[31] I argue that between 1450 and 1800 Europe could best be characterized as a "late-developer" civilization. And as the, albeit 'national', theory of late-development tells us, late-developers enjoy the many "advantages of backwardness."[32] This refers to the fortuitous situation whereby late-developers benefit from the advanced technologies that were pioneered previously by the early developers. The key early-developers of central significance here were the Muslims, North Africans, Indians and Chinese.[33] The Europeans, having begun to access Islamic scientific ideas around 1085, resorted to working with them more urgently, which in turn helped promote the Renaissance and later on the scientific revolution. This then coincided with Europe's development of military power during its military revolution between 1550 and 1660, which centred on the deployment of the gun, gunpowder and cannon. But these were in fact invented much earlier during China's military revolution (c. 850-c.1290), and were subsequently assimilated and then later adapted to higher ends as the Europeans became intent on conquering other parts of the world. Then, from the late seventeenth century the Europeans began to voraciously consume Chinese ideas and technologies, which in turn directly promoted the agricultural and British industrial revolutions.

It is certainly the case that Chinese ideas had been relayed back to Europe mainly via the friars who visited China in the thirteenth century (with Marco Polo being the most famous). But there was a clear lag in terms of these inventions either reaching Europe or in Europeans adopting and refining them. This lag, I would suggest, occurred as a function of the points that first, Europe had not yet developed the aggressive and acquisitive mentality to use them, and second because Marco's reports appeared incredible to the then backward "red-haired barbarians" at the time. However, as the Eurocentric identity of Europe emerged aggressively after 1453/1492 (which was initially manifested in a religious/civilizational sense) eastern resource portfolios became increasingly viewed as resources to steal—insofar as the Europeans, who borrowed eastern portfolios but then claimed western originality—ultimately, so as to promote Europe's catch-up drive.

As we also saw earlier, it was during the Age of the Enlightenment that many philosophies drew on Chinese ideas. The Europeans fed off the many pamphlets and books that flooded Europe in the seventeenth century, which in aggregate revealed the manifold technologies and advanced features of Chinese civilization. Moreover, numerous Europeans travelled to China to learn of their inventions and industrial/agricultural production processes. And, of course, some of the technologies were directly relayed back. These rapidly multiplying transmission circuits provided a crucial knowledge base that helped promote the British agricultural and industrial revolutions. And in the end the Europeans adapted some of these resource portfolios to higher ends.

While the British did indeed have an autonomous input here it was less one of exceptional originality and more one that was based more on a type of Churchillian bull-dogged problem-solving mentality. Indeed most of the significant technologies were developed over long periods of time through this relentless problem-solving drive—the steam engine, from Newcomen in 1705 to Trevithick almost exactly a century later, being an obvious example. *In toto*, this saw them draw on all their energies, as well as the Islamic scientific knowledge that they had adapted to higher levels, in order to adapt Chinese technologies, techniques and ideas, albeit belatedly, to higher industrial/agricultural ends. And, of course, this is what one expects from an adaptive late-developer civilization, though Europe was no ordinary example of one. For ultimately, this was fuelled by a restless Eurocentric drive—though this was not simply led by the state but permeated down to, and infused the mentalities of, various members of British and European society—in order to catch up with the East, and then to move ahead at any cost, not least to confirm the idea of European superiority. Sadly this cost was borne by the British working classes—men, women and children—at home, as well as the many colonial peoples of the world, since imperialism was the second major weapon that enabled British industrialization.

Thus the internal drive found its external expression in the drive to imperialism as a rapidly rising racist identity, that emerged tentatively in the eighteenth century but took off in the nineteenth century, fuelled by the western desire to exploit eastern resources—land, labour, raw materials, land-saving products, bullion, and markets—all of which were vital to supplying the British Industrial Revolution. Moreover, in the British case, this was supported by a highly fiscal-militarist interventionist state that applied heavy protectionism at home and tolerated protectionism and wars in continental Europe, while duplicitously imposing free trade, backed up by naval cannon, on the imperial eastern economies.[34]

This argument can be reinforced by briefly considering China between 1100 and 1800. As I explained elsewhere, in this period China was not only the leading power in the world but it had the material capacity to colonise parts—perhaps even large parts—of the world.[35] Moreover, it had extensive international political linkages through the tribute system. At first sight the Chinese international tribute system appears to exhibit similar properties to the European colonial system. But while China was the leading power for much of the second millennium, its identity led it to choose foregoing imperialism/colonialism. Certainly its identity was hierarchical, with China imagined as the "civilised Middle Kingdom" in contradistinction to all other outlier races that were perceived as 'barbarians'. But despite this superficial similarity the fact is that the Chinese international tribute system was radically different to western imperialism. It was more voluntary than forced and moreover, at virtually no point did the Chinese state try and culturally convert or even exploit its so-called vassal states.[36] The tribute system was designed more to lure 'vassals' towards China not least through holding out genuinely lucrative economic gains, for in agreeing to participate in the tribute system, vassal states then gained access to China's burgeoning economy. Ultimately, China's identity was more a defensive construct that was designed to both maintain Chinese cultural autonomy in the face of potential 'barbarian' invaders (e.g. the Mongols, Manchurians) and to secure its domestic legitimacy in the eyes of its own population. The latter point is issued by the fact that the tribute system enabled Chinese emperors to proclaim that they held the allegiance of the barbarian world, thereby in turn securing the idea that the state had secured the Mandate of Heaven. In sum, then, the Chinese chose to eschew imperialism even though China was the leading power in the world for most of the second millennium.

All in all, then, it is obviously the case that by about 1800 the West had managed to take the lead in terms of material-military power. And this was no less obviously an important factor in the colonization of the East. But there was nothing inevitable about the imperial role that the Europeans chose to undertake in the world. We have seen this in relation to the construction of China's identity. Ultimately the Europeans did not seek to remake the world simply because 'they could' (as in materialist explanations). They sought to remake the world because they *believed they should.* That is, their actions were significantly guided by their Eurocentric identity that deemed imperialism to be a morally appropriate policy. In short, there is no innate relationship between imperialism and superior material power, for what ultimately made Europe imperialist, in contradistinction to China, was its specific identity. And this in turn fed into the internal drive that propelled Europe towards modernity, pushing the Europeans to borrow manifold resource portfolios from the East and then adapt them to higher ends. This also implies that the Messianistic drive that spurred on European development, internally and externally, was ultimately lacking in China. Put differently, ultimately the Chinese withdrew not from global trade but *abstained* from the imperial power politics that would grip the Europeans after 1492.

Conclusion

In this chapter I have sketched one possible framework for rethinking the rise of the West by applying the paradoxical concept of 'cosmopolitan-Eurocentrism' that I believe has underpinned Europe's identity during its formative phase. Of course, the Eurocentrism that I am referring to should not be read as a timeless property for it has taken different forms. Eurocentrism emerged formally after about 1750, but was 'complemented' by racism in the nineteenth century. Previously there had been a kind of Christian Eurocentrism that later on became transformed into a modern secular version during and after the Enlightenment. In turn, Europe's cosmopolitanism can be gleaned through the dialogue of civilizations while at the same time, various forms of Eurocentrism also underpinned these dialogues while also nurturing western imperial appropriation of eastern resources. In sum, then, the postcolonial-inspired conception of Europe as a Eurocentric/Orientalist imperial civilisation obscures the point that Eurocentrism also reached out to, and promoted, the dialogue of civilisations which in turn promoted the rise of the West. Conversely, however, cosmopolitan-inspired scholars tend to reify the cosmopolitan face of Europe's identity, thereby failing both to accommodate the Eurocentric face on the one hand while failing to recognise the link between the cosmopolitan dialogues and Europe's Eurocentric face on the other. Thus we can correct both polarities in this debate by recognising the paradox of Europe's cosmopolitan—Eurocentric identity, which in turn underpinned the rise of the West more generally.

Notes

1. James M. Blaut, *The Colonizer's Model of the World* (London: Guilford, 1993); Andre Gunder Frank, *ReOrient* (Berkeley: University of California Press, 1998); Kenneth Pomeranz, *The Great Divergence* (Princeton: Princeton University Press, 2000).
2. Cf. Gerard Delanty (ed.), *Europe and Asia Beyond East and West* (New York: Routledge, 2006); Ibn Warraq, *Defending the West* (Amherst, NY: Prometheus, 2007).
3. Rémi Brague, *Eccentric Culture* (South Bend, Indiana: Saint Augustine's Press, 2002); Peter O'Brien, *Fragile Ego* (New York: Palgrave Macmillan, 2009). Cf. John M. Hobson, *The Eastern Origins of Western Civilisation* (Cambridge: Cambridge University Press, 2004).
4. Edward W. Said, *Orientalism* (Harmondsworth: Penguin, 1978/2003), xxii.
5. Edward W. Said, *Power, Politics, and Culture* (London: Bloomsbury, 2004).
6. Said, *Power, Politics, and Culture*, 260-1.
7. Said, *Power, Politics, and Culture*, 424.
8. See also Arun Bala, *The Dialogue of Civilizations in the Birth of Modern Science* (Houndmills: Palgrave Macmillan, 2006).
9. Mary Louise Pratt, *Imperial Eyes* (London: Routledge, 1992).
10. Samuel P. Huntington, *The Clash of Civilizations and the Remaking of World Order* (London: Touchstone, 1996).
11. Jan P. Nederveen Pieterse, *Empire and Emancipation* (London: Pluto, 1990).
12. Bernard Lewis, *The Muslim Discovery of Europe* (London: Phoenix, 1994), 19-20.
13. Marc Bloch, *Feudal Society*, I (Chicago: University of Chicago Press, 1961), 3.
14. María Rosa Menocal, *The Ornament of the World* (London: Back Bay Books, 2002).
15. Martin Bernal, *Black Athena*, I (New York: Vintage, 1991).
16. Bernal, *Black Athena*, I.
17. John M. Hobson, *The Eastern Origins of Western Civilisation*, 173-83; Jack Goody, *Islam in Europe* (Cambridge: Polity, 2004), 56-83; S.M. Ghazanfar, *Islamic Civilization* (Lanham, Maryland: Scarecrow Press, 2006); Bala, *The Dialogue of Civilizations in the Birth of Modern Science*; C.K. Raju, *Cultural Foundations of Mathematics* (New Delhi: Pearson Longman, 2007).
18. Bala, *The Dialogue of Civilizations*, 91.
19. Bala, *The Dialogue of Civilizations*, ch. 7.
20. Cited in George Saliba, *A History of Arabic Astronomy* (London: New York University Press, 1994), 64.
21. Hobson, *The Eastern Origins of Western Civilisation*, ch. 8.

22. Hobson, *The Eastern Origins of Western Civilisation*, ch. 9.
23. Joseph Needham and Wang Ling, *Science and Civilisation in China*, IV (2) (Cambridge: Cambridge University Press, 1965), 135-6, 225-8, 369-70, 387, 407-8, 411; Pomeranz, *The Great Divergence*, 61-2.
24. J.J. Clarke, *Oriental Enlightenment* (London: Routledge, 1997); Hobson, *The Eastern Origins of Western Civilisation*, ch. 9.
25. Goody, *Islam in Europe*, 48.
26. Cited in Francesca Bray, *Science and Civilisation in China*, VI (2) (Cambridge: Cambridge University Press, 1984), 377.
27. Hobson, *The Eastern Origins of Western Civilisation*, ch. 10.
28. See Janet L. Abu-Lughod, *Before European Hegemony* (Oxford: Oxford University Press, 1989); Blaut, *The Colonizer's Model of the World*; Frank, *ReOrient*; Pomeranz, *The Great Divergence*. See also Hobson, *The Eastern Origins of Western Civilisation*, ch. 13, for summary.
29. Hobson, *The Eastern Origins of Western Civilisation*, esp. chs 8, 10-11
30. Tzvetan Todorov, *The Conquest of America* (Norman: University of Oklahoma Press, 1984).
31. Frank, *ReOrient*.
32. Alexander Gerschenkron, *Economic Backwardness in Historical Perspective* (Cambridge, MA: Harvard University Press, 1962).
33. Hobson, *The Eastern Origins of Western Civilisation*, chs 2-4.
34. Hobson, *The Eastern Origins of Western Civilisation*, chs 10 and 11.
35. Hobson, *The Eastern Origins of Western Civilisation*, ch. 3.
36. Hobson, *The Eastern Origins of Western Civilisation*, ch. 3; David Abernethy, *The Dynamics of Global Dominance* (New Haven: Yale University Press, 2000), ch. 10.

9

The EU in the Eurasian Space: An Alternative to the USA?

Jyrki Kakonen

The main concern in this paper is with the CFSP (Common Foreign and Security Policy) of the European Union. However, when we talk about EU's CFSP, we are dealing with an aspect of European integration in which the EU is seen, by and large, as rather weak. It is even assumed by some that the EU is simply incapable of achieving a CFSP and therefore labelled as a dwarf in so called high politics and a giant in economy. This did appear to be the case in the context of the crisis caused by the disintegration of Yugoslavia in the 1990s, when the USA and NATO were needed to deal with the problems.[1] And that seems to be the case in the crisis in the Middle East.[2]

It has been difficult for the EU to define and carry out a coherent external policy when different international actors or conflicting partners have diverse expectations from the EU. The bottom line in this regard was quite obvious in the case of the US war on Iraq, when the European Union was split into two major camps: those who supported the US action and those who opposed it.[3] On the other hand, we should note that since the Rome Treaty of 1957, the Community has had a coherent policy towards the developing countries associated to the European Union, and it has been able for successive enlargement and this has to be seen as one aspect of foreign policy as long as the accession of the candidates is factual. In both these areas, we deal with external policy on which the Commission has been responsible.[4]

The EU's external policy is something that is constantly in construction. And that is how we might like to approach and evaluate it. This might also enable us to better explore what EU's external policy actually is, what it could be and what it should be. And this is precisely my intention in this essay. Here my interest lies in EU's policy towards Asia and the role EU tries to envisage for itself in Asia. At the same time, the EU is constructing its own identity as a global actor. It is within such a dynamic context that I seek some answers to the following questions:

- What are the EU interests in Asia? How does the EU see its own role in Asia?
- Does the EU construct for itself a role in Asia that is distinct from the USA?
- Can the EU emerge as an alternative to the USA's role in Asia and thereby contribute towards the construction of a less violent future in Asia, or for that matter, in a wider Eurasian space?5[5]

In my view, while we seek answers to the questions raised above, history is a factor that we should not forget. These questions also remind us of past practices when outsiders shaped the Asian social and political space.[6] This might still be the US interest but it can not be the EU interest, especially in case the EU wants to be an alternative to the USA in an Asian, or even wider, global geopolitics. When we talk about the future of Asia and wider Eurasia, we need to critically reflect on the question of whose Asia or whose Eurasia we are actually talking about. Whose interests are likely to matter the most in the discourses as well as practices aimed at re-visualizing or re-shaping the future of Asia/Eurasia?

Theoretical Perspectives

Since my intention in this essay is to treat Eurasia as a single geographical and social space, my theoretical starting point will be the classical geopolitics, especially as propounded by both Mackinder and Spykman.[7] The division of Eurasia into two distinct continents has been the European invention in order to distinguish itself from Asian despotism on the one hand and to facilitate its rise to the top of the world order on the other. However, the European history and civilization have always been closely connected to Asia and it is rather difficult to imagine Europe without Asia.[8] Classical geopolitics is interesting also in the sense that it tells us a good deal about how power and hegemony operate in the international system and how they produce certain kinds of geographical knowledge from time to time. What is common to the geopolitical theories propounded by both Mackinder and Spykman is that that both entertain the belief that "whoever controls Asia will control the entire world." Mackinder's version required first and foremost the control of the Eurasian heartland, whereas Spykman's emphasized the control of the Eurasian rimland. But in both the versions, the access to and control over Asia and its resources were considered to be the most critical factor for claiming and sustaining the leadership in the world.

In my view, one of the key defining features of classical geopolitics is that it treats the Eurasian landmass as one space for international rivalry. This is in contrast to the imagination that has divided Eurasia in two distinct parts, often seen as alien to each other. Europe presented itself as more civilized and democratic than Asia. And Asia saw itself far more spiritual in comparison to 'materialistic' Europe.[9] To me it is important to see Eurasia as one social space because that gives an option to construct Eurasian space as a zone of peace instead of being a zone of conflicts and theatre for the war on terrorism.

Classical geopolitics was closely connected to Nazi policy and German war politics in the inter-war period. Therefore it lost most of its popularity in the Cold War period. The so-called new or critical geopolitics has brought geopolitics back.[10] The problem with classical geopolitics, a political praxis based on it, is that it is always connected to power politics and rivalry for hegemony in the international system. This further means that the approach has a close connection to conflicts and war-generating politics. It is difficult, if not totally impossible, to connect classical geopolitics to the ideal of international cooperation and construction of zones of harmony and peace in the international system. So why should one start from classical geopolitics with all its historical baggage or legacies?

To my understanding it is the politics itself that has given a second chance to the classical geopolitics. When I say this I do not imply that politics or grand strategies of political actors are based on classical geopolitics. The decision makers do not even need to know sophisticated academic theories and still it is a theory that gives us a chance to make some sense about what is going on. At the beginning of the twenty-first century, it seems promising to use classical geopolitics in order to make sense out of what is going on in Asia. However, this does not mean that classical geopolitics provides bases for solving the problems. On the contrary, analysing the contemporary political complexities and challenges on the basis of classical geopolitics might lead us to a conclusion that the solutions are in fact beyond it.

At this point, I would like to briefly refer to some factors, which suggest that cotemporary Asia is still not outside the confines and considerations of the classical geopolitics paradigm:

- Essential world energy resources are in the Asian rimland and partly in the heartland; i.e. in Central Asia (BP 2008, 7);
- Two most important emerging powers, China and India, are the rimland as well as the EU;
- Many of the potential new nuclear powers i.e. Iran and North Korea, are in the rimland, besides China, India and Pakistan;
- Some of the most threatening conflicts are in the rimland and there are potential conflicts in the heartland.

To say the least, it is possible to agree with the scholars who argue that the second 'Great Game' is going on in Asia and the future world order will be shaped there.[11] However, this time the actors in the 'New Great Game' are not just external powers but also Asian powers engaged in the pursuit of their own interests.[12]

In the context of the classical geopolitics of this region it is possible to say that after the collapse of the Soviet Union, and the end of the Cold War, Russia lost control of the heartland. Russia had vested interest in the heartland or Central Asia.[13] But on the other hand, it is possible to understand the new situation in a way that there was a power vacuum in the heartland and it provided a chance to the rimland powers (or powers controlling the rimland) to expand into the heartland. This was an option the USA was ready and willing to use after the 9/11 terrorist attacks. This is the framework in which one could make sense of the US war on terrorism, invasion of Afghanistan, the war on Iraq and finally, may be the invasion of Iran. Terrorism and proliferation of the weapons of mass destruction are simply a pretext provided by the Muslim fundamentalists and the states labelled by the USA as rogue states.

From the perspective of classical geopolitics it is possible to conclude that the USA is involved in the struggle for hegemony in both the rimland and the heartland of Eurasia. And in the process of constructing the future world order, and its own continuing dominant position as the 'undisputed' world leader, the USA provides a violent future for Asia. Its policy is basically conflict prone. And just here we come to the question whether the EU can facilitate a different kind of a future and alternative for Asia and the wider Eurasian social-cultural space. And of course another question is whether it is in the EU's interest to plan and pursue a politics that is different from US politics. At least this seemed to be the case in the Middle East where the EU had an interest to find a peaceful solution to the aggression in Lebanon in 2006, and to get the UN involved into the peace process while the USA continued to support Israel's hard line.

In principle, the EU should be able to contribute towards constructing a Eurasian zone of peace. This option is very much present in EU's own ideals for its CFSP. As early as 1970, in the so called Luxemburg report, the EU stated that it shall have an international identity distinct from the USA.[14] This idea was clearly repeated in 1973 in the EU's Document on European Identity.[15] However, at the same time these documents mention EUs loyalty to the allies. And this might be one of the problems in constructing EU's CFSP. In a way it is possible to say that as a strong US ally the UK sticks to EU's own principle as well as do the members opposing the US global policy. This has to be understood in the way that UK presents the commitment to the ally, and others are committed to the idea of their own identity as distinct from that of the USA.

Additionally, the bases for EU's alternative Asian policy can be found in its own principles for its CFSP. These principles have been repeated several times in various EU documents throughout the 1990s and especially in the 1993 Maastricht and the 1999 Amsterdam treaties, as follows:

- to defend principles of representative democracy, rule of law, social justice and human rights;
- to promote peace, international security and international cooperation;
- to strengthen democratic principles—respect for human and minority rights;
- to promote regional stability and settlement of conflicts;
- to fight arms proliferation, terrorism and traffic in illicit drugs;
- to promote and support good governance.

During the Cold War, the policy of staying loyal to the allies prevented the EU from establishing and asserting its autonomy and difference vis-à-vis the USA beyond a point. Between the USA and the Soviet Union there was no other 'third way' except the Non Aligned Movement (NAM). The end of the Cold War gave a chance for the EU to formulate its own CFSP. But it is a different thing whether the EU has been able to formulate such a policy and act as a single unit despite the various national foreign policies of the member states.

USA in Asia

In order to assess how different is the EU's CFSP, compared to the US policy in Asia, it is useful to reflect first on what is the US policy in Asia, or what kind of Asia does it visualize geopolitically. And even if the CFSP of the EU turns out to be different and distinct from the US policy in principle, it does not necessarily guarantee that it would eventually emerge as an alternative to the US role in Asia. In this essay, as stated earlier, the US Asian policy is being analysed in the context of classical geopolitics. This might give the impression that we have already come to some kind of a conclusion, as far as the US unilateral assertions for hegemony and world leadership are concerned. Of course this need not be the case. A different theory could lead to a different kind of a picture and conclusions. However, in this case, the function of the theory is to make explicit something that is not necessarily explicated directly in various US foreign policy documents. Or else, examine a theory that gives tools for interpreting texts in a context where the text gets a new meaning.

I would also like to emphasize at this point that I am not stating that the contemporary US foreign policy is relying exclusively on the theory of classical geopolitics. The architects of US foreign policy do not necessarily need to know any theories of international politics. But that does not mean that a scholar could not make an effort to make sense out of the practical geopolitics of the USA in the context of classical geopolitical doctrines. In other words, my contention is that it is possible to approach and analyse the US foreign policy and behaviour within the framework of classical geopolitics irrespective of whether such a framework is an intended or a non-intended base of the politics.

I do not intend to go further back in history and would like to restrict myself to a few observations on the US Asian policy during the Cold War period. As mentioned earlier, although classical geopolitics after the World War II was almost a banned theory, the US foreign and security policy in Asia did maintain a close connection to classical geopolitics under different theoretical umbrellas. The policy of containment[16] of the Soviet Union in Asia can be understood in the way that the USA tried to prevent the heartland power USSR from extending its influence into the rimland of Eurasia. We can find almost similar elements and reasoning at work even beyond the so-called domino theory.[17] According to that theory the USA had to prevent the Eurasian rimland states from falling into the hands of communist forces. Consequently, the USA was involved in several armed conflicts in Asia during the Cold War.

In the wake of the collapse of the Soviet empire, the situation changed quite dramatically in Asia. But the shadow of classical geopolitics remained. As pointed out earlier, during the Cold War, the USA was active in the rimland. After the Cold War, Russia, as the heir of the Soviet empire, lost control of the Eurasian heartland. New weak states were born in Central Asia, i.e. in the heartland of Eurasia. Suddenly there was some kind of a power vacuum in the heartland. At the same time, Central Asian oil became an important object in international politics and economy. Not only were Russia and the USA interested in where this oil would flaw, the rising Asian powers, China and India, also perceived a stake in the Central Asian oil resources.[18]

Accordingly, the Eurasian rimland once again became the focus of world politics. And this happened only because of the presence of the two new emerging global economic powers there. It was also due to the fact that Islamic fundamentalism, now seen as a new threat to international security, came from the rimland. Yet another threat rising from the rimland was the so-called rogue states. Both these threats were connected to the potential proliferation of weapons of mass destruction. Whereas Pakistan and India had become nuclear power states towards the end of the 1990s, North Korea, Iran and Iraq remained potential nuclear states. However, the most threatening scenario was (and still is) that weapons of mass destruction might fall into the hands of terrorist organizations. At the same time, we cannot forget that the world's major fossil fuel energy resources are still located in Asia, i.e. in the Middle East.

The US economy and the 'US way of life' are critically dependent on energy resources located outside the USA. In 1999, USA imported 60 per cent of consumed oil.[19] That means that the so-called 'vital' US security interests extend far beyond the borders of the country.[20] The US security requires global stability as a basis for a free world economy. In the post-Cold War era, Central Asia as well as large areas of the Eurasian rimland became 'uncontrolled' and were seen as zones of trouble and instability. It is in this context that we need to understand and analyse the US policy in Asia. This is also reflected in the US' official security and foreign policy documents. According to those documents from the Bush Jr. Presidency, the threat to US security comes from the uncontrolled, 'disconnected' areas ruled by tyrants.[21] And in various US strategic maps the trouble zone stretches in Asia from the Middle East via Central Asia to North Korea.[22] This is precisely the strategic space that has to be controlled, pacified and democratized.

In the geopolitical context outlined above, 9/11 was a gift for the USA provided by Muslim fundamentalists and Al Qaeda. This does not refer to any kind of a conspiracy. But it was an opportunity for the neoconservatives in the Bush administration to push their geopolitical vision and agenda further. The tragic event (and equally tragic events to follow) opened the window for US Asian strategy, which had already been drafted by the neocons but was difficult to put into practice without an excuse. The terrorist attack gave a chance for the USA to invade Afghanistan and deploy forces in Central Asia. Or in the classical geopolitical context, the USA got the opportunity to make a move into the heartland of Eurasia. An aggressive pursuit of geostrategy in Asia was considered as essential to seize and stabilize the most strategic Asian spaces according to perceived US interests.

The Iraq operation was the next in the ordering of Asia and accordingly, an imagined threat of weapons of mass destruction was used as an excuse. The next in this direction might be Iran. This has become more probable since the Israeli invasion of southern Lebanon in 2006. After this event Iran seems to have found it increasingly difficult to give up the option of acquiring its own nuclear capability. On the whole it is possible to say that the US war on terrorism is not by its essence a war on terrorism, but a grand strategy for controlling both the heartland and the rimland of Eurasia. The war on terrorism justified every now and then by the Bush administration on the grounds of ensuring security to US citizens, has enabled the hyperactive Superpower to establish its footprint in Eurasia; from the Middle East to Central Asia. And very few actors have actively opposed the US policy since most of the world, and in this case most of Asia, is a partner in one way or the other, in the war on terrorism.

Simultaneously, with the new aggressive policy in Asia the USA has changed its partnership or alliance geopolitics. Since Pokhran nuclear tests by India in 1998, especially in the wake of 9/11, India has become the main US partner in Asia. The role of Pakistan is on the decline. This shift has also influenced the Kashmir conflict. On the other hand, Pakistan and China have become closer to each other than they have been in the past. China appears to have understood that the USA needs India to balance China's increasing power in Asia and even at the global level China is seen to be the major challenger of the USA hegemony.[23] As a nuclear state, India can be a balancing factor in Asia. But for the USA it is still just a regional power. On the other hand, both China and India have their own geopolitical and geoeconomic interests in Asia and neither of them is willing to leave the future of Asia once again in the hands of a non-Asian hegemonic state, although USA will remain one of the major actors in Asia.

One interesting aspect in US Asian policy is that in the course of its war on terrorism it has constructed certain camps[24] or zones of exceptions.

This means that in Asia there are areas where law have been left to the discretion of outlawed actors. In dealing with such a category of territories and actors, the USA does not need to respect any laws or international norms. The enemy, once identified, is totally dehumanised, like the Jews were in the Nazi concentration camps. And Israel has taken the same liberty for itself under the banner of the 'war on global terrorism'.

The Problems for the USA

In the context of classical geopolitics, it is possible to come to the conclusion that the US policy of dominating the Eurasian space is integral to its project of controlling Asia and dictating the emerging international order. The same theoretical approach points to some serious threats to the position of the hegemonic power. Basically there are two obvious threat scenarios that the hegemonic power might face in the times ahead: first, the potential alliance or close cooperation of the rimland powers; or, second, an alliance or cooperation of the rimland and heartland powers.

From the standpoint of an extra territorial hegemonic power it is important to try and prevent any formation of the above-mentioned alliances.

The war on terrorism has given a chance for the USA to create different kinds of unholy alliances around itself. Several Eurasian states are facing the challenge of either an armed opposition for demanding autonomy vis-à-vis state power, or an assertion of minority rights or movement for 'self-determination' and independent 'nation'-state. All such armed opposition movements can be labelled as 'terrorist' organizations by the state concerned. Joining the international war on terrorism has further given the justification to some of the Asian states to crush opposition and not to negotiate with it. Russia has Chechens, India has Kashmir, China has Uigurs, Caucasus and Central Asian states as well as Philippines have their Muslim fundamentalists.

In a way, the war on terrorism could function as a means to further strengthen the US hegemonic bid on Eurasia. On the other hand, there are signs of the construction of balancing alliances in Asia. The Shanghai Cooperation Organization (SCO) is one of them. It has brought together Russia and China. On the one hand this organization is for fighting terrorism. But on the other hand, it is connected to the new Central Asian oil and water policy. On top of it all, it does bring together Russia as a strong regional heartland power and China as a new global power in the Eurasian rimland.

Although India has gained an observer status in the Shanghai Cooperation Organization (SCO) it has a different role in the US Asian strategy. In the so-called second or 'New Grand Game' in Asia the USA needs strong allies and India appears far more promising than any of the old US partners in Asia, like Saudi Arabia or Pakistan.[25] India might also see this as a new opportunity to strengthen its own position in world politics. The nature and scope of the emerging USA-India partnership could well be quite decisive in shaping the future Asian space.

In the context of US threat perceptions, increasing EU interests in Asia are of considerable importance to USA.[26] It is essential for the USA to know whether the EU acts in Asia as a partner or whether the EU has a geopolitical agenda of its own, aiming at increasing cooperation between the Eurasian rimland powers. In case the EU provides an alternative vision for Asia it is likely to be seen as a challenge to the US hegemony in Asia. However, until now it is possible to say that the EU has functioned more or less as a little brother in Asia. In Afghanistan the EU's NATO members are taking over the cleaning up operations after the USA has mainly done the dirty work. And there seem to be the same kind of development going on in Iraq. The USA has an interest to free its fighting forces and replace them with the NATO forces in Iraq.

The EU as an Alternative

The major problem in the EU's CFSP is that it has not explicitly stated whether it is in its interest to support the US global policy or to have its own; one that is distinct from the US policy. In this respect, one of the major objections is that the EU is divided between traditional and new Atlantic-oriented and more Eurocentric states. On the other hand, we have to understand that the construction of the EU's international identity and its CFSP are both closely interconnected and still in the process of making. But simultaneously this is what makes it possible to evaluate whether the EU can be an alternative to the USA in shaping the future Eurasia.

In the context of this essay we first of all have to appreciate that the EU is one of the major Eurasian rimland powers. And in the bipolar world it was a close ally of the USA although it had an interest to become a third force between the USA and the Soviet Union. But it was the end of the Cold War that made it possible for the EU to define and construct a place of its own in world politics. It is again a different thing whether the EU has been able to use this opportunity effectively. At least in the Middle East it has not been successful[27] and partly it has failed even in the context of violent conflicts in Europe.

In order to assess whether the EU could be an alternative to the USA in shaping the Asian future we have to find out as to what kind of an identity the EU is constructing for itself in Asia and whether it is supporting the alternative vision of making Eurasia a zone of peace instead of the aggressive US policy. However, this does not necessarily mean that the EU is simply challenging the USA as a hegemonic power in Eurasia. The conclusion very much depends on how the EU is both willing and able to deal with the Asian powers, i.e. as a master or as equal partner. Here we can refer to how the English school in international studies has defined alternative international systems:[28]

- The Hobbesian (the realist) system is a system of enemies that introduces various elements of anarchy into to entire international system. In the US perception and policy there are enemies to be disciplined and pacified in Asia. And in order to do so the USA needs allies in Asia.
- The Lockean (rationalist) system is a system of competitors. In case of the USA, China is currently seen as the only serious competitor and again in order to balance China, the USA needs strong regional allies in Asia; i.e. India and Japan.
- The Kantian (revolutionist) system is a system of friends who have a common interest to construct a stable international system for co-operation, in which actors can and do respect diversity.

In analysing the manner in which the EU's policy in Asia has been articulated so far, my interest is to find out whether there are elements, which could tell us about the construction of a system of friends in the Eurasian space. In principle the EU should be able to do it in case it understands fully its own potential as a factor for peace.[29] European integration and the enlargement process of the EU is basically understood as a peace project, aimed at constructing a European zone of peace. Or one could even say that the European integration has constructed already some kind of a democratic zone of peace.

The EEC was founded as a civilian power. And the EU still is, first and foremost, a civilian power,[30] which still has difficulties in using military power. And that is an area where it is still not a match to the USA. However the EU has successively used its economic and normative power. This has been possible in Europe because a number of states outside the integration community have expressed an interest in joining the EU and therefore have Europeanized voluntarily their internal socio-economic and political systems. And still there are states, which are hoping to become members of the EU and therefore willing to Europeanize their societies. This gives a chance for the EU to expand the European zone of peace. But the enlargement is also a problem for the EU. Enlargement increases the heterogeneity of the Community and thus makes it a weaker international actor. On the other hand, an alternative for indefinite enlargement is to organize its relations with Asian and African countries on the basis of common interests and cooperation without discrimination.

The EU in Asia

The main question here will be whether the EU is seriously providing elements for an alternative order in Asia than the USA offers at present, or does the EU aim at becoming a hegemonic power in Eurasia, with a dominant position in the international system? My arguments below are based on five different EU documents expressing the EU's interests in Asia:

- EU's Russian Strategy from 1999;[31]
- Europe and Asia: Strategic Framework for Enhanced Partnership document from 2001;[32]
- EU-China Policy Paper from 2003;[33]
- Partnership with South-East Asia Document, also from 2003 (COM2003: 399/4);[34] and
- EU-India Partnership Paper from 2004.[35]

These documents as such already tell two interesting things. First, they divide the Asian countries at least into two different categories: partners (India and ASEAN) and others (the rest). Second, if we read the documents in the context of classical geopolitics, it appears that the EU's interests are basically in the rimland, indicating an intention to form some kind of an alliance among the Eurasian rimland powers.

These documents also reveal that although the EU is not neglecting totally the Eurasian heartland, it does not have any great interest in the heartland. Alternatively, it is possible to say that in the Eurasian heartland, the EU does not have any active role in conflict transformation or peace building. It is absent from the trouble zone, in a sharp contrast to the presence of the USA, Russia and China. But it is also possible to speculate that the EU might have left the heartland for Russia. In case the EU and Russia can improve their relations and find common interests, the EU might let the heartland be controlled by Russia. So in a way Russia would function as a proxy for EU interests in Asia. This possibility can be supported by the fact that the the EU sees Russia as a regional power with an important role to play in Eastern Europe and in Asia. But the EU does not take it as a global power.

In its own global policy, the EU has given a place and a role to Russia. However, this does not mean that Russia is in agreement with the EU on it. First of all the EU has an interest to support the stabilization of Russia. That can be achieved by strengthening democracy and market economy in Russia. Secondly, the wider interest of the EU in respect to Russia is to construct a common European socio-economic space. From the EU's perspective this is a strategy to integrate Russia into Europe without giving it a membership in the EU. Russia is seen more as a partner than a future member of the EU. But it remains rather unclear as to how Russia is seen as a partner. The most likely aspect is that Russia would be one element in the multi-polar world. The other aspect could be the cooperation in the EU's Asian policy since in Eastern Europe the EU barely needs Russia as a partner. At least it is not easy to define a role for Russia in the pacification and democratization of Eastern Europe.

Whereas Russia is a regional power for the EU, both China and India are seriously taken as global powers. Their influence on world politics is seen as not only as regional but global. In this respect, they both are seen as EU's partners in the global policy. Together with the EU, China and India favour a multilateral international order. This could be understood as an attempt to construct an alliance between the major rimland powers. As indicated earlier, this is one of the possible threat scenarios for US hegemony in Eurasia. In the context of classical geopolitics it is possible to conclude that the EU tries to build in Asia its own identity as distinct from the USA interests. But it does not say anything on whether the EU has an interest to replace the USA as a hegemonic power in Eurasia or whether it really provides an alternative for equal partnership for the Asian powers.

Although China and India are both taken as global powers, the documents also emphasize differences between those two Asian powers. In the case of China the EU points out some serious problems. The EU emphasizes human rights and democracy problems in China. India on the contrary is seen more as an equal. India, which is no longer considered simply a developing society, is presented as an old civilization but a modern society. The EU even stresses similarities between the EU and India and underscores the point that both these societies have a lot to learn from each other. Based on EU documents it is possible to conclude that India is seen as the major Asian partner by the EU. Unfortunately the

EU might be already late since India now appears more interested in forging a durable partnership with the USA than with the EU.

The documents clearly outline why Asia is considered as important for the EU. China, India and also ASEAN, are all essential economic factors. The potential for economic growth in two primary forms: more than 60 per cent of the world labour force (people in the productive age) is in Asia and it is here that future markets and consumers in international economy are located. Asia is important also because fossil fuel energy resources are located there. Asia, and especially the rimland, are important also because of those factors which cause problems for the future international order.[36]

China and India together are already now major sources for CO_2 emission and therefore the main factors in causing global warming. They both are also fast growing economies with increasing energy needs. Therefore their CO_2 emission is likely to increase in the future. Another factor that is likely to cause instability in the international system is poverty. More than 60 per cent of the world's poorest people live in Asia[37] and most of them can be found in the rimland: China, India and ASEAN. The economic growth does not change the situation overnight and, on the other hand, the gap between the wealthy and the poor seems to be widening. Poverty as such is already a problem. But in a wider international scale we have to remember that poverty is a factor that fundamentalist movements can use to justify even terrorism. However, though there is a connection between terrorism and poverty, this does not mean that poverty is a cause for terrorism. This means that the fight against terrorism can never be won on the battlefield but is as much, if not even more, a struggle to eliminate extreme poverty.

The fight against poverty is exactly the area where the EU may be able to do more than the USA has been able to do until now. In this respect the announced goal of the EU in Asia is to promote sustainable ecological and social development. In a way it is possible to say that the EU has extended its European strategy into Asia by encouraging and supporting a peaceful transition of Asian societies. Further, it is expected that the adapted policy of the EU will increase stability and contribute to peace in Asia by civilian means, in sharp contrast to the USA which basically aims for the same goals, but by military means.

The EU as a Model—White Man's Burden?

The EU has interests in the Eurasian space similar to the USA. But as a civilian power without military means it does offer an alternative to the

USA in Asia. It acts according to its own principles and implicitly participates in the construction of a Eurasian zone of peace. At the same time the EU is clearly engaged in promoting its own values in those Asian states which the EU has somehow accepted as partners in international politics. In fact it often presents itself as a model for its Asian partners. It is a model not just in democracy and human rights issues but also in multiculturalism and in constructing unity in diversity; an old Indian geopolitical discourse. It also presents itself as a model for regional integration, both in South East Asia and in South Asia. In this respect it is not necessarily an alternative to the USA and a hegemonic order.

The hegemonic aspect in the EU's Asian policy cannot be totally neglected. It has already been indicated above that the further development of the EU or EU member states is strongly dependent on Asia. This is clear in case of resources, markets and even labour force. The latest evidence about this is that blue-collar work is moving to India. For instance the US and also European call centre services are moving to India. India's advantage in services is also related to its competence in the English language. In Indian education, and especially in higher education, the language of communication is English. Somehow it has become possible to say that Asia can survive without Europe or even the USA but the EU cannot survive without Asia.

In a way it seems possible to argue that without a well defined and formulated Asian policy, one that is distinct from the US Asian policy, the EU does not have any chance of becoming a meaningful actor in global politics. And even further, it cannot be a meaningful partner for China or India without a coherent CFSP. As one united international actor, instead of several different national sovereign member states, the EU can develop a meaningful role for itself in Asia or in Eurasia. It is worth mentioning in the passing that the EU would further expand into Asia provided Turkey becomes a member of the Community.[38] Turkey on its side has a strong interest in Central Asia.

Already it is possible to conclude that the EU has an interest in Asia. It is also increasing its Asian connection. But its direct interests seem to be first of all in the rimland. This reminds us about the past history of colonialism. The European powers have never been able to penetrate into Asia directly, but rather via the rimland. On the other hand, history does not need to be repeated since the EU is still a civilian power. Therefore it can offer a partnership rather than try to pursue the project of mastering the future Asian space. However this can change in case the EU decides to establish itself also as a military power.

Therefore it is understandable that the Asian powers do not necessarily take the EU as an alternative to the USA and they might have a strong interest in shaping Asia according to their own interests without any outside partnership.

And So What?

It seems rather obvious that the EU offers itself as a partner for Asian powers. However, there is no strong evidence as yet of a collective political will on the part of the EU to construct a Eurasian zone of peace. There are no real reasons either to suggest confidently that in the Eurasian space there would be a transition from the state-centric policy to a people-centric policy. In this respect there are no reasons to talk about peoples' solidarity. In case there is some solidarity in Eurasia it is solidarity of some states to some other state, or solidarity within various religious entities.

Further it is difficult, if not impossible, to find any imagination of Eurasia in the EU documents. For the EU there is still a well-defined entity called Europe, beyond which lies Asia. Asia continues to be perceived as something different and alien to the EU. Therefore it is pertinent to ask as to in whose interest it would be to start to imagine a Euro-Asian space instead of Europe and Asia as two distinct continents. In imagining a Eurasian space there would be less 'Other' within the space. The most influential 'Other' would be the USA and that certainly is not in the US' interest. On the other hand the self-evident 'Other' in Asia for the USA is the various fundamentalist Muslim organizations and especially organizations labelled as terrorists.

On the basis of the above analysis it is also difficult to say whether the partnership policy that the EU offers to Asian powers would generate more cooperation than conflicts. The answer depends very much about whose Eurasia we are talking about. Or in whose interests the Eurasian space will be constructed. It is certain that the EU has a strong interest in Asia. Even peace and stability within the EU depends to a large extent on how the Asian space will be constructed. But the interest of the EU does not necessarily coincide with the interests of emerging Asian powers and it is not possible to ignore any more the interests and priorities of those powers. Therefore an interesting question is whether it shall be possible to carry out whosoever politics in Eurasia, i.e. the politics that could satisfy anybody's interests and nobody will be excluded.

In its own integration process the EU has adopted the Indian principle of 'unity in diversity'. Can the EU apply this principle in its Asian politics? The documents used in this analysis tell more about how the EU promotes its own values in Asia and less about meeting the diversity on an equal basis. The historically imagined gap between the materialist West and the spiritual East is still there and it seems difficult to overcome it, although it gets new forms more connected to historical situation. In this respect the EU is not necessarily capable of becoming an alternative to the USA.

Finally it is useful to ask whether the EU or USA have anything to offer to Asia. Asian people and powers have their own interests in shaping the Asian space. One possible scenario is that China and India become rivals in constructing the future Asian space without the EU or USA. As far as Pan-Asianism is concerned, it does not appear to be having a bright future. At least the historical experiments do not offer any great promises. But on the other hand, in case the EU and the USA join their forces in advancing and defending their vested interests in Asia, the Asian powers could find enough reasons to unite, in defence of their own interests in Asia. This kind of a scenario reminds us about the threat perceptions that arose in the beginning of the twentieth century, which, in turn, led to a discussion about the yellow threat to the white race.[39] And this kind of a scenario brings us back to the problem of the clash of civilizations.

Notes

1. See, for instance, Hazel Smith, *European Union Foreign Policy. What it is and what it does* (London: Pluto Press, 2002), 137.
2. Flora Kurikkala, *Representation of the Changing Self: An EU Performance in the Middle East* (Tampere: Tampere University Press, 2003), 72-90.
3. In these respect the US leadership divided Europe into two: the old Europe which opposed US policy on Iraq and the new Europe which supported the USA.
4. Smith, *European Union Foreign Policy*, 183-264; Charlotte Breterton and John Vogler, *The European Union as a Global Actor* (London & New York: Routledge, 1999), 109-68.
5. This is important in the sense that many scholars predict that changes in Asian geopolitics will generate tensions and even conflicts in the continent. One aspect in this is the ongoing US war on terrorism in Asia. In this respect see for instance Brahma Chellaney, *Asian Juggernaut. The Rise of China, India and Japan* (New Delhi: Harper Collins, 2006).
6. Andre Gunder Frank, *ReOrient: Global Economy in the Asian Age* (New Delhi: Vistar Publications, 1998).
7. Halford J. Mackinder, "The Round World and the Winning of the Peace," *Foreign Affairs* 21, no. 4; N.J. Spykman, *The Geography of Peace* (New York: Harcourt Brace and Company, 1944).

8. Marshall G.S. Hodgson, *Rethinking World History. Essays on Europe, Islam and World History* (Cambridge: Cambridge University Press, 1993); see also John M. Hobson, "The Paradox of Cosmopolitan-Eurocentrism in the Rise of the West: The Dialectical-Dialogues of Civilizations,"and Pekka Korhonen, "On the Metageography of Euro-Asia" in this volume.
9. Alstair Bonnet, *The Idea of the West. Culture, Politics and History* (Houndmills: Palgrave, 2004).
10. See for instance Gearoid Ò Tuathail and S. Dalby (eds), *Rethinking Geopolitics* (London: Routledge, 1998).
11. For instance Zbigniew Brzezinski, *The Grand Chessboard. American Primacy and its Geostrategic Imperatives* (New York: Basic Books, 1997).
12. For instance Challaney, *Asian Juggernaut*.
13. See Sanjay Chaturvedi, "Geopolitics of Domination and Clash of Imaginations in Central Eurasia: Continuity and Change," and Anita Sengupta, "Geostrategic Perspectives on Eurasia: Towards Multilateralism in Central Asia" in this volume.
14. See *Bulletin of the European Communities*, no 11 (November 1970).
15. See *Bulletin of the European Communities*, no 12 (December 1973).
16. For instance Karen Mingst, *Essentials of International Relations* (New York: W.W. Norton & Company, 1999), 50-51.
17. Mingst, *Essentials of International Relations*.
18. For instance Challaney, *Asian Juggernaut*, 89.
19. Emmanuel Todd, *Imperiumin jälkeen* (Helsinki: Rasalas kustannus, 2003), 165.
20. This is a problem I have discussed already in my study on imperialism. See Jyrki Käkönen, *Natural Resources and Conflicts in the Changing International System. Three Studies on Imperialism* (Aldershot: Avebury, 1988).
21. The solution to the problem is to support democratization and integration of 'outsiders' into the international community. See *The National Security Strategy of the United States of America* (March 2006).
22. Thomas P.M. Barnett, *The Pentagon's Map: War and Peace in the Twenty-first Century* (New York: G.P. Putnam's Sons, 2004).
23. Laurent Cohen-Tanugi, *The Shape of the World to Come. Charting the Geopolitics of a New Century* (New York: Cambridge University Press, 2008), 6, 12-13.
24. See the meaning of the camps in Giorgio Agamben, *Homo Sacer. Sovereign Power and Bare Life* (Stanford CA: Stanford University Press, 1998), 166-80.
25. See the *The National Security Strategy of the United States of America* (White House: Washington, March 2006), 39.
26. Currently EU has partnership agreements with all Asian countries bilaterally or regionally. See for instance http://ec.europa.eu/external_relations/sp

27. Kurikkala, *Representation of the Changing Self.*
28. Martin Wight, *International Theory. The Three Traditions*, Gabriele Wight and Brian Porter (ed.) (Leicester: Leicester University Press, 1991).
29. See for instance Arie M. Kacowicz, "Explaining Zones of Peace: Democracies as Satisfied Powers?" *Journal of Peace Research* 32, no. 3 (1995): 270.
30. Katja Keisala, *The European Union as an International Actor: Strengths of the European Civilian Power* (Tampere: Tampere University Press, 2004); R. Whitman, *From Civilian Power to Superpower? The International Identity of the European Union* (London: MacMillan, 1998).
31. *Common Strategy of the European Union of 4 June 1999 on Russia* (1999/414/CFSP).
32. *Communication from the Commission. Europe and Asia: Strategic Framework for Enhanced Partnership.* COM (2001) 469 final.
33. *Communication from the Commission. A Maturing Partnership: Shared Interests and Challenges in EU-China Relations.* COM (2003) 533.
34. *Communication from the Commission. A New Partnership with South East Asia.* COM (2003) 399/4.
35. *Communication from the Commission. An EU-India Strategic Partnership.* COM (2004) 430.
36. Challaney, *Asian Juggernaut*, 54-87.
37. *Communication from the Commission. Europe and Asia, 6.* COM (2001) 469 final.
38. See Ayla Göl, "Turkey's Search for Identity: A Eurasian and Islamic Country " in this volume.
39. See for instance Oswald Spengler, *Ratkaisun vuosia* (Helsinki: Otava, 1934), 203-26.

10

Conceiving the Project of Eurasia through EU-India Cooperation

Rajen Harshe

Diverse and wide ranging networks of ties, with the help of rapidly changing technologies, have been constantly reducing distances between states, societies and continents, under globalization. Such shrinking of spaces, in their turn, has unleashed the processes of establishing viable linkages through trade, commerce, information as well as political, diplomatic, strategic and military networks between different parts of the world. Indeed, the regional organizations, at one level, epitomize the essence of globalization on the regional scale. Several such organizations in the continents of Europe and Asia are currently engaged in negotiating with the challenges of globalization by building viable projects of regional cooperation. This has also opened up new possibilities of cooperation between regional organizations, on the one hand and between regional organizations and geographically and economically large-sized states like India and China, on the other. Also, the forthcoming decades are likely to witness growing and complex interdependence between the regional organizations and the states of Europe and Asia. Evidently, any conception of 'Eurasia' can hardly be indifferent to the possible ties between the European Union (EU) and India for, the EU has already absorbed as many as 25 member states and is expanding eastwards, while India is a major rising power in Asia, in general, and the dominant power in the South Asian region, in particular. This article begins by making a few preliminary observations on the nature of the EU and India by underscoring the apparent similarities and fundamental differences between them and then proceeds to locate India in Asia. Subsequently, it reflects on the possible trajectories of EU-India ties in significant areas such as development cooperation and security.

Apparent Similarities between the EU and India

More often, the entire experiment of European regional cooperation/integration, with most of its diversities and bewildering complexities, is held in some measure of awe in contemporary international relations. The experiment of regional economic integration in Europe began with the Rome Treaty which established the European Economic Community (EEC) in 1957. The EEC, initially, had six member-states but as regional cooperation/integration grew, gradually, the project of the EU that grew out of the EEC and has achieved remarkable success in promoting regional cooperation, over the past few decades, by grouping together as many as twenty five states. Indeed, the processes of widening and deepening regional integration have been simultaneously on the move. Hence the achievements of the EU in 'region building' by no means could ever be underestimated. By integrating a populace of almost 460 million people into a single market and developing a consciousness that is regional, the EU has left an indelible impression in contemporary world politics. It has also stimulated new ways of imagining the geographies of Europe.[1] The erstwhile ideological divisions which separated the western and eastern parts of Europe no longer hinder the drive towards integration in Europe. What is more, the association of Asia-Pacific, African and Caribbean countries with EU markets has allowed the EU to emerge as one of the major centres of world capitalism. Such association not merely rationalizes and promotes the international division of labour but also provides an avenue to diverse sets of countries—in terms of development—to be a part of the multilateral trading system.

Arguably, India is just a sovereign state and not an international organization of the EU's magnitude and strength. However, like the EU, India has demonstrated its capability to celebrate changing forms of diversities. It could as well be asserted that the socially plural society of India, with its sub-continental dimensions, houses a wide range of spiritual, religious, linguistic, regional as also class and caste-related diversities among its more than one billion inhabitants. Although independent India began on the note of a partition of the subcontinent, the area it commanded and the diversities and social complexities it absorbed have always been mind boggling for outsiders. Moreover, roughly the 250 million people who constitute the middle classes in India form a vibrant international market. With the initiation of economic reforms after 1991, the three engines of growth in India such as industry, manufacturing and services, have simultaneously registered high rates of growth. Perhaps, unlike in all other emerging markets, the unique characteristic of development in India has been the sustained growth of the service sector that has even bypassed the industrial phase. Consequently, India has already started developing as a global hub for outsourcing for many manufacturing companies.

Even if the mounting of the currency, such as the Euro in Europe, on a vast territorial space was a much celebrated affair, India always has had her currency, the Rupee, circulated and used across its vast territory which is comparable to the Euro zone. Indeed, India has been an old civilization and a multinational state. Due to its multinational character the talk of national integration through democratic social and political transformation has inevitably gained currency for the survival of India in its present form. Practically all social groups perceive a thread of unity weaving the diversity of India into a unique and perhaps indivisible pattern. However, under globalization uneven development between relatively developed geographical regions of the south and west, on the one hand, and the regions belonging to the northern belt, on the other, have accentuated inequalities between regions, sub-regions and hence citizens in India. Likewise, apparently even the EU region has a wide range of economic and social disparities among its various nations/regions from the west, central, eastern and south-eastern parts. Hence even purely at the level of integration the EU as a regional organization, and India as a multinational state, have a lot to gain from reciprocal interactions. Such interactions at multiple levels can firm up Indo-EU ties and the eventual project of Eurasia.

A Glance at Fundamental Differences

At the same time, it would be imprudent to carry any comparison between the EU and India too far since there are fundamental differences that clearly separate the two entities. First, the former constitutes an organization of sovereign member states that are involved in promoting the economic and political integration of Europe by bringing together democratic regimes that are committed to protect human rights. The latter is only a sovereign, independent and democratic state that has absorbed the diverse nuances of any plural society. Second, post-colonial India is a single entity with a common foreign and defence policy. In contrast, the EU, along with sovereign member states, has been involved in carving out a common security and defence policy for the EU, as a whole.

Finally, the entry of the Eastern European states into the EU has further added to the complexities in the functioning of the EU, involving the nature of development alternatives. For instance, the western part of Europe has been steeped in a developed capitalist system whereas the eastern economies are gradually replacing their erstwhile centrally planned economies through initiating measures to build a capitalist mode of development. Due to the relatively poor performance of the centrally planned economies of Eastern Europe the levels of economic and social development in the eastern and western parts of Europe show variations. It will also require longer term gestation period for the East European states and societies to internalize and implement forms of capitalism that suit their respective social conditions.

Besides, the non-territorial and transnational forces unleashed by globalization related to finance, technology, trade, information, knowledge and crime syndicates as well as terrorism have clearly made their presence all too obvious in the western parts of Europe. In Western Europe the youth is more aware of and devoted to EU as an entity. In contrast, the states in East Europe, especially after the fall of the former Soviet Union and Yugoslavia, during the nineties, are witnessing a resurgence of the forces of nationalism and ethnicity. The EU reflects the tensions associated with the processes of restructuring as well as reconstructing capitalism as a developmental alternative, where notions of development, planning and the status of the nation state, are getting constantly redefined. Nevertheless, the experiment of the EU has been inspiring several regional organizations in contemporary world politics and economy, helping to usher in an era of viable regional organizations to negotiate with globalization, more effectively. Having spelt out the areas of similarities and differences, between the EU and India, let me proceed to locate India in the context of Asia.

Locating India in Asia

In view of the relatively successful experiment of region building by the EU, several other parts of the world are busy in promoting regionalism as a strategy to negotiate effectively, with the phase of globalization. In the globalizing world, India is also facing the challenge of promoting region building through regional cooperation. It has been at the apex of regional organizations like the South Asian Association of Regional Cooperation (SAARC). South Asia primarily has been an Indo-centric region. Owing to its land mass, industrial and military development, trained manpower and social and cultural linkages with the neighbouring

South Asian states no project of regional cooperation in South Asia could easily be conceived without the active participation of the overwhelmingly powerful state, such as India. However, building projects of regional cooperation is feasible when the states in any region enjoy peaceful ties. Actually, the experiment of region building in Europe could take off because France and Germany resolved their traditional animosities and laid the foundation of the regional integration movement in Europe. Both these powers aimed at combating US dominance and fear of the likely Soviet expansion towards the West.

Unlike the Franco-German rapprochement since the mid-fifties, there is no semblance of harmony in relations between India and Pakistan, that happen to be the major powers of South Asia ever since these two states were born in 1947. In fact, India and Pakistan continue to be antithetical expressions of each other. So far, they have fought three major wars and two mini wars. Both these countries have produced their own nuclear arsenal and transformed South Asia into a theatre of conflict. The perpetual hostility between the two countries, especially over the intractable question of the status of Kashmir, has been foiling any constructive bid to bring about regional cooperation in South Asia on a sound footing. What is more, China's support to Pakistan in building its nuclear weapons programme, the Sino-Pakistan trade and China's occupation of some area of Kashmir with the help of Pakistan, has further compounded the prospects of regional cooperation in South Asia. The shadow of Sino-Indian rivalry and Sino-Pakistan friendship will have their impact in shaping the project of regional cooperation in the South Asian region. In spite of their rivalry, Sino-Indian trade has also been on the rise and China has emerged as one of the major trading partners of India during the past few years. To put it simply, irrespective of unresolved political differences, the phase of globalization can stimulate new configurations of trading partners in Asia and other parts of the world. India's efforts to build linkages with regional organizations such as the Association of South East Asian Nations (ASEAN), Bay of Bengal Initiative for Multi-Sectoral Technical and Economic Cooperation (BIMSTEC), African Union (AU) and South American Regional Trade Agreement, namely, MERCOSUR, are cases in point. Especially, while enhancing the prospects of cooperation in Eurasia, India's role in promoting new configurations of trading partnerships is going to be crucial, in the years ahead, due to its geographical location.

Geographically, India is connected to the central, west as well as south-eastern parts of Asia. That is why, whatever happens in Asia, affects

India and whatever happens in India, affects Asia. Actually, the two Asian giant powers, namely India and China, thanks to their geopolitical location, are well linked with all other major parts of Asia. Although Nehru used to describe India as a hub of Asia, perhaps geographical location and the land expanse, coupled with its growing economic prowess, make contemporary China a hub of Asia. Even India's stature as a major power, in the context of globalization, will also be determined by its multiple range collaborative ties with China, in the decades ahead. Besides, India has been virtually surrounded by states with predominant Muslim populations, on three sides. The Muslims also constitute the most dominant religious minority group in India. Obviously, while relating its foreign policy to different parts of Asia, India's policy makers have had to be sensitive to the sensibilities of its Muslim population in India.

Furthermore, as Pannikar had once remarked, India actually is a castle surrounded by the seas and capped by the Himalayas. Its peninsular position compels India to be a maritime power as well as a continental power. Especially, in the context of globalization, India has to promote its sea-borne trade to ensure its economic growth. During the past decade India's economy has grown consistently at the annual average rate of almost six percent and the growth is likely to be accelerated in the years ahead. While managing its economy efficiently, India will have to face the constant challenge of meeting its energy requirements. Evidently, India will have to link itself to the energy heartlands of West Asia, such as Iraq, Iran, and Saudi Arabia, as also countries in Central Asia that possess substantial deposits of natural gas. Like India, the European countries are also trying to link their economies with the energy heartlands of Asia.

One of the important similarities between most of the EU countries and India has been the fact that both these regions are dependent on the supply of oil from West Asian countries. Especially after the first oil shock of 1973, and the consequent formation of the Organization of Petroleum Exporting Countries (OPEC) the economies of India as well as most of the EU countries have been hostage to a steady and uninterrupted supply of oil from West Asia. Obviously, coming together to resolve rising energy demands through evolving mechanisms of cooperation would spring up as a major challenge to Indo-EU ties. The EU countries and even India do have the technological resources to exploit natural resources like oil. Of course, unlike India, the US and the European oil companies are much better entrenched in the energy heartlands. However, serving energy requirements can bind the regions of Eurasia. The politics related to the sharing and exploiting of oil and natural gas has and is going to involve all the major oil companies and states in the days ahead. Moreover, owing to its rapid economic growth, India's energy demands are going to rise sharply. This will pose challenges for the state in India as well as the Oil and Natural Gas Corporation (ONGC) of India in working out policies to ensure India's energy security. Such a policy would reflect interdependence between India, on the one hand, and some of the major oil companies, states of the EU and West Asia, on the other. They would require deft handling because in spite of efforts to build a pipeline between Iran and India, via Pakistan, the project still has not taken off. In addition to oil and gas the EU-India cooperation in the realm of energy is also likely to be promoted in other forms of power generation, such as coal, hydro, solar and nuclear power generation.

Paradoxically, the countries from the energy heartland today and its immediate neighbours, like Afghanistan and Pakistan, have been plagued by the proliferation of different terrorist outfits that have been using Islam as a political weapon to promote their demands. Indeed, the multinational terrorist organization, such as the Al Qaeda, led by Osama Bin Laden, has brought enormous insecurity on the planet. Besides, there are several other kinds of terrorist outfits that are impeding development processes and cooperation across Eurasia. Under these circumstances, the project of Eurasia as well as the likely trajectories of EU-India ties will be constrained to address issues related to development cooperation as well as security, simultaneously.

The EU-India Development Cooperation

The EU-India strategic partnership has been growing over the years. The EU's combined gross domestic product is 10 trillion Euros accounting for the world's fourth highest gross national product. Since the EU has been competing with the US, ties with Asia as a whole, is likely to be significant for the EU, in the days ahead. The Asian region produces 23 per cent of the global GDP and its GDP is rising every year. In fact, the EU has been extending its trade and investment ties with countries such as China, Japan and India. In the process, the EU has emerged as India's most significant trading partner. EU imports from India came to 18.9 bn Euros in 2005, covering mainly textiles and clothing and agricultural products, as well as chemicals. In fact the textile exports from India to the EU after the removal of textile quotas have grown to 5.2 bn Euros in 2005, as compared to 4.4 bn Euros in 2004, while the EU exports to India in 2005 amounted to 21.1 bn Euros, comprising machinery, chemical products, gems and jewellery. Since 2001, bilateral trade between the two has grown by 11 per cent on an average.[2] The trade of services between the two has also grown substantially. There is also reciprocity of flows of foreign direct investments (FDI) between the EU and India. The EU was the main destination of companies from India which invested one out of four dollars in the EU. Some of the prominent Indian companies such as Infosys, Tata Consultancy Services, HCL Technologies, Wipro and Birla Soft as well as a range of firms, including Thermax, Tata Telly, Compact Disk India Ltd., Mastek and Bank of India who by now have presence in the EU. The EU invested 1.1 bn Euros in India in 2004, which was 1.4 per cent of total EU outflows.[3] Obviously, the widening membership of the EU also has been among the major causes for the growth of such trade. However, India is still not among its very significant trading partners for the EU. The EU imports only 1.6 per cent of the total goods and 0.8 per cent of its services from India.[4]

Furthermore, there are burgeoning prospects of development cooperation between India and the EU in several other fields. India has already given its commitment to participate in EU's multibillion dollar Galileo-Satellite project. The project will come on line in 2008, as an alternative to the US Global Positioning System. China has put up about 230 million Euros to join it and India is likely to give 300 million Euros. Besides, India has an ever growing Information Communication Technology (ICT) sector since the 1990s. Its outsourcing capacity has already attracted countries like the US. The losses of jobs due to outsourcing have placed the economies of the advanced countries in some measure of discomfort. Likewise the budding, skilled as well as semi-skilled personnel from the ICT sector of India, can construe the EU as a potential source and destination for the job market. Moreover, the aging and even declining rate of the working population in European countries can also provide employment avenues for Indians in the EU countries. For, within the next decade the percentage of population of the youth in India, compared to EU countries, is likely to increase dramatically. India would get the advantage of capitalizing on this demographic dividend. EU-India development cooperation could be promoted even further through investments in infrastructure. India's policy to develop all-round infrastructures of roads, rail links, ports, airports and power sector facilities, provide potential avenues to firm up Indo-EU economic and technological ties.

Besides, key international agencies, like the World Trade Organization (WTO) have already become a medium to ameliorate trade cooperation between the EU and India, where problems related to goods, general agreement in trade, in services, agriculture, and textiles, new trade-related areas, in intellectual property rights and trade-related investment measures, are being thrashed out. The policy of offering substantial subsidies to farmers in the EU and other developed countries, at the moment, has prompted India and several other developing countries to fight within forums like the WTO for farmers of developing countries who are unable to compete in the world market. Moreover, any form of trade liberalization involves lowering and eventually abolition of trade barriers. However, such long-term ends could be served better if India is able to activate South Asian cooperation. In a word, the prospects of EU-India cooperation would appear brighter only if India is able to contribute to region building in South Asia.

In spite of the emergence of the SAARC since the eighties, regional cooperation in South Asia has moved ahead at a very slow pace. The trade between SAARC countries is still insignificant because their economies are competitive and not complementary. The major trading partners of these countries are the EU, the countries from the Asia-Pacific and the US. The twelfth summit of SAARC held at Islamabad has worked out a longer-term project of establishing a South Asian Free Trade Area (SAFTA) in 2004.[5] Considering the asymmetrical power relations between India and fellow SAARC countries, India will be constrained to take a lead in forging trade and development-related ties. In this context, the Gujral doctrine that rested on promoting non-reciprocity of relations between India and relatively less developed and weaker states, like Bangladesh, Nepal, Sri Lanka and Bhutan, has acquired added significance. India already has been stimulating trade with its weaker partners in South Asia by lowering tariff barriers for their goods and exercising positive discrimination in economic ties to integrate regional trade. Similarly, the sharing of Ganga waters through a 30 year agreement between India and Bangladesh in 1996, or the prospects of the Mahakali Treaty to share river waters with Nepal are enhancing South Asian cooperation in the domain of agriculture. South Asian cooperation could also forge closer ties with constant development of the transport infrastructure. The bus services between India and Pakistan have already heralded this process. Peaceful ties within the region would eventually promote development cooperation in crucial sectors, such as energy. For instance, the hydro power in Nepal and natural gas resources of Bangladesh have yet to be fully exploited in the pursuit of the development of the region. Besides, transport, agriculture, ICT, rural development, health care services, have also sprung up as potential areas of cooperation.

In spite of some efforts to promote regional cooperation in South Asia the range as well as the depth of such cooperation still leaves much to be desired. In order to promote better economic cooperation it is essential to harmonize macro-economic policies, integrate labour markets along with commodity and capital markets and achieve social integration. In the long run, if the project of SAFTA takes off under SAARC a possibility of exploring EU-SAARC cooperation could also be set on the rails. It still appears like a distant dream. For, in contrast to the EU experience of building a movement for regional cooperation, the region of South Asia is still bogged down with the security-related problems.

Security Related Problems and Perceptions

Security-related problems in South Asia, in general, and India, in particular, have had twofold dimensions. First, all these countries after attaining sovereign statehood are struggling to achieve national integration. Deprived regions or communities in all these countries still have a sense of discomfort along the existing borders of these countries. Like several other regions of the developing world, the borders of the states and nations do not correspond with each other in South Asia as well. Even developed capitalist countries like the UK, Canada and Spain, have had to face secessionist movements while negotiating with this problem. Such secessionist groups for the sake of either autonomy or even independence have been striving to carve out spaces for themselves in different parts of the world. In the context of South Asia, the break up of Pakistan and the consequent emergence of Bangladesh in 1971, was an extreme example in the latter category. Second, India has also witnessed the advent of secessionist movements with varying degrees of intensity and power. The secessionist movement launched by the Sikh extremists in the '80s have subsided over the years. However, movements in the states of Kashmir, Assam and the northeast have inevitably unsettled the security environment in India since the past two decades. Such movements have also facilitated the intervention of external powers, such as China, Myanmar, Pakistan, Bangladesh and Bhutan, in India's internal affairs. To keep the country together the legislative bodies and coercive apparatus of the state in India have had to use harsher measures, including Prevention of Terrorism Act (POTA) in areas prone to insurgency or terrorist activities.

In view of the role of the state in India, however, human rights organizations as well as different states in the EU have been unsparing in condemning human rights violation in India in areas such as Kashmir, and even Manipur. Plausibly, the EU countries need to understand the state–society ties in socially pluralistic societies like India, more imaginatively. The EU insistence on protecting human rights in the context of the democratic framework is quite legitimate. However, to establish such a framework requires a longer time span, where democratic institutions get built and prove sustainable, in the long run. Till such institutions are in place the ties between the state and civil society are in a state of flux. Under these circumstances, there is scope for violence. To establish its primacy over society state agencies can utilize repressive measures and commit excesses. At the same time, innocent citizens also can die, owing to terrorist violence. They, at times, do not find concrete support from human rights organizations of various hues. Ironically, human rights organizations are capable of defending the rights of individuals allegedly involved in terrorist activities. Thus, the concerns of the EU countries about human security and human rights need to be sensitively placed in the context of complex ties between the state and civil society in developing countries like India. The fact that among the Third World countries India still functions as a vibrant parliamentary democracy can seldom be underestimated while forging EU-India ties.

In fact, there is a growing menace to human security from several kinds of inter-linked terrorist outfits owing to the swift and sophisticated methods through which terrorist organizations operate. Consequently, neither the phenomenon of terrorism nor the notions of security could be perceived through narrow prisms of state security. It is evident that terrorist outfits such as Al Qaeda are operating very much within the context of globalization and to contain such organizations inter-state and inter-societal cooperation has become absolutely essential. What is more, apparently all the states today are supporting nuclear non proliferation or the use of nuclear energy for peaceful purposes. However, scientists in states like Pakistan have been accused of transferring nuclear technology to other states through clandestine operations. If the terrorist outfits get a hold over nuclear technologies the world would become even more insecure.

However, the EU countries' encounter with terrorism has become frequent only after 9/11. Countries such as Spain and Britain have already experienced terrorist violence overtly. In contrast, the spectre of terrorism has been haunting India since the eighties. Unlike the EU countries, the entire South Asian region has already become a theatre of conflict. Practically all the countries that surround India have problems with the former due to lack of a mutually acceptable international border, sharing of resources, including river waters and the flow of migrants, terrorists and refugees, across the borders. Particularly, the intractable dispute between India and Pakistan over the status of Kashmir has put Indo-Pakistan ties in a perennial mode of conflict. Pakistan has built a vast terrorist infrastructure and promoted terrorist outfits to liberate Kashmir from India's clutches. In its turn, India is attempting to suppress all forms of terror inside Kashmir to preserve its territorial integrity, sovereignty and secular nationhood. After the two countries joined the nuclear club, the danger of nuclear war in the subcontinent cannot be ruled out, entirely. The Inter Services Intelligence (ISI) of Pakistan is operating actively in countries like Nepal and even in the north-eastern states to hinder the functioning of democracy in India. Furthermore, Nepal has its own brand of terrorists who define themselves as Maoists. They also are linked up with diverse Maoist outfits in the states of Bihar and Andhra Pradesh in India. Similarly, India has had to encounter the terrorist outfit of Liberation Tigers of Tamil Elan (LTTE) over the past two decades. The LTTE group wants to secede from Sri Lanka and due to atrocities committed on the Tamilians in Sri Lanka India continues to face the problem of refugees that are flowing out of Sri Lanka into the state of Tamil Nadu in India. In substance, if the activities of terrorist outfits are mapped out within South Asia, it could be safely asserted that the burgeoning of such outfits due to intractable intra-and inter-state conflicts is halting the process of regional cooperation and development.

In view of the capabilities of terrorist organizations to operate on a global scale, fighting terror in all its forms can form one of the major objectives of EU-India ties ahead. So far, both the parties have shown an intent of cooperation and launched ritual condemnations of terrorist outfits and their activities. The EU-India joint declarations on terrorism of 2001 and 2004 respectively, are cases in point. Both the parties have similar views on the nexus between terrorism and organized crime, including narco-trafficking, money laundering, nuclear proliferation and weapons of mass destruction. The EU also has expressed support to India's draft, under consideration at the United Nations, on Comprehensive Convention on International Terrorism. It has also legally banned terrorist organizations such as the LTTE of Sri Lanka. Actually, seeking a legal solution to the political problem created by the Tamil ethno-nationalist movement may not help in resolving protracted insurgency in Sri Lanka.[6] India had tried to resolve the same problem by deploying the Indian Peace Keeping Force during 1987-90. However, the military solution to political problems also did not yield positive results. To contain terrorism, apart from legal or military means, more persuasive, long-term and humane methods are equally necessary. Perhaps people to people contacts through groups that promote peace activism can unleash spaces for carrying out peaceful negotiations between the contending parties. Nevertheless, the EU countries can gain from India's long experience in handling terrorist outfits. The India-EU Joint Working Group on Anti Terrorism eventually has to operate within the Joint Working Group on Security Cooperation.

Conclusion

The possible project of Eurasia can be translated into a reality on the ground as major powers and forces in Eurasia establish viable linkages among each other in multiple areas, under globalization. Obviously, EU-India ties in multiple areas of development cooperation would bind vast territorial spaces, their respective immediate neighbouring regions, as well as intermediary regions, into cooperative ventures. It also needs to be underlined that the projects of inter-state development cooperation are operating within the dialectics of globalization. Under the circumstances, such cooperative ventures could progress well only with the formation of multilateral counter-terrorist coalitions.

Notes

1. Ray Hudson and M. Williams, *Divided Europe Society and Territory* (London: Sage, 1999).
2. European Commission External Trade-Press Information Service, 13 October 2006. http://ec.europa.eu/trade/
3. European Commission.
4. European Commission.
5. See A.R. Kemal, "Regional Cooperation in South Asia," SAFMA Regional Conference, Dhaka, 20-21 August 2004. www.southasiamedia.net/conference/Regional_Cooperation/safta.
6. B. Raman, "Implications of EU Ban on LTTE," *International Terrorism Monitor*, Paper 63, 28 May. www.saag.org/papers19/paper1817.

Conclusion

Sanjay Chaturvedi and *Jyrki Kakonen*

Is Asia truly rising? If so, then some might wonder whether Europe is in fact ready for 'Rising Asia', and all that this rise might entail, in its bewildering variety. Howsoever difficult it might be to provide answers to these questions as of now, there remains little doubt that the centre of gravity of global geopolitics has shifted from Europe to Asia in recent years.[1] The key contributing factors include the rise of China and India (these two Asian giants being appropriately labeled as 'Planetary Powers' by the World Resources Institute, Washington D.C., due to the likely impact of what they choose to do, or otherwise, with regard to resource use and ecological conservation, at a planetary scale), gradual assertion by Japan of its military profile, and a significant shift in the US global force posture in favour of Asia-Pacific. Whether Asia will witness rising tensions and conflicts in the coming years with various powers jockeying for influence (both on land and at sea), or whether the forces of economic globalization and multilateralism will act as a catalyst for peace and stability remains to be seen. The historical juncture termed as 'crossroads' by us in this volume does pose dilemmas hitherto unimagined before the intellectuals and institutions of statecraft throughout Euro-Asia. And this is precisely what we wish to argue and illustrate in this chapter.

In our view, the rhetoric of 'Rising Asia' should be tempered with the appreciation that the major powers in Asia, such as China, India and Japan are still rising and facing wide-ranging issues; including those that any rising power in the international system is likely to confront.[2] It is also useful to bear in mind that many Asian countries, with the exception of India, are in a demographic situation similar to or even worse than Europe.[3] By the year 2030, due to a substantial graying of the population,

China may have nearly as many senior citizens (65 years of age or older) as children under fifteen. But what is beyond any measure of doubt is the fact that all major players in the international system, including EU, are now re-assessing their policy options vis-à-vis Asia as a new balance of power struggles to emerge in the region. A complex geopolitics of re-orientation is visible among the foreign policy establishments throughout Euro-Asia and beyond.

While the US still remains the predominant power in Asia, the rise of China and India can no longer be ignored in the region. Japan, as Takako Hirose points out, "has finally taken a positive interest in India," as a part of its new Asia policy, and "finally taken its own defence and security matters seriously under a drastically changed environment. The relationship with an emerging China, the immediate threat from North Korea and ever-present terrorism has forced the Japanese nation to discuss defence and security issues, which were long held as taboo in post-war Japan, more openly."[4] And it is becoming increasingly difficult to maintain US military bases in Japan against the backdrop of what Hirose calls "a drifting US-Japan Alliance."[5]

In many ways, while globally, the international system remains largely uni-polar, in Asia-Pacific a multi-polar regional order is gradually taking shape. According to a neo-realist understanding of global politics, multi-polar systems are inherently unstable because they generate uncertainty and make it difficult for states to distinguish clearly between allies and adversaries. In the process, miscalculations about one another's motives, especially when the deficit of mutual trust and confidence is considerable, can and do occur. Any conflict between two of the powers in the system is more likely to escalate to general war as the other powers might be tempted to join in. Minor powers are also more likely to play great powers off against each other. Power imbalances, argue realists, are more common in a multipolar world and far more difficult to predict.

Can EU as a normative-civilian power provide an alternative to the United States in Asia both in terms of the theory (i.e. critiquing the dominant realist paradigm) and practices of international relations? Jyrki Kakonen's analysis in volume has mapped out at some length the complex nature of this question. As hinted at by him various scenarios are plausible if one looks at contemporary Asia. From one perspective, Asia remains a multi-polar region where the US remains the predominant power. From another, the American primacy is increasingly being challenged by China and so this makes the region very susceptible to future geopolitical uncertainty and strategic instability. China's possible future conduct remains to some extent a matter of conjecture as well as the source of regional uncertainty. Other regional players are rethinking their strategic agenda with various possible scenarios in mind. Everyone seems to be aware of the rise of China in one sense or the other but few could predict the precise trajectory of this overall ascendance. The US has started to re-define its strategy for the Asia-Pacific. Japan and India, two of the biggest powers in the region, are also re-evaluating their policy options.

It will be some time before the implications of all these transformations mentioned will become clear. But what is certain is that the strategic landscape of Euro-Asia, including the Eurasian Rimland[6] will undergo profound changes in the next few years with equally profound consequences. One of the central messages of this volume has been that there are no 'final' or 'settled' understandings of what 'Asia' is, or for that matter what 'Europe' stands for in terms of exclusive, inward looking values or norms. Constructions labeled 'Asia' and 'Europe' are historically contingent and the outcome of various competing geopolitical visions and imaginations; each trying to impose its own map of meaning on diverse continental as well as oceanic landscapes. The chapters by Pekka Korhonen and Rudolf Wastl in this volume have reminded us of the need to return to human-cultural geographies of the continent shared by both Europe and Asia and thereby acknowledge the open-ended opportunity to explore and articulate alternative imaginations of spaces, places and peoples of Euro-Asia based on both historical possibilities, as ably shown by Hobson in his chapter.

The fatal attraction of classical state-centric geopolitics continues to rest in its reductionism but not without inviting critique and resistance.[7] The clash of imaginations in the case of Central Eurasia, analysed by Sanjay Chaturvedi in this volume, is a good example of how certain intellectuals and institutions of statecraft through imaginative geographies can (and do) depoliticize places and turn them into security commodities. Our two case studies in this volume by Ayla Gol and Daragh McDowell have underlined the importance of paying due attention to details, contingencies and specificities. In short, they suggest that one of the most effective antidotes to excessive geopolitics lies in a return to human and cultural geographies, with meticulous attention paid to details. This volume has argued in a collective sense that Euro-Asia should stay a hyphenated concept, so as to remind us constantly that both 'Asia' and 'Europe' are highly heterogeneous places sharing the same continent. Also, Europe and Asia are 'constructions', always in the process of becoming, both spatially and temporally. The hyphenation is also a subtle but significant reminder to those who often talk of 'European' and/or 'Asian' values without even an iota of acknowledgement to various dialectical-dialogues of civilizations that have taken place on the vast continent, as pointed out by John M. Hobson in this volume.

May be the time has come to rid the label 'Eurasia' from some of its historical-strategic baggage by giving it a new, more open-ended, inclusive content, as forcefully argued by Anita Sengupta in this volume.[8] The normative appeal for Euro-Asian cooperation and dialogue has increased in recent years, since the relationship between these two ends of the Eurasian continent can no longer be viewed as of secondary importance. Much of the need to improve relations among Eurasian actors has to do with commercial reasons. The EU, for example, has a vested interest in being present in the expanding Asian markets and influencing their development. On the Asian side, European presence is likewise important, particularly in the form of investments and development assistance. As emphasized by Rajen Harshe in this book, the EU as civilian power (looking for partners rather than enemies) can also serve as a model—and, at times, as an inspiring example—for its Asian partners who are going through processes of regional integration and modernization similar to those experienced in Europe.

Perhaps the greatest challenge of all in the long term has to do with environmental degradation and climate change, for both Europe and Asia will need to find alternative, more sustainable ways to maintain the predominant model of development, the spreading of which now seems so inevitable also in Asia. The Euro-Asian connection is also to be understood in terms of a larger, world political context, where Europe and Asia are now taking a more active role. This could also mean creating a counter-balance at times when American power, especially in view of the invasion of Iraq by the Bush administration, is seen to be more destructive than constructive.

According to Immanuel Wallerstein (2006), looking ahead, two kinds of trends are probable. "The first is a complete breakdown of nuclear non-proliferation, with the rise of one to two dozen small nuclear powers in addition to those already in existence. The decline of US power plus the competing interests of the multiple power centres virtually guarantee that those countries which ended such programmes in the period 1970-2000 will resume them, no doubt joined by others. This will both act as a deterrent to military actions in many zones of the world and make the consequence of such actions more dangerous."[9] Secondly, argues

Wallerstein, a multi-currency system is going to question, and eventually replace, the dominance of the US dollar, posing major economic dilemmas before the US in dealing with the existing national debt, and probably result in declining living standards.

According to the realists, great power politics is alive and well in Asia and Europe will have to learn to talk in a language, other than the normative, that it has tended to sideline because of its own historical reasons if it is to have a real strategic impact in shaping Euro-Asia's future. If so, then it implies the continuation of more or less the hegemony of realist approaches. On the other hand, it is possible to argue that rising powers in Asia, especially China and India, will create their own 'schools' of International Relations. We hope that this volume has provided us with an opportunity for not only critically reassessing the politics behind the written meta-geographies of Europe and Asia (the old and the new), but the underlying geopolitical narratives, but also for reformulating and conjoining them in ways that better reflect the reality of Euro-Asia and allow new kinds of practices and institutions to emerge in the future. What are needed are visions that not only shy away from critiquing various self-fulfilling hypotheses about conflicts, as the persisting interpretations about the 'New Great Game' in Central Asia or the much-talked-about thesis of Samuel P. Huntington on the clash of civilizations tend to generate, but also offer the blueprints for an alternative, more humane, and yet deeply argumentative worlds characterized by plural identities and forms of autonomy that, as pointed out so perceptively by Ranabir Samaddar in his contribution to this volume, that are "able to disconnect popular sovereignty and centralized state apparatus, and give rise to a new sociality."

Notes

1. K. Mahbubani, *The New Asian Hemisphere: The Irresistible Shift of Global Power to the East* (New York: Public Affairs, 2008); S. Mansingh, "Rising China and Emergent India in the 21st Century: Friends or Rivals?"*The Korean Journal of Defense Analysis* 19, no. 4 (2007): 117-42; M.S. Pardesi, "Understanding the Rise of India," *India Review* 6, no. 3 (2007): 209-31.
2. H. Pant, "Indian Foreign and Security Policy: Beyond Nuclear Weapons," *The Brown Journal of World Affairs* 11, no. 2 (2009): 225-38.
3. F. Zakaria, *The Post-American World* (London: Norton, 2008), 197.
4. T. Hirose, "Japanese Emerging Nationalism and Its New Asia Policy," in *Asian Security Dynamic: US, Japan and the Rising Powers*, V.R.

Raghavan, (ed.) (New Delhi: Delhi Policy Group and Promila Co. Publishers, 2008), 78.

5. Hirose, "Japanese Emerging Nationalism."
6. R.D. Kaplan, *Monsoon: The Indian Ocean and the Future of American Power* (New York: Random House, 2010).
7. G.O'Tuathail, Critical *Geopolitics: The Politics of Writing Global Space* (London: Routledge, 1996).
8. She has argued this point also in her recent book. See A. Sengupta, *Heartlands of Eurasia: The Geopolitics of Political Space* (Lanham: Lexington Books, 2009).
9. I. Wallerstein, "The Curve of American Power," *New Left Review* 40 (July/ August 2006): 92.

Bibliography

Abernethy, David. *The Dynamics of Global Dominance*. New Haven: Yale University Press, 2000.

Abu-Lughod, Janet L. *Before European Hegemony*. Oxford: Oxford University Press, 1989.

Agamben, Giorgio. *Homo Sacer. Sovereign Power and Bare Life*. Stanford CA: Stanford University Press, 1998.

Agnew, John. *Geopolitics. Re-visioning World Politics*. London and New York: Routledge, 1998.

Agnew, John and S. Corbridge. *Mastering Space*. London: Routledge, 1995.

Agnew, John *et al*. "Reading Gerry Kearns' ~~Geopolitics~~ and Empire: The Legacy of Halford Mackinder." *Political Geography*. 2010. doi: 10.1016/j.polgeo.2010.09.007.

Ahmad, Feroz. "Islamic Reassertion in Turkey," *Third World Quarterly*, 10, no. 2 (April 1988).

Alagappa, Muthiah. *Asian Security Practice: Material and Ideational Influences*. Stanford: Stanford University Press, 1998.

Alexandrov, M. "Uneasy Alliance: Relations between Russia and Kazakhstan in the Post—Soviet era, 1992-1997," *Contributions to the Study of World History*, no. 66 (1999): xiv, 327.

Allison, R. "Strategic Reassertion in Russia's Central Asia Policy." *International Affairs* 80, no. 2 (2004): 277-93.

Ashimbaev *et al* (eds). *New Challenges and New Geopolitics in Central Asia After September 11*. Almaty: Kazakhstan Institute for Strategic Studies, 2003.

Ateş, Toktamiş. *Dünyada ve Türkiye'de Laiklik* [*Laicite* in Turkey and the World]. 10th edition. Ankara: Ümit Yayincilik, 2000.

Atlas of the World. London: Times Books, 2000.

Aydin, Senem and Rusen Cakir. *Political Islam in Turkey*, Centre for European Policy Studies Working Document No. 265 (April 2007).

Bakshi, J. "Shanghai Co-operation Organisation (SCO): Before and After September 11." *Strategic Analysis* 26, no. 2 (2002): 265-76.

Bakshi, J. "India and Central Asia: Policy Review and Projecting into Future (2005-2025)." In *Emerging India: Security and Foreign Policy Perspectives*, N.S. Sisodia and C.U. Bhaskar (eds). New Delhi and Chicago: IDSA, Promilla & Company in association with Bibliophile South Asia, 2005.

Bala, Arun. *The Dialogue of Civilizations in the Birth of Modern Science.* Houndmills: Palgrave Macmillan, 2006.

Banerjee, D. "Central Eurasian Republics Today." *Strategic Analysis* (August 1994): 525-41.

Barnett, T.P.M. "The Pentagon's New Map." *Esquire* (March 2003). http://www.nwc.navy.mil/newrulesets/ThePentagonsNewMap.htm (last accessed 29 June 2003)

———. *The Pentagon's New Map: War and Peace in the Twenty-First Century.* New York: Berkley Books, 2004.

Bassin, Mark. "Inventing Siberia: Visions of the Russian East in the Early Nineteenth Century." *American Historical Review* 96 (1991): 1, 1-17.

———. "Russia between Europe and Asia: The Ideological Construction of Geographical Space." *Slavic Review* 50 (1991): 763-94.

———. "Civilizations and Their Discontents: Political Geography and Geopolitics in Huntington's Thesis." *Geopolitics* 12, no. 3 (2007): 351-74.

Bassin, Mark and Konstantin E. Aksenov. "Mackinder and the Heartland Theory in Post-Soviet Geopolitical Discourse." *Geopolitics* 11, no. 1 (2006): 99-118.

Berman, I. "The New Battleground: Central Asia and the Caucasus." *The Washington Quarterly* 28, no. 1 (2004): 59-69.

Bernal, Martin. *Black Athena. The Afroasiatic Roots of Classical Civilization. Vol. 1. The Fabrication of Ancient Greece 1785-1985.* New Brunswick, NJ: Rutgers University Press, 1987; New York: Vintage, 1991.

———. *Black Athena. The Afroasiatic Roots of Classical Civilization. Vol. 2. The Archaelogical and Documentary Evidence.* New Brunswick, NJ: Rutgers University Press, 1991.

Bhagat, G. "Central Asia and Energy Security." *Asian Affairs* 37, no. 1 (2006): 1-16.

Blank, Stephen. "The Shanghai Cooperative Organization: A Post Mortem," *Nordic Newsletter of Asian Studies* 3 (2002).

Blank, Stephen. "Which Way for Sino-Russian Relations?" *Orbis* (Summer 1998).

Blaut, James M. *The Colonizer's Model of the World.* London: Guilford, 1993.

Bloch, Marc. *Feudal Society*, 1. Chicago: University of Chicago Press, 1961.

Blouet, B.W. (ed.). *Global Geostrategy: Mackinder and the Defence of the West.* London: New York: Frank Cass, 2005.

Bonnet, Alstair. *The Idea of the West. Culture, Politics and History*. Houndmills: Palgrave, 2004.

BP. Statistical Review of World Energy. June 2008.

Bradshaw, Michael. *World Regional Geography*. 2nd ed. New York: McGraw-Hill, 2002.

Bradshaw *et al. Contemporary World Regional Geography*. 2nd ed. Boston: McGraw-Hill, 2007.

Brague, Rémi. *Eccentric Culture*. South Bend, Indiana: Saint Augustine's Press, 2002.

Bray, Francesca. *Science and Civilisation in China*, VI (2). Cambridge: Cambridge University Press, 1984.

Brenner, N. "Beyond State-Centrism? Space, Territoriality, and Geographical Scale in Globalization Studies." *Theory and Society* 28 (1999): 39-78.

Breterton, Charlotte and John Vogler. *The European Union as a Global Actor*. London & New York: Routledge, 1999.

Brezezinski, Z. *The Grand Chessboard: American Primacy and its Geostrategic Imperatives*. New York: Basic Books, 1997.

———. "A Geostrategy for Eurasia." *Foreign Affairs* 76 (1997): 5.

Bulletin of the European Communities, no. 11 (November 1970): 9-14.

Bulletin of the European Communities, no. 12, (December 1973): 118-22.

Capisani, G.R. *The Handbook of Central Asia: A Comprehensive Survey of the New Republics*. London: I.B. Tauris Publisher, 2000.

Carnegie Endowment for International Peace, Meeting Report 2, no. 8 (3 November 2000). www.ceip.org/files/events/gulomov.asp?EventID==218

Casanova, Jose. "Catholic and Muslim Politics in Comparative Perspective," *Taiwan Journal of Democracy* 1, no. 2 (December 2005).

———. "The Long, Difficult, and Tortuous Journey of Turkey into Europe and the Dilemmas of European Civilisation," *Constellations* 13, no. 2 (2006).

CEF Quarterly (February 2005).

Cem, Ismail. *Turkiye, Avrupa, Avrasya*. Vol. 1. Istanbul: Bilgi Universitesi Yayinlari, 2004.

———. "Turkey and Europe: Looking to the Future from a Historical Perspective." http://www.mfa.gov.tr. Accessed on 23.06. 2007.

Challaney, Brahma. *Asian Juggernaut. The Rise of China, India and Japan*. New Delhi: Harper Collins, 2006.

Chaturvedi, S. and J. Painter. "Whose World? Whose Order? Spatiality, Geopolitics and the Limits of World Order Concept." *Cooperation and Conflict* 42, no. 4 (2007): 375-95.

Chufrin, G.I. and Stockholm International Peace Research Institute. *Russia and Asia: the Emerging Security Agenda*. Oxford: Oxford University Press, 1999.

Clarke, J.J. *Oriental Enlightenment*. London: Routledge, 1997.

Clawson, David *et al. World Regional Geography*. 9th ed. Upper Saddle River: Pearson, 2007.

Cohen, S.B. *Geopolitics: The Geography of International Relations*. Lanham: Rowman & Littlefield, 2009.

Cohen-Tanugi, Laurent. *The Shape of the World to Come. Charting the Geopolitics of a New Century*. Cambridge University Press: New York, 2008.

Common Strategy of the European Union of 4 June 1999 on Russia (1999/414/ CFSP).

Communication from the Commission. COM (2001) 469 final. Europe and Asia: Strategic Framework for Enhanced Partnership.

—— (2003) 399/4. A New Partnership with South East Asia.

—— (2003) 533. A Maturing Partnership: Shared Interests and Challenges in EU—China relations.

—— (2004) 430. An EU-India Strategic Partnership.

Cornell, S.E. "America in Eurasia: One Year After," *Current History* (October 2002).

Cornell, Svante E. "Introduction," *Nordic Newsletter of Asian Studies* 3 (2002).

Crampton, W. Jeremy. (2001). "Maps as Social Constructions: Power, Communication and Visualization," *Progress in Human Geography* 25(2): 235-52.

Cressey, George B. *Asia's Lands and Peoples. A Geography of One-Third the Earth and Two-Thirds its People*. New York, Toronto and London: McGraw-Hill, 1951.

Cummings, S.N. *Kazakhstan: Power and the Elite*. London: I.B. Tauris, 2002.

Daniel Brumberg and Larry Diamond. Introduction. In *Islam and Democracy in the Middle East*, Larry Diamond, Marc F. Plattner and Daniel Brumberg, (eds). Baltimore: The Johns Hopkins University Press, 2003. *Freedom in the World,* http://www.freedomhouse.org, accessed on 15.05. 2007.

Davis, E.V.W. and R. Azizian (eds). *Islam, Oil and Geopolitics: Central Asia after September 11*. Lanham: Rowman and Littlefield Publishers, 2007.

De Blij, H.J. and Peter Muller. (2006). *Geography: Realms, Regions and Concepts*. 11th ed. (New York: John Wiley&Sons).

Delanty, Gerard (ed.). *Europe and Asia beyond East and West*. London and New York: Routledge, 2006.

Der Spiegel 41, 2004: 29

Dodds, K.J. *Geopolitics in a Changing World*. Harlow and New York: Prentice Hall, 2000.

Dunden Bugune Anayasa Mahkemesi: 1962-2007, 45. Yil Albumu, 2007, p. 177-178, <http://www.anayasa.gov.tr/images/loaded/pdf_dosyalari/mahkeme/dundenbuguneaym.pdf> Accessed on 07.07.2007.

East Asian Summit. East Asia Summit Declaration on Avian Influenza Prevention, Control and Response. (2005). http://www.mofa.go.jp/region/asia-paci/eas/joint0512-2.html, visited 10.01.2006.

East Asian Summit. Kuala Lumpur Declaration on the East Asia Summit. (2005). http://www.mofa.go.jp/region/asia-paci/eas/joint0512.html, read 10.01.2006.

Eisenstadt, S.E. "Multiple Modernities," *Daedalus*, 129, no. 1 (Winter 2000).

Elden, S. "Missing the Point: Globalization, Deterritorialization and the Space of the World." *Transactions of the Institute of British Geographers* 30 (2005): 8-19.

Ferguson, Y.H. and R.W. Mansbach. *Remapping Global Politics: History's Revenge and Future Shock*. Cambridge: Cambridge University Press, 2004.

Fesharaki, F. "Energy and the Asian Security Nexus." *Journal of International Affairs* 53, no. 1 (1999): 85-99.

Filali-Ansary, Abdou. "Muslims and Democracy." In *Islam and Democracy in the Middle East*, Larry Diamond, Marc F. Plattner and Daniel Brumberg (eds). Baltimore: The John Hopkins University Press, 2003, 193-207.

Foucault, Michel. *Essential Works of Michel Foucault, 1954-1984*. Vol. 3. New York: New Press, 2001.

Frank, Andre Gunder. *ReOrient: Global Economy in the Asian Age*. Berkeley: University of California Press, 1998.

Funk, N.C. and A.A. Said. "Islam and the West: Narratives of Conflict and Conflict Transformation." *International Journal of Peace Studies* 9 no. 1 (2004): 1-28.

Gallup World Poll. *Special Report: Muslim World, Islam and Democracy* (Princeton: Gallup Organisation, 2006). http://media.gallup.com/WorldPoll/PDF/GALLUPMUSLIMSTUDIESIslamandDemocracy030607.pdf, accessed on 07.07.2007.

Gardner, H. *American Global Strategy and the "War on Terrorism"*. Aldershot: Ashgate, 2005.

Gellner, Ernest. *Muslim Society*. Cambridge: Cambridge University Press, 1981.

Gerschenkron, Alexander. *Economic Backwardness in Historical Perspective*. Cambridge, MA: Harvard University Press, 1962.

Ghazanfar, S.M. *Islamic Civilization*. Lanham, Maryland: Scarecrow Press, 2006.

Gholizavareh, G.R. *The Political Geography of Central Asia*. Qome: Islamic Press, 1995.

Gismondi, M. "Civilization as Paradigm: An Inquiry into the Hermeneutics of Conflict." *Geopolitics* 9 no. 2 (2004): 402-424.

Gleason, A. "Eurasia: What is it? Is It?" *Journal of Eurasian Studies* 1 (2010): 26-32.

Gleason, G. "Foreign Policy and Domestic Reform in Central Asia." *Central Asian Survey* 20, no. 2 (2001): 167-82.

Göle, Nilufer. "Authoritarian Secularism and Islamist Politics: the Case of Turkey" In *Civil Society in the Middle East*, A.G. Richard (ed.). Vol. 2. Leiden, Netherlands: Brill, 1996.

Goody, Jack. *Islam in Europe*. Cambridge: Polity, 2004.

Gray, C. "In defence of the Heartland: Sir Halford Mackinder and his critics a hundred years on." In *Global Geostrategy: Mackinder and the Defence of the West*, Brian W. Blouet (ed.). London: New York: Frank Cass, 2005, 17-35.

Gregory, D. *The Colonial Present: Afghanistan, Palestine, Iraq*. Oxford: Blackwell, 2004.

———. "Imaginative Geographies." In *The Dictionary of Human Geography*, D. Gregory, R. Johnston, G. Pratt, M.J. Watts and S. Whatmore (eds). Chichester: Wiley-Blackwell, 2009.

Guang, Pan. "China-Central Asia-Russia Relations and the Role of the SCO in the War against Terrorism," *SIIS Journal* 9, no. 2 (May 2002).

Guang, Pan. "The New SCO Observers: Making a Leap Forward in Cautious Augmentation," *CEF Quarterly* (July 2005).

Harkavy, R. "Strategic Geography and the Greater Middle East." *Naval War College Review* 54, no. 4 (2001): 37-53.

Harris, L.C. "Xinjiang, Central Asia and the Implications for China's Policy in the Islamic World." *The China Quarterly* 133 (1993): 111-29.

Heper, Metin. "Islam and Democracy in Turkey: Toward Reconciliation?" *Middle East Journal*, 51, no. 1 (Winter 1997).

Herodotus. *Herodotus*. c. 440 BC. Loeb Classical Library, Cambridge, Mass. and London: Harvard University Press, 1990.

Hirose, T. "Japanese Emerging Nationalism and Its New Asia Policy." In *Asian Security Dynamic: US, Japan and the Rising Powers*, Raghavan, V.R. (ed.). New Delhi: Delhi Policy Group and Promila Co. Publishers, 2008.

Hobson, John M. *The Eastern Origins of Western Civilisation*. Cambridge: Cambridge University Press, 2004.

Hodgson, Marshall G.S. *Rethinking World History. Essays on Europe, Islam and World History*. Cambridge: Cambridge University Press, 1993.

Huasheng, Zhou. "China, Russia and the United States: Prospects for Cooperation in Central Asia."

———. "The SCO in the Last Year," *CEF Quarterly* (July 2005).

Hudson, Ray and Williams, M. *Divided Europe Society and Territory*. London: Sage, 1999.

Hunter, S. *Central Eurasia since Independence*. Washington Papers 168. Washington DC: Centre for Strategic and International Studies, 1996

Hunter, S. "Iran, Turkey and Central Asia: The Islamic Connection." In *Islam, Oil and Geopolitics: Central Asia after September 11*, E.V.W. Davis and R. Azizian (eds). Lanham: Rowman and Littlefield Publishers, 2007.

Huntington, S.P. *The Clash of Civilizations and the Remaking of World Order*. New York: Simon and Schuster, 1996.

Hurd, E. Shakman, "Negotiating Europe: The Politics of Religion and the Prospects for Turkish Accession," *Review of International Studies* 32 (2006): 401-18.

Hyman, A. "Central Asia's Relations with Afghanistan and South Asia." In *The New Central Eurasia and its Neighbours*, P. Ferdinannd (ed.). London: The Royal Institutional Affairs; Pinter Publisher, 1994, 75-94.

Ilkenberry, G.J. and A.M. Slaughter. "Forging a World of Liberty under Law: U.S. Security in the 21st Century." Final Report of the Princeton Project on National Security. The Woodrow Wilson School of Public and

International Affairs, Princeton University, 2007. http://www.princeton.edu/~ppns/report/FinalReport.pdf 2006, accessed on 15 November 2010.

Isingarin, N. *Kazakhstan i Sodruzhestvo: problemy ekonomicheskoi integratsii: uchebnoe posobie*. Almaty: BIS, 2000.

Ismagambetov, Talgat. "Some Geopolitical Peculiarities of Central Asia, Past and Present." In *Oil, Transition and Security in Central Asia*, Sally N. Cummings (ed.). London and New York: Routledge-Curzon, 2003.

Israeli, R. "Return to Source: The Republics of Central Eurasia and Middle East." *Central Eurasian Survey* 13, no. 1 (1994): 19-31.

Ivanov, I.S. *Novaìa rossiiskaìa diplomatiìa: deciat' let vneshnei politiki strany*. Moskva: Olma-Press, 2002.

Iwashita, Akihiro. "The Shanghai Cooperation Organization and Its Implications for Eurasian Security: A New Dimension of 'Partnership' after the Post Cold War Period." In *Slavic Eurasia's Integration into the World Economy and Community*, S. Tabata and A. Iwashita (eds). Sapporo: Slavic Research Centre, 2004.

Jackson, Patrick Thaddeus. *Civilizing the Enemy. German Reconstruction and the Invention of the West*. Ann Arbor: The University of Michigan Press, 2006.

Jung, Dietrich. *Turkey's Future: EU Member of 'Islamist Rouge State'?* Danish Institute for International Studies Brief. DIIS: Copenhagen, January 2007.

Junichiro, Koizumi. Press Conference by Prime Minister Junichiro Koizumi following the ASEAN+3, Japan-Asean and EAS Summit meetings. 2005. http://www.mofa.go.jp/region/asia-paci/eas/press0512.html, visited 10.1.2006.

Kacowicz, Arie M. "Explaining Zones of Peace: Democracies as Satified Powers?" *Journal of Peace Research* 32, no. 3 (1995): 265-76.

Käkönen, Jyrki. *Natural Resources and Conflicts in the Changing International System. Three Studies on Imperialism*. Aldershot: Avebury, 1988.

Kaplan, R.D. *The End of the Earth: A Journey into the Frontiers of Anarchy*. New York: Random House, 1996.

———. *Monsoon: The Indian Ocean and the Future of American Power*. New York: Random House, 2010.

Kassimeris, Christos. "Turkey's foreign policy options: Europe, the USA or Central Asia?" *Contemporary Politics* 16 (2010): 3, 321-36.

Katzenstein, Peter J. "Multiple Modernities as Limits to Secular Europeanization?" In *Religion in an Expanding Europe*, Timothy A. Byrnes and Peter J. Katzenstein (eds). Cambridge: Cambridge University Press, 2006.

Kavalski, E. "Coming to terms with complexity of external agency in Central Asia." *Journal of Eurasian Studies* (2010). In press.

Keisala, Katja. *The European Union as an International Actor: Strengths of the European Civilian Power*. Tampere: Tampere University Press, 2004.

Kemal A.R., "Regional Cooperation in South Asia," SAFMA Regional Conference, Dhaka, 20-21 August 2004. www.southasiamedia.net/conference/Regional_Cooperation/safta

Kiernan, Victor. *The Lords of Human Kind. European Attitudes to Other Cultures in the Imperial Age*. London: Serif, 1995.

Kimmage, D. "'Sovereign *Democracy*' in Almaty and Moscow," *RFE/RL Newsline*, 2006.

———. "Kazakh President Touts 'friendship' with Russia, rejects talk of Union," *RFE/RL Newsline*, 2006.

Kindersley, Dorling. *Student Atlas*. 4th ed. London, 2006.

Kissinger, H. *Diplomacy*. New York: Simon & Schuster, 1994.

Klare, M. "The New Geography of Conflict." *Foreign Affairs* (May-June 2001): 46-61.

Klett-Perthes. *Perthes World Atlas*. 1st ed. Gotha, 2006.

Kolesnikov, A. "Upheaval of All Liberties—Russia Prods Asia to Give America an Ultimatum," *Kommersant* (translated and reprinted in *the Current Digest of the Post-Soviet Press*), 2005.

Korhonen, Pekka. *Japan and the Pacific Free Trade Area*. Routledge: London & New York, 1994.

———. *Japan and Asia Pacific Integration: Pacific Romances 1968-1996*. London and New York: Routledge, 1998.

———*Ajia no Nishi no Sakai*. Kyoto: International Research Center for Japanese Studies, 2000].

———. "The Political Geography of Okakura Tenshin." *Nichibunken Japan Review*, no. 13 (2001): 107-27.

———. "Asia's Chinese Name." *Inter-Asia Cultural Studies* 3, no. 2 (2002): 253-70.

———. "Aasiaksi nimetty tila." *Kosmopolis* 33, no. 1 (2003): 9-37.

———. "On the Metageography of Euroasia: Are there 'Two' or 'Three' Continents on the Eurasian Landmass?" Paper presented at the international conference *Revisiting "Euro-Asia" Cultures, Connections and Conceptualisations*, Chandigarh, India, 13 February 2006.

———. "The Concept of Asia." In *At the Crossroads of Europe, Asia and Africa*, Zeki Kütük (ed.). Turku: University of Turku, Department of Contemporary History Researches 29, 2006.

Krause, Joachim. "Multilateralism: Behind European Views," *The Washington Quarterly* 27, no. 2 (Spring 2004).

Kristof, Ladis K.D. "The Image and the Vision of the Fatherland: The Case of Poland in Comparative Perspective." In *Geography and National Identity*, D. Hooson (ed.). Oxford: Blackwell, 1994, 221-48.

Kristof, Ladis K.D. "Mackinder's Concept of Heartland and the Russians." Unpublished article.

Kunzweiler, W.R. "The New Central Eurasian Great Game." *Strategic Review* 22, no. 3 (1998): 14-33.

Kurikkala, Flora. *Representation of the Changing Self: An EU Performance in the Middle East*. Tampere: Tampere University Press, 2003.

Lacoste, Y. "Rivalries for Territory." *Geopolitics* 5, no. 2 (2000): 120-58.

Laumulin, Murat. *The Security, Foreign Policy, and International Relationship of Kazakhstan After Independence, 1991-2001*. Almaty: Kazakhstan Institute of Strategic Studies and Freidrich Ebert Shiftung, 2002.

Lefebvre, H. *The Production of Space*. Oxford: Blackwell, 1991.

Legvold, R. and American Academy of Arts and Sciences, *Thinking Strategically: the Major Powers, Kazakhstan, and the Central Asian Nexus*, American Academy Studies in Global Security. Cambridge: American Academy of Arts and Sciences, MIT Press, 2003.

Lewis, Bernard. "Islamic Revival in Turkey," *International Affairs*, 28, no. 1 (January 1952).

Lewis, Bernard. "Why Turkey is the Only Muslim Democracy?" *Middle East Quarterly* (March 1994). Also available at http://www.meforum.org/article/216, accessed on 31.05. 2007.

Lewis, Bernard. *The Muslim Discovery of Europe*. London: Phoenix, 1994.

Lewis, Martin W. and Kären E. Wigen. *The Myth of Continents. A Critique of Metageography*. Berkeley: University of California Press, 1997.

Lichtenberger, Elisabeth. *Europa—Geographie, Geschichte, Wirtschaft, Politik*. Vienna: Primus, 2005.

Lieven, Anatol. "The End of NATO," *Prospect* (December 2001), cited from Khamzayeva, Anar. "Novaya Strategiya NATO? Ee Posledstviya Dliya Tsentralnoi Azii," *Kazakstan i Sovremennie Mir* 1, no. 2 (2002).

Lipset, Seymour Martin. "Some Social Requisites of Democracy: Economic Development and Political Legitimacy," *The American Political Science Review*, 53 (March 1959): 69-105.

Macapagal Arroyo, Gloria. Chairman's Statement of the Second East Asia Summit. 2007. http://www.mofa.go.jp/region/asia-paci/eas/state0701.html, visited 22. 04. 2007.

MacFarlane, S. Neil "The United States and Regionalism in Central Asia," *International Affairs* 80, no. 3 (May 2004).

Mackinder, Halford J. "The Round World and the Winning of the Peace," *Foreign Affairs* 21, no. 4 (1943).

Mahbubani, K. *The New Asian Hemisphere: The Irresistible Shift of Global Power to the East*. New York: Public Affairs, 2008.

Mahmood, A. "Central Asia's Great Game." *Current Affairs* (2000). http://defencejournal.com/globe/2000/june-july/contents-june-july2000.htm

Mamadouh, V.D. "Geopolitics in the Nineties: One Flag Many Meanings." *Geo Journal* 46 (1998): 237-53.

Mammone, A., E. Godin, and B. Jenkins. "The Extreme Right in Contemporary Europe." (Editorial). *Journal of Contemporary Europe* 16 no. 3 (2008): 323-26.

Mansingh, S. "Rising China and Emergent India in the 21st Century: Friends or Rivals?" *The Korean Journal of Defense Analysis*, 19, no. 4 (2007): 117-42.

Mardin, Serif "Religion in Modern Turkey," *International Social Sciences Journal*, 19, no. 2 (1977).

Marston, Sallie *et al. World Regions in Global Context*. 3rd ed. Upper Saddle River: Pearson, 2008.

Mattoo, Amitabh. "United States of America and Central Asia: Beginning of the Great Game." In *Central Asia the Great Game Replayed, an Indian Perspective*, Nirmala Joshi (ed.). Delhi: New Century Publications, 2003.

McNally, Rand. *Atlas of World Geography*. Chicago: Rand McNelly&Company, 2005.

Meiirzhan, Mashan. "Regional Security as a System Factor in Central Asian Integration." In *Peace and Security in Central Asia*, Jasjit Singh (ed.). New Delhi: IDSA, 2000.

Menocal, María Rosa. *Ornament of the World: How Muslims, Jews and Christians Crated a Culture of Tolerance in Medieval Spain*. New York, London: Little, Brown and Company, 2002.

Mesbahi, M. "Regional and Global Powers and the International Relations of Central Asia." In *The Making of Foreign Policy of Russia and New States of Eurasia*, A. Dawisha and K. Dawisha (eds). Armonk: M.E Sharpe, 1995, 215-45.

Midlarsky, Manus I. "Democracy and Islam: Implications for Civilisational Conflict and Democratic Peace," *International Studies Quarterly*, 42, no. 3 (September 1998): 485-511.

Mihelic Pulsipher, Lydia *et al. World Regional Geography*. 2nd ed. New York: W.H. Freeman, 2002.

Mingst, Karen. *Essentials of International Relations*. New York: W.W. Norton & Company, 1999.

Ministry of Foreign Affairs, Tehran (2010), Weekly briefing of the Foreign Ministry Spokesman, http://www.mfa.gov.ir/cms/cms/Tehran/en/NEW/258891.html. Accessed on 15 November 2010.

Mohsenin, M. "Iran's Relation with Central Asia and the Caucasus." *The Iranian Journal of International Affairs* 2 (1995): 217-32.

Moore, P. "Kremlin Theoretician Develops Ideas on Democracy," *RFE/RL Newsline*, 2006.

Morozov, S. *Diplomatiya V.V. Putina: vneshnreaeia politika Rossii, 1999-2004*. Sankt-Peterburg: Izmaæilovskiæi, 2004.

National Geographic Society. *Concise Atlas of the World*. Washington D.C.: National Geographic Society, 2003.

National Geographic Society. *Family Reference Atlas*. Washington D.C.: National Geographic Society, 2007.

Nederveen Pieterse, Jan P. *Empire and Emancipation*. London: Pluto, 1990.

Needham, Joseph, and Wang Ling. *Science and Civilisation in China*, IV (2). Cambridge: Cambridge University Press, 1965.

Neumann, Iver B. *Russia and the Idea of Europe. A Study in Identity and International Relations*. London and New York: Routledge, 1996.

Neumann, I.B. "Regionalization and Democratic Consolidation." In *Democratic Consolidation in Eastern Europe*, J. Zielonka and A. Pravda (eds). Oxford: Oxford University Press, 2001.

Nye, J.S. *Soft Power: the Means to Success in World Politics*. New York: PublicAffairs, 2004.

ÓTuathail, G. "The Bush Administration and the 'End' of the Cold War: a critical geopolitics of US foreign policy in 1989," *Geoforum* 23 (1992): 437-52.

———. *Critical Geopolitics: The Politics of Writing Global Space*. London: Routledge, 1996.

ÓTuathail, G. and S. Dalby (eds). *Rethinking Geopolitics*. London: Routledge, 1998.

O'Brien, Peter. *Fragile Ego*. New York: Palgrave Macmillan, 2009.

Okara, A. "Sovereign Democracy: A New Russian Idea or a PR?" *Foreign Affairs* 2 (July & September 2007.)

Oudenaren, John Van. "What is Multilateral," *Policy Review* 117 and "Unipolar Versus Unilateral," *Policy Review* 124.

Oxford School Atlas. 30th ed. New Delhi: Oxford University Press, 2000.

Oxford School Atlas. 31st ed. New Delhi: Oxford University Press, 2006.

Pant, H. "Indian Foreign and Security Policy: Beyond Nuclear Weapons," *The Brown Journal of World Affairs* 11, no. 2 (2009): 225-38.

Pardesi, M.S. "Understanding the Rise of India," *India Review* 6, no. 3 (2007): 209-31.

Parker, W.H. "Europe: How Far?" *Geographic Journal* 126 (1960): 278-97.

Peet, R. "From Eurocentrism to Americentrism." *Antipode: A Radical Journal of Geography* 37 (2005): 936-43.

Peimani, H. *Regional Security and the Future of Central Asia*. Westport: Praeger, 1998.

Pomeranz, Kenneth. *The Great Divergence*. Princeton: Princeton University Press, 2000.

Pratt, Mary Louise.: *Imperial Eyes*. London: Routledge, 1992.

Raeff, Marc. "Russia's Perception of Her Relationship with the West," *Slavic Review* 23 (1964): 13-19.

Raju, C.K. *Cultural Foundations of Mathematics*. New Delhi: Pearson Longman, 2007.

Raman , B. "Implications of EU Ban on LTTE." International Terrorism Monitor: Paper 63, 28 May 2006. www.saag.org/papers19/paper1817

Redmond, John. "Turkey and the European Union: Troubled European or European Trouble?" *International Affairs*, 83, no. 2 (2007).

Rizvi, H.A. "Domestic Politics, External Linkages, and Security." *Sworn & Plough Shares* 10 (1996): 17-23.

Roberts, S., A. Secor, and M. Sparke. "Neoliberal Geopolitics." *Antipode* 35 (2003): 886-97.

Ross, M.H. "The Political Psychology of Competing Narratives: September 11 and Beyond." In *Understanding September 11*, Calhoun Craig, Paul Price and Ashley Timmer (eds). New York: New Press, 2002.

Roy, Oliver. "Turkey: a World Apart, Or Europe's new Frontier?" In *Turkey Today: A European Country?* Olivier Roy (ed.). London: Anthem Press, 2005.

Ruggie, John Gerard (ed.). *Multilateralism Matters, the Theory and Praxis of an Institutional Form*. New York: Columbia University Press, 1993.

Rumer, B.Z. (ed.). *Central Eurasia in Transition: Dilemmas of Political and Economic Development*. Armonk: M.E. Sharpe, 1996.

"Russia Needs Friend, Long-term Partner," *ITAR-TASS*, 2007.

Rywkin, M. "Central Asia in the Forefront of Attention." *American Foreign Policy Interests* 24 (2002): 35-42.

Said, Edward W. *Orientalism*. London: Penguin, 2003 (1978).

———. *Power, Politics, and Culture*. London: Bloomsbury, 2004.

Saliba, George. *A History of Arabic Astronomy*. London: New York University Press, 1994.

Samaddar, R. *A Biography of the Indian Nation, 1947-97*. Delhi: Sage, 2001.

———. *The Politics of Dialogue*. Aldershot: Ashgate Publishing, 2004, chs. 5, 6, 7.

Samaddar R. (ed.). *The Politics of Autonomy*. New Delhi: Sage, 2006.

Samsun'da Cumhuriyet Mitingi, BBC Turkish Service, 20 Mayis 2007; http://www.bbc.co.uk/turkish/news/story/2007/05/070520_turkey_update.shtml Accessed on 10. 06.2007.

Samsun'da Miting Coskusu, CCN Turk, 20 Mayis 2007; http://www.cnnturk.com/TURKIYE/haber_detay.asp?PID=318&haberID=349478. Accessed on 10. 06.2007.

Schlesinger, Stephen. "The United States and the World: Is a Return to Multilateralism Possible?" In *United Nations: Multilateralism and International Security*, C. Uday Bhaskar and others (eds). Delhi: Shipra Publications, 2005.

Schwab, Raymond. *The Oriental Renaissance. Europe's Rediscovery of India and the East, 1680-1880*. 1950. New York: Columbia University Press, 1984.

Sen, A. *The Argumentative Indian: Writings on Indian History, Culture and Identity*. New York: Picador Publishers, 2006.

Sengupta, Anita "Region, Regionalization, Regionalism: The 'Myth' of Tsentralnaya Aziia Revisted." In *Central Asia since Independence*, K. Warikoo and Mahavir Singh (eds). New Delhi: Shipra Publications, 2004.

———. *Russia, China and Multilateralism in Central Asia*. Delhi: Shipra, 2005.

———. *Heartlands of Eurasia: The Geopolitics of Political Space*. Lanham: Lexington Books, 2009.

Shambayati, Hootan. "The Rentier State, Interest Groups, and the Paradox of Autonomy: State and Business in Turkey and Iran," *Comparative Politics* 26, no. 3 (April 1994): 307-31.

Shams-ud-Din. "India and Central Asia." *World Focus: Monthly Discussion Journal* 19, no. 3 (1998): 15-17.

Shams-ud-Din. "The New Great Game in Central Asia." *International Studies* 34, no. 3 (July-September 1997): 329-41.

Shaolei, F. "Chinese-Russian Strategic Relations: The Central Asian Angle." In *Islam, Oil and Geopolitics: Central Asia after September 11*, E.V.W. Davis and R. Azizian, (eds). Lanham: Rowman and Littlefield Publishers, 2007, 203-16.

Shlapentokh, D.D. "Putin's Neo-Eurasianism, or Models of the Construction of a New Russian Identity and Their Implications," *Prague Watchdog*, 2007.

Singh, K.R. "Geo-strategy of Commercial Energy," *International* Studies 39, no. 3 (2002): 259-88.

Singh, Manmohan. Media Briefing by Prime Minister Dr. Manmohan Singh on-board Special Aircraft to Kuala Lumpur to attend 4th India-ASEAN Summit and 1st East Asia Summit. 2005. http://meaindia.nic.in/, visited 10.1.2006.

Smith, Hazel. *European Union Foreign Policy. What it is and what it does.* London: Pluto Press, 2002.

Solzhenitsyn, A. "Conversations with Aleksandr Solzhenitsyn," *Komsomolskaya Pravda,* 1996.

Soysal, Mumtaz "The Future of Turkish Foreign Policy." In *The Future of Turkish Foreign Policy*, Lenore G. Martin and Dimitris Keridis (eds). Cambridge: The MIT Press, 2004.

Sparke, M. "Geopolitical fears, geoeconomic hopes, and the responsibilities of geography," *Annals of the Association of American Geographers* 97, no. 2 (2007): 338-49.

Speech by Minister of Foreign Affairs of the Russian Federation Igor Ivanov at the Joint Session of Federation Council and State Duma Foreign Affairs Committees, 12 February 2004. Russian Ministry of Foreign Affairs, http://www.russianembassy.org.

Speech by the State Secretary-Minister of Foreign Affairs of the Republic of Kazakhstan, "Vestupleniye Kasymzhomarta Tokayeva na Transaziatskom Parlamentskom Forume PA OSCE vorba protiv terrorizma: ucpekhi, noviye ugrozi," *Kazakhstan i Sovremennie Mir* 2, no. 5 (2003).

Spengler, Oswald. *Ratkaisun vuosia*. Helsinki: Otava, 1934.

Spykman, N.J. *The Geography of Peace*. New York: Harcourt Brace and Company, 1944

Stepan, Alfred C. "An Arab More than a Muslim Electoral Gap," *Journal of Democracy,* 14, no. 3 (2003): 30-44.

Stepan, Alfred C. "Arab, not Muslim, Exceptionalism," *Journal of Democracy* 15, no. 4 (2004): 140-6.

Strabon. *The Geography of Strabo*. 8 vols. 24 AD. Loeb Classical Library, Cambridge, Mass. and London: Harvard University Press, 1968-82.

Stralenberg, Philip Johan. *Das Nord und Ostliche Theil von Europa und Asia, in so weit solches das ganze Russische Reich mit Sibirien und der grossen Tatarey in sich begreiffet, in einer Historisch-Geographischen Beschreibung der alten und neuern Zeiten, und vielen andern unbekannten*

Nachrichten vorgestellet, Nebst einer noch niemahls ans Licht gegebenen TABULA POLYGLOTTA von zwei und dreyssigerley Arten Tatarischer Völcker Sprachen und einem Kalmuckischen Vocabulario, Sonderlich aber einer grossen richtigen Land-Charte von den benannten Ländern und andern verschiedenen Kupfferstichen, so die Asiatisch-Scythische Antiqvität betreffen; bey Gelegenheit der Schwedischen Kriegs-Gefangerschafft in Rußland, aus eigener sorgfältigen Erkundigung, auf denen verstatteten weiten Reisen zusammen gebracht und ausgefertiget von Philipp Johann von Strahlenberg, Stockholm, in *Verlegung des Autoris*, 1730; republished *in toto* as Ph. J. von Strahlenberg. *Das Nord und Ostliche Theil von Europa und Asia*. Studia Uralo-Altaica 8. Szeged: Attila József University, 1975.

Suny, R.G. "The Pawn of Great Powers: The East-West Competition for Caucasia," *Journal of Eurasian Studies* 1 (2010): 10-25.

Sutton, P.W. and S. Vertigans. "The Established and Challenging Outsiders: Resurgent Islam in Secular Turkey," *Totalitarian Movements and Political Religion,* 3, no. 1 (Summer 2002): 64.

Takmil-Homayon, N. "A Glance at Asia: Understanding Central Asia," *Central Eurasia and Caucasus Review* 1, no. 3 (1993): 21-47.

Talbott, Strobe. "A Farewell to Flashman: American Policy in the Caucasus and Central Asia." Speech at the Central Asia Institute, School of Advanced International Studies, The John Hopkins University, 21 July, 1997.

Tauasarov, Assylbek. "SHOS Priobretaet Realnie Ochertaniya," *Kazakhstan i Sovremennie Mir* 2, no. 5 (2003).

Tehranian, Majid. "Disenchanted Worlds: Secularisation and Democratisation in the Middle East." In *Democratisation in the Middle East: Experiences, Struggles, Challenges*, Amin Saikal and Albrecth Schnabel (eds). Tokyo: United Nations University Press, 2003.

Terent'ev, A. *Vybory v Kazakhstane: Ukroshenie "Oranzhevoy" Volny*. Mirovaya Ekonomika i Mezhdunarodnaya Otnoshenniya, 2006.

The National Security Strategy of the United States of America. White House: Washington, March 2006.

Therborn, Goran. "Entangled Modernities," *European Journal of Social Theory* 6, no. 3 (2003).

Therborn, Göran. "Post-Western Europe and the plural Asias." In *Europe and Asia beyond East and West*, Gerard Delanty (ed.). London and New York: Routledge, 2006, 24-44.

Todd, Emmanuel. *Imperiumin jälkeen*. Helsinki: Rasalas kustannus, 2003.

Todorov, Tzvetan, *The Conquest of America*. Norman: University of Oklahoma Press, 1984.

Tolipov, Farkhod. "East Vs West? Some Geopolitical Questions and Observations for the SCO," *CEF Quarterly* (July 2005).

Tolipov, Farkhod. "Multilateralism, Bilateralism and Unilateralism in Fighting Terrorism in the SCO Area," *China and Eurasia Forum Quarterly* 4, no. 2 (2006).

Toprak, Binnaz. "Islam and Democracy in Turkey," *Turkish Studies* 6, no. 2 (June 2005).

Traynor, I. "US Campaign behind Turmoil in Kiev," *The Guardian*, 2004.

Trenin, Dmitri. "Russia and the Shanghai Cooperation Organization: A Difficult Match," *CEF Quarterly* (July 2005).

Tully, A. *Uzbekistan: US Sharpens Call for Independent Probe of Andijon Bloodshed, while Russia objects*, 2005. www.eurasianet.org.

Turan, Ilter. "Unstable Stability: Turkish politics at the Crossroads?" *International Affairs* 83, no. 2 (2007).

Ulsever, Cuneyt. "An Analysis of the AKP," *Turkish Daily News*, 26 May 2007. http://www.turkishdailynews.com.tr/article.php?enewsid=74056. Accessed on 30.05.2007.

Vladimir Putin and Nursultan Nazarbaev: Nachalo vstrechi s Presidentom Kazakhstana Nursaltanom Nazarbaevym. 5 July 2005. www.kremlin.ru.

Vladimir Putin: Vystuplenie na tseremonii otkrytiya Goda Rossiya v Kazakhstane, 9 January 2004. www.kremlin.ru

Vladimir Putin: Vystuplenie na vstreche s sekratryami sovetov bezopasnosti gosudarstv-uchastnikov Organisatsii Dogovora o kollektivnoi bezopasnosti, 21 March 2003. www.kremlin.ru.

Wallerstein, I. "The Curve of American Power," *New Left Review* 40 (July/August 2006).

Warraq, Ibn. *Defending the West*. Amherst, NY: Prometheus, 2007.

Weitz, Richard. "Terrorism in Eurasia: Enhancing the Multilateral Response," *China and Eurasian Forum Quarterly* 4, no. 2 (2006).

Wen Jiabao. China's Peaceful Development: An Opportunity for East Asia. 2005. http://www.fmprc.gov.cn/eng/wjdt/zyjh/t228273.htm, visited 10.1.2006.

Westermann. *Diercke Weltatlas*. Vienna, 2002.

Whitman, R. *From Civilian Power to Superpower? The International Identity of the European Union*. London: MacMillan, 1998.

Wight, Martin. *International Theory. The Three Traditions*. Gabriele Wight and Brian Porter (eds). Leicester: Leicester University Press, 1991.

Yu Jincheng. "Emerging Strategic Triangle," *China Daily* (17 November 2010). http://www.chinadaily.com.cn/opinion/2010-11/17/content_11560684. htm. Accessed on 18 November 2010.

Yuan, Jing-dong. *Asia-Pacific Security: China's Conditional Multilateralism and Great Power Entente*. Carlisle, Pennsylvania: Strategic Studies Institute Publication, 2000.

Zakaria, F. *The Post-American World*. London: Norton, 2008.

Zhengji, Hung "The Irresistible Multipolarity Trend of the World," *International Strategic Studies*, no. 4 (1997).

Zhurkin, V. "Russia and the Enlargement of NATO." In *The Emerging New Regional Order in Central and Eastern Europe*, T. Hayashi (ed.). Sapporo: Slavic Research Centre, 1997.

Zygar, M. "Beer without Friendship is a Waste of Money," *Kommersant*, 2005.

Internet Sources

A.K. Party Official Web Site at http://eng.akparti.org.tr/english/chairman.html, accessed on 10.07. 2007.

European Commission External Trade-Press Information Service, October 13, 2006, http://ec.europa.eu/trade/

European Monetary Union:http://www.austria.gv.at/site/6638 (29.01.09).

http://ec.europa.eu/external_relations/sp

Ministry of Foreign Affairs, China, www.fmprc.gov.cn/eng

NATO: http://www.nato.int/structur/countries.htm (25.01.09)

Organization for Security and Cooperation in Europe: http://www.osce.org/ (25.01.09)

Russian Ministry of Foreign Affairs, http://www.russianembassy.org.

Schengen Agreement: http://europa.eu/index_de.htm (25.01.09)

Union of European Football Associations: http://www.uefa.com/index.html (25.01.09)

Contributors

Editors

Jyrki Kakonen is Jean Monnet Professor of International Relations and European Studies in the Institute of Political Science and Governance, Tallinn University, Estonia. He was the Research Director of Tampere Peace Research Institute (1988-98), Jean Monnet Professor, University of Tampere (1998-2007) and the Director of Jean Monnet European Centre of Excellence, University of Tampere (2000-2007). He has extensive experience in peace research, environmental studies, political theory and IR. He is author and editor of over 200 publications, including (with S. Chaturvedi) *Globalization: Spaces, Identities and (In)Securities* (South Asian Publishers 2005), and *Politics and Sustainable Growth in the Arctic* (Dartmouth 1993), and *Green Security or Militarized Environment* (Dartmouth 1994).

Sanjay Chaturvedi is Professor of Political Science and Honorary Director of Centre for the Study of Mid-West and Central Asia at Panjab University, Chandigarh. He was awarded the Nehru Centenary British Fellowship, followed by highly coveted Leverhulme Trust Research Grant for post-doctoral research at University of Cambridge, England (1992 to 1995). A Fellow of India-China Institute (2010-2012) at the New School, New York and an Associate Fellow of Asia Society (2010-2013), New York, he serves on the editorial board of *Geopolitics* (Routledge), *Political Geography* (Elsevier) and *Co-operation and Conflict* (New York: Sage). His research has been published in peer-review journals such as *Third World Quarterly*, *Australian Journal of Political Science*, *Cooperation* *and Conflict, Geopolitics, Journal of the Indian Ocean Region, Ocean Year Book, Terra: Journal of Geographical Society of Finland, and Journal of Social and Economic Geography.*

Anita Sen Gupta is Fellow at the Maulana Abul Kalam Azad Institute of Asian Studies, Kolkata. She works on Central Asia, with Uzbekistan being her area of specific interest. She is the author of *Heartlands of Eurasia: The Geopolitics of Political Space*, Lanham, Boulder, New York, Toronto, Oxford: Lexington Books, 2009; *Russia, China and Multilateralism in Central Asia*, New Delhi: Shipra Publications, 2005; *The Formation of the Uzbek Nation-State: A Study in Transition*, Lanham, Boulder, New York, Toronto, Oxford: Lexington Books, 2003 and *Frontiers into Borders: The Transformation of Identities in Central Asia*, Delhi and London: Hope India Publications and Greenwich Millennium Press Ltd, 2002.

Authors

Pekka Korhonen, is Professor of World Politics in Jyväskylä University, Department of Social Sciences and Philosophy. Research interests: the conceptual and rhetorical basis of world politics, especially the image construction of Asia. He is the author of *Japan and the Pacific Free Trade Area*. Routledge, London & New York, 1994 and *Japan and Asia Pacific Integration: Pacific Romances 1968-1996*, London and New York: Routledge, 1998. He was a visiting Associate Professor at International Research Centre for Japanese Studies, Kyoto (1999-2000) and a visiting fellow at International Christian University (Tokyo), Peace Research Center; Australian National University, Australia-Japan Research Centre; Institute of Southeast Asian Studies, Singapore; Waseda University (Tokyo), Department of Social Sciences; Institute of International Relations, Taipei, Republic of China and Lingnan University (Hong Kong), Centre for Asian Pacific Studies.

Rudolf Wastl has studied Geography at McNally, Rand University of Klagenfurt in Austria and made his PhD in experimental cartography regarding the usability of different map types for way-finding and creating mental images. Today he is military geographer in a provincial military command. He is teaching basics of cartography and development of rural areas at University of Klagenfurt as well as military geography and environmental protection at the Austrian military academy. He has several publications in this field and is member of the board of directors of the military specialty group of the Association of American Geographers.

Ayla Göl, a PhD from London School of Economics and Political Science (LSE), is lecturer in the Department of International Politics, Aberystwyth University, UK, with particular interest in Middle Eastern and Islamic Studies. Before she joined the Department of International Politics at Aberystwyth University in 2005, she lectured at the Department of International Relations, LSE between 2003 and 2005. She was the inaugural John Vincent Visiting Fellow at the Department of International Relations, Research School of Pacific and Asian Studies, Australian National University (ANU) in 2002. Dr Göl holds awards and scholarships from Australia, Turkey, the UK and the USA. She was most recently a Visiting Scholar at the Centre of Middle Eastern and Islamic Studies, University of Cambridge, November 2009 and March 2010.

Daragh McDowell is a DPhil student at the University of Oxford, currently researching the development of Russia's relationships with the former Soviet republics within a framework of 'post-Imperialism.

Ranabir Samaddar, a founder of the CRG and its journal, *Refugee Watch*, was earlier a professor of South Asia Studies, and then was the founder-Director of the Peace Studies Programme at the South Asia Forum for Human Rights, Kathmandu. Known for his critical studies on contemporary issues of justice, human rights, and popular democracy in the context of post-colonial nationalism, trans-border migration, community history, and technological restructuring in South Asia, he has recently completed a three-volume study of Indian nationalism, the final one titled as, *A Biography of the Indian Nation, 1947-1997* (2001). Besides being the editor of three well-known volumes on issues of identity and rights in contemporary politics, *Refugees and the State* (2003), *Space, Territory, and the State* (2002), and *Reflections on Partition in the East* (1997), he is also the editor-in-chief of the *South Asian Peace Studies Series*. His current work is on theory and practices of dialogue, a question critical to the politics of justice and reconciliation.

Dr. John M. Hobson is currently Professor of Politics and International Relations in the Department of Politics at the University of Sheffield, UK. He gained his PhD from the LSE (1991) and taught at La Trobe University, Melbourne (1991-97) and the University of Sydney (1997-

2004). His work is principally involved in carrying forward the critique of Eurocentrism in World History/Historical Sociology, and International Relations. Some of his recent publications include *Politics of the World Economy* (Cambridge: Cambridge University Press, 2007), co-edited with Len Seabrooke; *The Eastern Origins of Western Civilisation* (Cambridge: Cambridge University Press, 2004); 392pp. 8th reprint in English (2009). Out in Arabic, Greek, Korean, Turkish,Chinese, Croatian, Spanish and Swedish.

Rajen Harshe is currently the Vice Chancellor of the University of Allahabad, India. A Ph.D. from Jawaharlal Nehru University (J.N.U.), New Delhi, he was a Fulbright scholar at Columbia University New York (1985-86). He is the author of Pervasive *Entente France and Ivory Coast in African Affairs* (Arnold -Heinemann 1984 and Humanities Press 1984), *Twentieth Century Imperialism Shifting Contours and Changing Conceptions* (Sage 1997). He has edited a book entitled *Interpreting Globalisation: Perspectives in International Relations* (New Delhi and Jaipur, ICSSR and Rawat publishers, 2004) and co-edited a volume entitled *Engaging with the World: Critical Reflections on India's Foreign Policy,* (New Delhi, Orient Longman, 2005). In addition, he has published over seventy five papers in major national and international journals and prestigious anthologies. One of the significant contributions of Prof. Harshe to policy oriented issues appeared when he completed a monograph on 'Stakeholder Participation in the Andhra Pradesh Reform Process' (2001) for the World Bank.

Index